Saint of
Circumstance

Also by Sheila Weller

Hansel & Gretel in Beverly Hills
Marrying the Hangman: A True Story of Privilege, Marriage and
  Murder
Amy Fisher: My Story
Raging Heart: The Intimate Story of the Tragic Marriage of O.J. and
  Nicole Brown Simpson

Saint of Circumstance

THE UNTOLD STORY BEHIND THE ALEX KELLY RAPE CASE:

GROWING UP RICH AND OUT OF CONTROL

SHEILA WELLER

POCKET BOOKS

New York   London   Toronto   Sydney   Tokyo   Singapore

POCKET BOOKS, a division of Simon & Schuster Inc.
1230 Avenue of the Americas, New York, NY 10020

ISBN: 0-671-01437-4

First Pocket Books hardcover printing December 1997

10 9 8 7 6 5 4 3 2

POCKET and colophon are registered trademarks of
Simon & Schuster Inc.

Printed in the U.S.A.

For John and Jonathan,
my heroes

AUTHOR'S NOTE

Rape cases in close-knit, notoriously private communities engender a constant tension between anonymity and disclosure. And so does the process of reporting on them.

With the exception of Adrienne Bak Ortolano, who chose to go public with her name and image after Alex Kelly's June 12 conviction, the names of Alex Kelly's alleged sexual assault victims have been changed. In addition, some sources agreed to be interviewed only on the condition that their names as quoted sources (though not as case or trial principals) would not be used.

The following names in this book are pseudonyms:

Valerie Barnett
Mr. Arenberg
Julia West
Jay Bush
Jamie
Jim Hunter
Rick Dawson
Margaret
Louise
Kathy Bishop
Cory Johnson
Jillian Henderson
Emily Meehan
Nick
Darcy

AUTHOR'S NOTE

Reed
Kimberly Marengo
Diane Sales
Briana

I attempted to interview Joe, Melanie, and Alex Kelly, but all requests were denied through Alex's lawyer Thomas Puccio.

—Sheila Weller
September 17, 1997

Saint of Circumstance

PROLOGUE

ON BRILLIANT EARLY MORNINGS IN THE WINTER OF 1989, a breezily outgoing, handsome, and apparently very wealthy twenty-year-old telemark skier with almost waist-length hair, known locally as American Alex, would take the gondola lift up glacier-encrusted Mont Blanc Massif's south face with his friend Canadian Mark. The two young men were opposites— Alex boisterous and wired; Mark thoughtful and calm—but they were both prodigious skiers, favoring the Norwegian free-heel form which demanded greater attention and afforded greater thrills. In telemarking, the ski connects to the foot only at the toes. One's mooring is unstable. If you slip, it is almost impossible to break the fall.

On those mornings, the sun would be striking the mountain with an intensity that would soon bake its north-face snow to avalanche-hazard consistency. Mont Blanc is the highest mountain in Europe, and, after their ascent to the 4,807-meter-high Aiguille du Midi ("needle of midday"), Alex Kelly and Mark Hanson would slip their sheepskins over their skis and start their hike. A few hours later, they'd remove the skins and, for three or four hours, "drop down" the unregulated north face ridges that make this region—the Chamonix valley, at France's Alpine juncture with Switzerland and Italy—the world capital of daredevil "extreme" skiing. Extreme skiers flock to Chamonix from the regulated slopes of the United States and Canada because, as they often approvingly say, "The French do not baby-sit you." Instead, the cool Gallic policy is: Ski your hearts out wherever you want—but we are not liable if you die.

If they'd thought hard about it, Alex Kelly's old buddies from high school, who knew him as a hyper-adrenalined jock and limit-pushing wild man, might have predicted that he would someday end up here, where every single day is a physical rush. And where, come to think of it, so many aspects of life— the wearing of identical down-stuffed nylon suits and face-obscuring caps and goggles; the relinquishment of last names (people were known as Australian Richard, Kiwi Patrick, French Paul); the collective fixation on a single activity—just happen to rub out particularities of identity, thus making it easy to hide.

Hiding was a distinct priority for Alex Kelly now.

Some of the ridges that American Alex and Canadian Mark encountered were "death chutes": if you took an unfortunate step, your chance of hitting a crevasse and plunging to your doom was over 50 percent. Whenever they heard the clatter of a distant ambulance-helicopter (a sign that a fellow skier had been unlucky), the two young men wisecracked about their own fate. Alex Kelly may have been known to fellow international ski-bum pub crawlers as the ultimate obnoxious American (always bragging about his descents and occasionally spraying the others with mouthfuls of beer), but on these outings—marked as they were by stillness, rigor, and the landscape's humbling majesty—"Alex," Mark Hanson says, "was different. He was reflective and vulnerable. He had a sensitive side, which most people didn't know, and he showed it to me."

He would talk about his life. He told Mark about how he had recently served in the Peace Corps. He spoke of his hometown—Vail, Colorado. Of his wealthy investment banker father, who was with a large corporation and kept an apartment in New York. Sometimes Alex would fly from Vail to New York—just for a Grateful Dead concert! He talked with palpable concern about his older brother, Chris, a drug addict, who had mixed speedballs of heroin and cocaine. Recently, Chris and two friends had been arrested; the other young men had been tried, convicted—and given twenty-year prison sentences. But Alex and Chris's father, with his prominence and his connections, had hired a powerful lawyer for Chris and that lawyer had gotten Chris off.

Perhaps because he was such a guy's guy, it was always his brother and his father that Alex Kelly talked about. Curiously, Mark remembers, he never talked about his mother—except to say that she was the one who sent him all those gifts of ski clothes and equipment. Unlike the other young skiers on the funky Chamonix–La Grave axis, Alex had all the newest gear and clothes—and only North Face and Patagonia, the best brands. He was frank about being a rich kid, supported on the slopes by his parents; he often, generously, bought everyone a round of beer. Mark was sure that, given Alex's wealth, athletic prowess, and stamina (he could drink tequila all night, then get up at dawn, ready to hit the slopes) he would make it onto a Mount Everest expedition one day. Meanwhile, he and Mark climbed and skied, and Alex told Mark of his life. The stories were moving. They were vivid. They were heartfelt.

The only trouble is—they weren't true.

Alex Kelly was not from Vail, Colorado (although he and his family had vacationed there), but from Darien, Connecticut, a wealthy, proper town in which he'd lived all his life, but a place whose name he never uttered on those ski slopes. Alex's father was, indeed, a successful man, but he was not an investment banker, or connected to a corporation, although most of Alex's Darien peers' fathers were, and Alex's mother had come from such a family. Alex's father was a plumber—a plumber who serviced the homes of those investment bankers and corporate executives whose children were Alex's friends and girlfriends.

Alex had never served in the Peace Corps. There was no New York apartment. Alex's experience in that city was pretty much limited to the precious metals dealers to whom he had fenced the stereo parts and heirloom silverware he had stolen from neighbors' homes during his junior year. And although his older brother, Chris, had fought a serious drug dependency, and indeed mixed and consumed speedballs, it was not *Chris* Kelly who had recently beaten a serious criminal charge with the probable help of his father—it was Alex. Two charges, in fact. Of first degree sexual assault. And he had not actually beaten those charges but fled them. In mid-February 1987, on the eve of the first day of his scheduled double-rape trial, he had boarded a plane and run away.

Mild-mannered Canadian Mark did not know it, but his carefree, high-living American friend was—right down to the Interpol postings, the FBI list, and the several segments devoted to him on *America's Most Wanted*—a fugitive from justice.

Twenty years old was very young for a man—a *boy*—to have a hidden life and an extensive criminal past, but wholesome-seeming, handsome, happy Alex Kelly did indeed have both.

While Alex Kelly was trying to avoid death on Mont Blanc, Adrienne Bak*, the daughter of a corporate executive from Darien, was a student at Boston's Northeastern University. On

---

*Adrienne Bak (now Adrienne Ortolano) is the victim's real name. After the June 12, 1997, conviction of Alex Kelly, she chose to break her anonymity. In keeping with general news-media practice, however, the author is not identifying any other of the alleged sexual assault victims by their real names but is giving them, instead, pseudonyms. Some others in this story, too, requested pseudonyms before agreeing to be interviewed. A complete list of pseudonyms appears in the "Author's Note."

the surface, she seemed like any other affluent, well-bred, athletic, and very attractive communications major at the college: a young woman whose life had been comfortable, unchallenging, and pleasantly unremarkable; who was on a secure and unquestioned track from schooling to marriage and beyond. You would not have taken her as someone who had barely survived an extreme violation and was halfway through an unnerving eleven-year battle for justice and peace of mind.

Yet while Alex Kelly zoomed down the Chamonix slopes, Adrienne was struggling to construct for herself a normal outlook on life against the backdrop of a memory that gave her regular nightmares and still defined her days—a memory that made her physically unable to get in a car with any adult male.

Adrienne didn't even allow close friends from high school to find out where she lived. To get in touch with her, friends had to call her parents, who would then call her in Boston. Only then would Adrienne return their calls. Every so often she would come to the police station in her hometown, Darien. "Whenever she gave us a new address," former Detective Rebecca Hahn Nathanson says, "she made us swear up and down that we wouldn't reveal it to anyone. She was always afraid she would walk around the corner in Boston and run into Alex Kelly. Or that he'd knock on her door."

On February 10, 1986, five days after her sixteenth birthday, at about 11:30 at night, in a cul-de-sac yards from the Kellys' stately yellow home and across the road from Wee Burn Country Club, Darien's most exclusive club, Adrienne Bak had been brutally choked and raped by Alex in the back of his girlfriend's parents' Jeep. Afterward, he threatened her: "If you tell anybody, I'll do it again, and then I'll kill you."

Adrienne *did* end up telling her family what had happened. And, after some equivocation—Adrienne was afraid to leave the house, even to seek needed medical attention, fearing Alex would see her walk out and assume she had told someone of the rape—she and her mother informed the police. But even then, because of her fear of reprisal, the family put off pressing charges.

Three days after Adrienne's rape, during the period of time that the Bak family was deciding whether or not to press charges, Alex Kelly allegedly took a second victim. She will here be called Valerie Barnett.* Valerie and Adrienne had never met or even heard of one another, but the alleged rape Valerie reported to the Darien police on the night of February 13 took place in a strikingly similar manner, vehicle, and location as the one Adrienne reported. It was accompanied by a similar kind of violence and by exactly the same death threats.

However, this rape, according to Valerie's police statement and hospital report, also included an act of forced anal intercourse.

The day after Valerie Barnett reported her rape to the police, Alex Kelly was arrested, in the morning, on his way to Darien High. He appeared surprised—according to one arresting officer, "wide-eyed."

The cases against Alex Kelly were joined—the two separate rape charges were to be tried together as a double rape at one trial. As similar as the two incidents appeared to be, the prosecution's stated reason for joining the cases—"expediency" for the court system and Connecticut taxpayers—suggested, indeed, a rather striking disregard for the primacy of defendants' rights, which must be the first concern in any criminal trial. Presented as a double rape case, the likelihood of Alex Kelly's conviction was high, and, if convicted, the eighteen-year-old's sentence could have been ninety years.

The idea of spending all his vital years in prison must have been unsupportable to him. Alex Kelly's parents may have felt as much pain at that possibility as he. The joinder of both rape

---

*"Valerie Barnett" is a pseudonym.

cases into one trial and the unfairness it posed to him as a
defendant is, contend his lawyers, what had made Alex Kelly
flee.

At the time of his arrest in February 1986, and even at the
time of his flight one year later, most of the boys in Alex Kelly's
circle took his side. They could not believe he had raped
anybody. "Rape" was the word for an atrocious crime performed by fiends, lowlifes, *outsiders*. And "rape" was about
wanting sex and not being able to obtain it in the normal
fashion. Alex Kelly was a star-athlete senior—maybe the best-
looking senior boy. He could have any girl he wanted—and his
girlfriend, Amy Molitor, was the prettiest girl in the junior
class. Why would he force someone to have sex? Since he
could not possibly need to do that, the charges against Alex
Kelly could not be true. The first girl had exaggerated, the
second girl had leveled a "copy-cat" accusation, and the police
and prosecutor were coming down hard on a rich white boy
for political reasons, the boys concluded.

The Darien parents had nursed their own baffled questions.
Why would people as decent and upright as Joe and Melanie
Kelly—he, a self-made man with working-class values, unpretentious enough to go out on house calls when his customers'
pipes froze; she, a warm if private woman, active in Republican town politics and a sustaining member of the Junior
League—give their tacit blessing to a son fleeing justice on a
double rape charge? Or, worse, why would they—as it increasingly came to be rumored—be abetting him and supporting
him in his fugitive life abroad?

There were many lax, licentious parents in Darien—people
who went on two-week business trips or cruises, leaving the
kids to open their houses to marathon keg parties. But the
Kellys were not among this group. They were not even
members of one of the town's three country clubs—only of
unexclusive "starter club" Middlesex Swim, and, at that, only
when their boys were younger.

And if commuter fathers and frequently absent mothers were viewed as contributors to their children's problems— well, here again, the Kellys did not fit the bill. Joe Kelly worked in town, one of a minority of fathers who did in this bedroom community where fully half of the population of 18,200 commuted to New York City every day. And Melanie was one of those mothers who was always making cookies and inviting the neighborhood kids in. As one neighbor and longtime friend, Ann Brown, puts it, "They were definitely family people. There were *a lot* of people in Darien who, in terms of being involved in their own lives rather than their kids', were far worse parents—far, *far* worse."

Besides, Alex Kelly just didn't seem to fit the profile of a rapist. The Darien community certainly did not consult the clinical literature to form their commonsense assumption, but if they had, they would have found their hunch affirmed. Sexual offenders are characterized as having poor social skills, a far cry from Alex Kelly, who was popular—indeed considered "charismatic"—among his peers. Rapists were often sexually abused as children—and that seemed highly unlikely in his case. Many in Darien knew that Alex Kelly had always been a wild, rule-flaunting kid—but violent *sexual* offenses, as the community understood them, are pathologies of a different order from other "bad kid" crimes.

Alex Kelly *could not* be a rapist, many in the town had concluded back then.

Indeed—even years later; even at thirty—Alex Kelly, when viewed up close, looks so sweet, so innocent—so disarmingly boyish. There is not a trace of hardness in his face.

Yet ten months of research reveals that he is not only a rapist but, quite possibly, a serial rapist.

What the townspeople of Darien did not know is this: There were a number of Darien girls who, upon hearing about Alex Kelly's arrest for rape, had silently said to themselves, "Of *course* he did it." They felt this way for a simple reason:

According to them, he had raped or attempted to rape them, too. These were not "date rapes," in which consensual affection had escalated to the point that the girl's ultimate "no" went unheeded or unheard. These were incidents of forcible, sometimes violent sexual assault.* (In addition, just before the rape and alleged rape of Adrienne and Valerie, Alex Kelly allegedly raped a girl in Vermont. And while he was awaiting trial, he allegedly committed another rape, in the Bahamas. That girl was thirteen. That makes one proved and three alleged rapes by Alex Kelly in 1986 alone.)

At the time, none of the Darien girls reported their attacks to anyone but their best friends. As one puts it today, "After Alex raped me, I just kept my mouth shut. A lot of the time, in that town, people keep their mouths shut." Other girls were said to be frantic about not letting the news out. So although they were neighbors and friends of one another, almost none of these girls knew what they had in common.

In January 1995, Alex Kelly, in an arrangement negotiated by Thomas Puccio, the defense attorney who had won Claus von Bülow's acquittal, turned himself in in Zurich, Switzerland. The two rape charges—of Adrienne Bak and of Valerie Barnett—would no longer be joined because of a change in Connecticut statute. This severing meant that the existence of a second rape charge could be kept out of the first trial.

Alex was brought back to Darien in handcuffs. His parents raised the million-dollar bail required to keep him out of jail. His former friends had stopped feeling loyal. During Alex's eight years evading the law, the teenagers within his crowd

---

*Three of these women recounted their attacks to this author and each account was corroborated through the author's interviews with people to whom the women had reported the incidents after they occurred. A fourth woman's experience was described to the author by two men: one who had intercepted the attempted attack, another who had aided the alleged victim immediately afterward. In every case, the corroborating witnesses were located and interviewed first, in two instances without their knowing how to find the woman whose twelve- to sixteen-year-ago attack they recalled.

9

had become young adults. Some had endured sleepless nights over what they had always known but had never revealed to the police. To others, the blatant reward for evading the law which Alex's parents had endowed upon him had left them disgusted. As one young woman who had been in the inner circle of Darien teenagers of the 1980s, and whose family remained very close to all the Kellys, puts it dryly: "I'd love to have *my* parents finance an eight-year ski vacation. But then again, *I* didn't do anything bad."

For many of Alex Kelly's peers, the endless party that had been their youth had come to exact an enormous price. There had been breakdowns, trips to rehabilitative clinics, a stint or two in jail. There were many abortions, a baby given up for adoption. There were deaths of siblings and best friends in drunk driving accidents. There were long benders after these deaths of loved ones, and, for the people who had been driving the death cars, a new appreciation of life, which now would never be the same. During the years that Alex Kelly was away skiing down mountains, his own brother Chris had died of a drug overdose that was almost certainly a suicide.

To some in Darien, it seemed as if life in their town had become a soap opera. For all their privilege in the extreme, they were forced to reassess their youth and the town's values in light of these sobering events. To the young people, who had spent their teen years following the Grateful Dead, it was perhaps (to borrow an expression from the group's decade of origin) karmic: as if Alex's lack of conscience had rematerialized into *their* penance; his renunciation of accountability transformed into a bad debt left on their collective doorstep. A favorite Grateful Dead song describes a charismatic young man who is able to make himself look good in any situation and who has the knack of turning things his way. Yet this young man is really using others, draining something from the shared pool of luck. This character harbors a dark side which can turn him into a "tiger in a trance." With the charmingly fatuous symbolism favored by male adolescents, the song is called "Saint of Circumstance."

Back in Connecticut, Alex Kelly underwent a physical transformation. Gone was the waist-length mane of his skiing days in Europe. His hair was cut properly short. For court dates, he religiously wore a blue blazer, khaki pants, dark tie: the standard-issue "preppy" costume that in fact, although most members of the larger public did not know it, he had rarely worn before his arrest. As he mounted the Stamford courthouse steps, the features of his handsome face—the deep-set eyes, short upturned nose, square jaw—were fixed in a vague, distracted frown. In these photographs he looked like what many of his peers had turned out to be: a young stockbroker on his way to a meeting with a client at a country club. The media designated him "the Golden Boy," "the All-American."

These labels were as superficially plausible—and as deeply inaccurate—as Alex's own depiction of himself and his family to his ski friend Mark Hanson. And yet, as some who grew up in his hometown believed, it was this very dissonance between appearance and essence that made Alex Kelly a true son of Darien.

On June 12, 1997, the lucky Alex Kelly ran out of good fortune: He was convicted of the rape of Adrienne Bak. When the verdict was recited Alex, who had not said a word through either trial, half shouted, half whimpered at the jury: "Are you serious? But I'm not guilty! I'm not guilty! I'm not guilty!" Then he angrily and incredulously shouted at Adrienne: "Why are you doing this to me?!"

On July 24, Alex Kelly was sentenced to sixteen years in prison, thirteen of which he must serve before he is eligible for parole. (His trial for the rape of Valerie Barnett is scheduled to start in November, though a plea agreement is considered far more likely.) Before Judge Tierney delivered the sentence and

Alex was ushered into the prison van, Alex made a statement, crying as he spoke. Two sentiments have resonance. "I now know you can't run from your problems," he said. And: "The teenagers of eleven years ago have grown up. . . . I hope we can stop destroying ourselves."

The truth in these statements is something that Alex Kelly will spend the best years of his life in jail for, for coming to too late.

The lesson Alex finally learned about not being able to run from one's problems is one that only parents can enforce—in part by living by it themselves, even (especially) when that requires looking painfully inside the family to examine why a child is disturbed. Alex Kelly's parents, despite their ostensible embodiment of many outstanding values, failed him here.

As for Alex's acknowledgment of his friends' maturing after what he suggested was destruction within their Darien social group: well, that is what this story is all about. Constructed through interviews with over fifty Darien insiders, as well as other sources, *Saint of Circumstance* is the story of how a rapist with a pretty face could emerge from within a traditional, all-American family and thrive, unchecked, as the most popular, charismatic boy in his class in a community of gleaming order and fabled rectitude. It is the story of how one young man was able to run away from the consequences of his acts while everyone around him kept running into theirs. It is about the emotional and sexual baggage and the hard lessons that America's young leadership-class adults are carrying with them as they marry and raise children of their own.

And, finally, it is a story about growing up male and female in one of America's last remaining enclaves of glamorous, genteel elitism—suggesting that those privileged, perfect childhoods that the rest of us may envy and romanticize look very, very different at close range.

CHAPTER 1

THERE IS ALMOST NO SUCH THING AS A CHARMLESS
street name in Darien, Connecticut.

Lyrical appellations that developers would pay an advertising agency handsomely to conjure—Pear Tree Point, Christie
Hill Road, Nearwater Lane—are printed in small letters on
wooden and metal signs. But these rural evocations—Holly
Lane, Berry Lane, Pasture Lane; these signposts of Revolutionary army marches—Five Mile River Road, Red Coat Pass, Tory
Hole Road—are *literal* descriptions, not sales-pitch lures.
They underscore the heritage and ethos of the town: To be
stalwart, proper, moral; to appear graceful at all times. Partridge Lane, Hummingbird Lane: They are soothing names,
narcotic names—lulling one to the dream of a perfect life
along the curling, leaf-draped roads.

Set back on stately mounds of grass behind centuries-old
stone walls and smartly tailored hedges are colonials, salt-
boxes, and other primly serious homes, from the three-
bedroom "starters" on a half acre priced at $250,000 to the
5-million-dollar mansions backed by private woods. The wa-
terfront estates in Tokeneke and Long Neck Point are braced

by pines and open out to the flat blue sound, where, farther out, lie the seriously private homes on Delafield and Contentment Islands. The kitsch, bombast, and banality of the rest of America are resolutely absent.

If it's been said that every generation gets the scandal it deserves, then it might also be said that every town or city breeds just the type of crime its peculiarities can best accommodate. Why did serial rape by a handsome and gifted young resident emerge from, and for over a decade bedevil the image of, this sublime place? Rape is a crime in which ultimate stealth joins ultimate entitlement. And acquaintance rape is a crime in which appearance and essence, prelude and act could not be more different from one another. It should not be a surprise that Alex Kelly grew up in this town whose estimable moral heritage veered over time into opposite values; whose focus on decorum is extreme—and extremely functional. And a place where cruelty and mayhem are camouflaged, but not erased, by loveliness and order.

Old King's Highway and Hollow Tree Ridge Road were the names given the town's only two trails soon after the settlers bought the territory from the Siwanoy Indians, in 1596 for twelve coats, twelve hoes, twelve hatchets, twelve glasses, twelve knives, four kettles, and four fathoms of white wampum. Eminent citizen Captain Isaac Weed's Weed Pond House bestowed its name on the town beach. The town's name itself exemplifies the era's and region's laudable modesty. Civic elder Thaddeus Bell, for whom the town was to be named, chafed at the prospect of living in "Bellville." Recalling a sailor's remarks that the area's contours (wedged as it is between the Noroton River and Long Island Sound) reminded him of a land mass he had seen during his journeys, Bell had it named instead for what that isthmus (of Panama) was known as back then: the Isthmus of Darien.

But the town's most preeminent hero was Dr. Moses Mather,

the ardently patriotic proindependence minister of Middlesex Parish's First Congregational Church, who was twice captured by Tory neighbors, the second time as one of fifty men seized during a dramatic 1781 raid on his church, then rowed across the sound and imprisoned in New York. The elderly Dr. Mather barely survived, enduring, as one account put it, "intolerable conditions of filth, cold, starvation and disease" until he was released.

Moses Mather's name and parish became the names of Darien's two middle schools, Mather and Middlesex. It was hoped that the integrity, courage, and the deferral of gratification that Mather embodied would guide future generations of Darien youth.

These values would be mocked by many of the students of Alex Kelly's generation—and mocked in the extreme by Alex himself.

Darien is so determinedly peaceful, it is hard to see how crowded it is, but there is little undeveloped land left in this fifteen-square-mile town, thirty-six miles and forty commuter-train minutes from New York. Beyond the Darien station, the Manhattan-originating train makes few express stops; for this reason, Darien (whose nineteenth-century residents were so against the railroad's coming, some townsfolk barricaded Old King's Highway in protest) has been in demand for much of this century. During these years its flinty New England integrity became mixed with other values.

Darien was the favored bedroom community of the martini-sipping advertising executives whose aplomb was glamorized in such 1940s and 1950s Hollywood movies as *Mr. Blandings Builds His Dream House* and *The Man in the Gray Flannel Suit*. By the 1960s, when U.S. corporations started moving their junior executives around the country like chess pieces, the transferred-from-Winnetka managers at IBM and Colgate vied with the Madison Avenue Northeasterners as the town's archetypal heads of household.

For both groups, drinking was the lubricant of life. Photographer Donal Holway, who grew up in Darien in the 1950s and early 1960s, remembers as a boy "standing at the train station in early evening and watching the men, who'd been drinking in the club car all the way from Manhattan, step off the train—and be handed cocktails by their wives *on the platform.*"

The late social critic Vance Packard detailed the new Darien resident in his 1972 book, *A Nation of Strangers.* Packard termed Darien the ultimate haven for ambitious "high-mobile corporate" families. Like career-military households, these families were forced to manage the difficult feat of being both constantly peripatetic *and* deeply traditional: picking themselves up whole and moving every two or three years while somehow succeeding to *look* as if no jarring dislocation had been suffered. In that conformist corporate culture—where the wife's "flexibility" and "adaptability" were as much a prerequisite for the husband's promotions as his own talents— the ability to erect an airtight facade of serenity over an undercurrent of chaos was crucial. "In describing past experiences in moving, one [Darien woman] said she had moved 22 times in the 25 years of her marriage," Packard wrote. "Another had moved 15 times in 31 years of marriage . . . another, eight times in nine years. . . . " It took inordinate psychic discipline to survive such chronic uprootings with grace. Those who were too emotional or idiosyncratic, too inept at polished artifice were weeded out, and Darien filled up with only those able to keep up appearances against enormous challenge.

In Darien—the town's young adults, educators, and police officers say—unpleasant things are covered up or euphemized. Says a school administrator: "I've always thought the town motto should be: 'Welcome to Darien, where *nothing* is what it seems.'"

* * *

Darien's architecture—like that of other aesthetically zoned towns, such as Santa Barbara, California, and Princeton, New Jersey—is itself euphemistic. Along the pink-clapboard store-lined Boston Post Road, some things do not look like what they are: A dignified, modern brick edifice houses the town's pizza parlor; the Darien Car Wash is an elegant building resembling a Rolls-Royce showroom. Others project nostalgia: Griebs Pharmacy could have been lifted off Disneyland's Main Street; the movie theater has a quaint marquee. Some shop names— The Complete Kitchen, The Complete Angler, Jack and Jill's Children's Clothing—reflect the self-satisfaction of bygone decades. The inevitable Starbucks, where young blond wives sip lattes, is the town's one nod to upscale mass culture; a Dunkin' Donuts, its sole plebeian venue. (The tanning salon, hidden on a back street, hints at the surrender, of some in town, to mall-level vanity.)

A casual tour of Darien starts where everyone (except the despised two-commuter Yuppie couples) buys the morning papers: at the reassuringly musty Darien News Store, under the railroad trestle and around the corner on Tokeneke Road. The shop's owner, once-dashing Bill Frate, is Darien Old Guard: aristocratic, wistful, gossipy—a renegade from an Updike story. Frate used to be a Wall Street stockbroker and before that was Ted Kennedy's college roommate; his state-senator father convened political meetings in the News Store's back room. Frate holds forth behind the counter in his lived-in shetland crewneck, decrying the town's rising taxes in a timbre so muted it's almost inaudible and exuding the melancholy courtliness of a weathered deb-ball escort stranded at the Stork Club. As if to stay in character, he sometimes visits very long hugs on select customers.

The under-thirty-five Darien crowd own, bartend, and hang out at Moody's, Back Street and, on Friday nights, across town line at Stamford's Jimmy's Seaside. If one marker of that disappearing civic entity, the self-contained small town, is the fact that the owners, staff, and regulars at its favorite watering holes all knew each other in high school, then Darien doubly qualifies; *its* most infamous resident's inner circle of high-school intimates actually, to this day, *bartend* at these places: Alex Kelly's diehard-loyal lifelong friend Junie Clark, at Jimmy's Seaside; Alex Kelly's former close friend (and running buddy on the night of the rape for which he was convicted)-turned-witness-*against*-him Tom Kelly (no relation), at Back Street; and Alex's implacable fiancée, Amy Molitor, at Moody's. For a town whose older generation doth protest so much about privacy, the stubborn nightly appearance, in these key venues, of the young star supporting players in the town's long-running soap opera speaks volumes for rebel exhibitionism.

These bars are a companionable jumble of three kinds of people: those who've partied so long, they never quite got it together to abandon either the area or the presumption that nursing a buzz and shooting the shit are a worthy day's centerpiece; those who have gone on to appropriately adult lives and who've stayed local out of a combination of a disinclination to flee or rebel and the amazing good luck of being able to afford to live almost as well as their parents; and those who will tell you they barely escaped from the town in one piece yet who nevertheless find themselves rooting homeward at what they freely acknowledge to be suspiciously frequent intervals.

The women at these bars look like bridesmaids at Hyannis Port weddings. Some of the men sport ponytails, two initials for first names, and voices that dip and swoop in light renditions of *Wayne's World* vowels. Here, everyone radiates good manners and a certain undiminishable wholesomeness. Here, everybody has a sister who used to date somebody else's brother. Here, someone's always just come back from Colorado, Lake Tahoe, New Zealand, or Florida. Here (with that unique vocational wingspan of upper-upper-middle class society), you're either a stockbroker or else you're a carpenter. Or you're in advertising or media sales, or a sales rep for a trendy leisure-goods company like Perrier or North Face. (Darien's young people cluster in business and finance—not law, medicine, the arts, or academia.) If you're not any of the above, you and your spouse are restoring a two-hundred-year-old house, managing a working farm, or are poised to take over the several-generations-old family business. Many of the young men and women at these bars have attended 60 to 110 Grateful Dead concerts. To the Back Street crowd, the day Jerry Garcia died is right up there, remember-where-you-were-when?-wise, with the day of the O. J. Simpson verdict.

These, then, are the Alex Kelly people.

Straight down Boston Post Road, the Darien Sport Shop, owned by highly regarded Steve Zangrillo (the generations-old Italian families, now landed-gentry-proper, rule the town's infrastructure), is a large, awninged building, its name emblazoned in 1950s script. Here's where Darienites buy their sports clothes, now that the Corner House, from which women used to purchase pastel shirts and skirts with jaunty rows of tiny whales, has been shuttered. Today, the favored clubwear is not of that so-easily ridiculed variety, and today people know enough to claim they rank and covet clubs not on the basis of social cachet but, rather, on the degree of challenge of their golf courses.

Still, the pinnacle club, Wee Burn—with its stringent and mysterious exclusivity, its five-figure membership fee, its casual power of anointment (any incoming CEO of IBM is almost automatically waved in), even its archly kilt-by-the-fireplace name—is as intriguingly cloistered as a feudal city. Members' rankings in its bowling matches and golf and tennis tournaments are cheerily chronicled in the Wee Burn *Burr*, yet the club is so grandiosely private, photographs taken on its golf course are allowed to be printed in publications that reach beyond its (unexpectedly) hacienda-style stucco walls *only* on the condition that the club's name *not* appear in the caption.

For years, Wee Burnites secretly enjoyed what one country club daughter calls "rocking social lives." The Fortune-500-leading husbands and their tanned, frosted-blond wives cocktail-partied with one another copiously and indulged, with various degrees of discretion, in affairs with one another's spouses. In the 1980s, this young woman continues, "You'd come home from a party, and find your mother in a totally compromised situation with someone else's father from the club." Sometimes Tokeneke families who'd lived in adjacent estates while raising their families would, once the kids left for college, divorce and recombine—like nineteenth-century European dynasties in Brooks Brothers shirts and tennis whites. "It was so weird: Your next-door neighbors would become your stepbrothers and stepsisters. The families married each other."

Recently, one club member was apprehended at Zangrillo's store for shoplifting. It was not her first time. She was banned from the Darien Sport Shop. But she was not banned from Wee Burn.

Up the Post Road is the Black Goose Grille, in whose old-fashioned wooden booths the lunching fortyish women may be discussing their tennis serves, their mammograms, or recent gossip: The friend who finally left her husband for her lover after seeing Meryl Streep in *The Bridges of Madison County*, the patriarch of a major Darien family who got into all that trouble with the IRS because of a falsely declared Manhattan residence, or the woman from Old Farm Road who claimed that her executive husband had one long-term mistress and more than fifty other affairs and repeatedly kicked her, choked her, threw sharp objects at her, threatened to kill her and hurled her down the stairs. She had starved herself down to eighty pounds and filed for divorce under the auspices of the federal Violence Against Women law. In the Darien tradition of protecting "privacy," this woman's horrifying complaint was made anonymously—just as many girls Alex Kelly allegedly attacked never pressed charges.

Across the street sits the Sugar Bowl, where the folks who do not regularly enter Wee Burn or Woodway or Country Club of Darien quietly hold forth. Opened in 1959 as the town's teenagers' malt shop, it's the kind of luncheonette they don't make anymore: pin-neat, Wedgwood plates and ceramic hens dotting its pine-paneled walls. While au pairs keep their charges from squirming off the plastic chairs at the front tables, the local public-works guys, mailmen, and veteran cops gather by the back window.

You might catch them comparing the town's current tight DUI-enforcement with the recent past, when mayor (the actual title is First Selectman) William Patrick—known to the cops as "Whiskey Bill"—drunkenly ranted into his car's police radio that a garbage truck had almost run him over. (As always, Bill was eased home by the cops that night; no one officially said not to arrest certain people, but the message was implicit.) Or they might be waxing sentimental over now-deceased Bill Ward, whose hole-in-the-wall tavern, The Post, was so congenial, cops didn't even mind bellying up to the bar with the preppy kids they were always arresting. Kids like Billy Hughes, whose good looks, blue-collar millionaire parents, and status as Darien High's star wrestler and football player were outshone only by his notoriety as a brawler and drug user. Hughes' most notable contretemps occurred in another of the area's bars, Lock, Stock and Barrel, when (according to the arresting officer) he flung over the top of the men's room stall the bags of cocaine he had left in his pants that he couldn't flush down the toilet.

Darien has always had a secret history of boys like Hughes: young champion-athlete criminals. Alex Kelly wasn't the first, the Sugar Bowl fellows know. He probably won't be the last one. And the tony folks in town have always turned straight to the local paper's Police Blotter first thing Thursday morning.

"Still," an ex-officer says, "the mandate from the town government to the police is: Keep these people happy; keep up this image of this quiet little New England town where we have no crime. I used to joke, 'If they could get away with not having a police department here that's what they'd do, because if you have a police department that means you have crime, and they don't want that word spoken.' In Darien, image is everything."

Proceeding south, there's Town Hall on Renshaw Road, where Jackie Kennedy Onassis's cousin Shella Crouse, a droll, gravelly-voiced woman who knows everyone and everything, sits at the information desk. Here, records reveal what Darien is very good at:

Darien ranked first in the state for supplying blood to the Red Cross. It has a completely teenager-staffed emergency medical service, Post 53, which is the lauded prototype for other such services nationwide. Learning from its sad recent past, its Safe Ride allows inebriated teenagers to anonymously call other teens to drive them home from parties. Its Committee on Drugs and Alcohol (CODA) attempts to keep all these kids clean and sober. The town's sewers, shores, bridges, and roads are relentlessly upgraded. A tax-initiative-funded school expansion is underway (though balked at by the town's frugal empty-nesters). Darien's beautiful, computer-filled modern public library is the state's busiest on a per-capita basis. The town is changing in other ways, too, Town Clerk Marilyn van Sciver will tell you: There are more two-career families. Fathers, not just mothers, take their children to and from school. And a stop by the railroad station at 6:45 P.M. reveals that the invariably briefcase-clasping commuters are today about 75 percent male, not the 100 percent of the past. But it is steel-jawed, white-haired, vigorously patrician men that that train disgorges in almost dizzying quantity.

Darien is a holdover, a relic: a sophisticated town that is airtightly homogeneous. It is the most Republican wealthy town that is also almost all white Christian and that lies within a short train commute from Manhattan.

Politically, Darien's residents are overwhelmingly (seven to two) registered Republicans; there were more "unaffiliated" than Democratic registered voters in 1995. Darien voted for Dole over Clinton two to one in the 1996 election (while the nation at large voted for Clinton over Dole, 45 million to 37 million). Darien's political persuasian runs deep—its Darien Women's Republican Association is the oldest Republican women's club in the nation—and wide: If Darien were a county, it would be the most Republican county in America.

In terms of prosperity, the town ranks second highest in per-capita and median-household income of all the towns in Fairfield County (only neighboring New Canaan is higher), and Fairfield is the county with the highest per-capita income in prosperous Connecticut and one of the richest counties in the country. Darien's average per-capita income, according to the 1990 census, is $51,795, and its average median household income is $89,395*: wealthy even by wealthy-town standards. Moreover, although Darien has struggling, two-paycheck, lower-middle-class families, there are almost *no* poor people in Darien: Of its 18,200 residents, in 1994–1995, twelve individuals and six families qualified for welfare.

As for the town's complexion: When Arthur Ashe was invited to speak at Darien High School in the early 1970s, he stood on the stage and told the students that he would never live in Darien because, a, he'd be all alone, and, b, he wouldn't be allowed in. He was not overstating by much. Aside from the brief tenure of a black doctor and his family, no black families (in two dozen young people's and educators' memories) owned a home here. A few families adopted nonwhite children and some employed live-in housekeepers of color whose

---

*New Canaan's average per-capita income is $52,692, and its average median-household income is $91,951.

children attended town schools. Darien High has long had a program called ABC (A Better Chance) for minority students from outside the area; they live together in a supervised home. Says a thirty-two-year-old woman: "The only black people you ever saw were working on someone's lawn."

Even in the 1980s and early 1990s, the Darien Police Department would receive phone calls: "'There's a black person, standing on the Post Road,' in the middle of the day," recalls a former patrolman. "We'd get these calls sometimes up to three calls a week, though not on a consistent basis." In this town in which the police are expected to appease, rather than contradict, the higher-social-class residents, such callers were gently asked by a desk officer: "Is there a bus stop where they're standing? Are they *at* the bus stop, ma'am?" Sometimes this explanation was not enough to placate the caller, and police officers were compelled to drive out to make sure nothing untoward was going on.

But the police's private eye-rolling at such callers did not make life any easier for African Americans who happened to be in the town. Black employees told their employers they dreaded standing at Post Road bus stops. A white woman was on a date with a black man; their car was pulled over by a Darien police officer who asked her if everything was all right. It was said that you could get stopped in Darien for the misdemeanor of WWB: Walking While Black. (Things have improved a bit since Alex Kelly went to high school here; for one thing, there are now three black officers—two patrolmen, one lieutenant, including a father and son—on Darien's fifty-member police force.)

Still, the form of bigotry which is the biggest thorn in Darien's side is its perceived anti-Semitism, most famously presented in the 1947 Academy Award–winning movie *Gentlemen's Agreement*. "When that movie came out people were saying it was *really* about New Canaan," says a seventy-year-old Darien resident. But the movie was about Darien (however much New Canaan may have shared its policies). Recalls one former resident, "When my parents bought their house in Darien in 1953, the deed contained a covenant (which they did not intend to observe) prohibiting them from selling it to members of the Jewish faith." Today, says a Jewish woman who recently house-hunted, "there *is* a Jewish community in New Canaan, but when I told a realtor we wanted to be near a synagogue she said, 'Then you don't want Darien.'"* A woman whose husband was in real estate in the 1980s says, "The Darien realtors' attitude was: The Jews are in Westport and Stamford. If Jewish families want to look in Darien, show them houses that aren't quite what they're looking for."

A young woman who grew up in the town says, "Anti-Semitism will always exist there—Jews still can't join Wee Burn. But it's loosened up a bit; the younger generation are a bit more cosmopolitan. I noticed a Jewish name on a sign outside a house on Long Neck Point the other day and my mother said, 'That's nice. Because once they start taking the big plots in Darien, they're just going to *have* to accept them.'" Another, who graduated a few years before Alex Kelly, says,

---

*In the Darien Chamber of Commerce's "Darien Facts and Figures", a brochure sent to people inquiring about the town, there is this notification: PLACES OF WORSHIP: Baptist, Christian Science, Congregational (United Church of Christ), Episcopal, Interdenominational, Methodist, Presbyterian, Roman Catholic. In the "Town of Darien 1994 Government Directory" (mailed out by the Chamber of Commerce in the summer of 1997 to an inquirer about the town) is this notification: RELIGIOUS FACILITIES: United Methodist Church, St. John's Roman Catholic Church, St. Luke's Episcopal Church, St. Paul's Episcopal Church, Talmadge Hill Community Chapel (Interdenominational), First Church of Christ Science, St. Thomas More Catholic Church, Calvary Baptist Church, Noroton Presbyterian Church, First Congregational Church. A separate one-page flysheet, "Places Of Worship" (Xeroxed from a publication called DISCOVER DARIEN 1991, also sent out in the packet to inquirers, starts with the sentence "Newcomers and visitors to Darien and Rowayton have many houses of worship to choose from within the two communities and in nearby towns. . . ." After listing (and providing times of services for) 12 churches, under the separate boldfaced designation "Nearby churches and temples" are, in this order, similar entries on a Unitarian church in Stamford, a Jewish temple in Norwalk and a Jewish temple in Stamford.

"By the time I had graduated Darien High, I had *never met* a Jewish person!"

Two young people who attended Mather Middle School in the early 1980s vividly remember the harassment of the school's one Jewish teacher. "It was disgusting—one girl would throw pennies at Mr. Arenberg, to see if he'd stoop to pick them up, and everyone in the class laughed," says the young woman. The young man recalls classmates "taping Hitler mustaches on their lips" and on a Jewish holiday one boy taking the yarmulke Mr. Arenberg was (uncharacteristically) wearing off his head "and playing Frisbee with it. Mr. Arenberg was practically in tears."

When Mr. Arenberg, who still teaches in Darien, was called to comment, he said, after a pause, "Throwing pennies? Anything may have been done behind my back but I don't remember it." He said he never wore a yarmulke to class; thus, "Your sources are unreliable. Their remembrances are far from accurate."

When told of Mr. Arenberg's reply, the former students, bewildered by his denial, firmly reiterated their accounts and named the offending students to help jog his memory. In a very Darien response to unpleasantness, Mr. Arenberg declined to comment.

What happens to youth in a town that is so homogeneous?

Educators say that the subtle pauses for clues about how someone is going to respond to a remark or an action are dispensed with. With a high school population of many backgrounds, no one can be too sure of what it takes to make someone else mad. While diversity may not always engender the racial harmony and cross-group friendships its proponents seek, it does provide a humbling dose of uncertainty: a sense that something less than the whole world is known and can be taken up and conquered.

But take a completely homogeneous group of youths, add privilege to the mix—and a smug recklessness can take root. A guidance counselor who worked both at Darien High and at a more heterogeneous high school says that it always amazed her: At Darien High proms, the kids *arrived* drunk— miserably, wantonly, "vomiting-and-peeing-on-the-bathroom-floor drunk: including those adorable little girls, in their prom dresses!" At a mixed-group school "the kids wouldn't dare arrive drunk. They couldn't afford to lose so much control so early in the evening."

There is another reason the guidance counselor found so much drunkenness at Darien's proms: The town has a history of parental complicity in teenage drinking, going back more than thirty years. The death of the seventeen-year-old daughter of an airline vice-president on a long-ago summer night and the events that ensued exemplify this. The incident also reveals how good Darien is at hiding unpleasant facts, how hard some in town can fight to duck responsibility, and how blithely they can disregard the courts. If a place's more toxic values can be said to metamorphose over time into different families and forms, then this saga from Darien's recent past casts a shadow right up to the Kelly family's door.

On June 23, 1964, Nancy Hitchings left a debutante party with eighteen-year-old Michael Smith in her family's station wagon. Smith had been drinking at two parties hosted by parents. The car crashed into a tree and Hitchings was killed. Smith, slightly hurt, told police he didn't remember if he had been driving.

The coroner ruled Hitchings' death a criminal act and said evidence showed that Smith had been at the wheel. Charged with negligent homicide, Smith pled not guilty; his parents hired experts to prove that it was the now-dead girl who'd been driving.

The judge presiding over the nonjury trial, one Rodney Eielson, chastised the young defendant and, shortly before finding Smith guilty (and sentencing him to sixty days in jail), he ordered the arrest of all thirteen adults who had served liquor to teenagers at the parties in question. The arrests made

The New York Times's front page. An accompanying photo showed a corporate executive, a lit cigarette tipped cavalierly downward in his right hand, leaving court after making what the *Times* called "an emotional plea for 'consideration and understanding'" to get out of the $250 (that's about $2,000 today) fine. All the others, rather than consider the fine a small conscience sop for their indirect, partial responsibility for a tragedy, vowed to fight the charges. In the midst of their battle, a *second* teenage drunk-driving death after another parent-sanctioned summer party was, to quote the *Times*, "uncovered" after having been, curiously, hidden for four months. Finally, the trial against one of the liquor-serving adults was called off. Why? Most of the witnesses happened to be away at college, and the witness whom Judge Eielson had singled out for praise had just been arrested for drug possession.

Judge Eielson's arrest of the Darien adults exposed the petty self-interest behind the town's proper facade, but even he wasn't able to recognize one of the biggest factors contributing to the town's mystique, an attitude he held himself: sexism. While the judge was lambasting the community for enabling teenage drinking, he was at the same time banning from his courtroom women who wore slacks. Other past critics of Darien culture shared the same myopia. Vance Packard despaired at the corporate upper middle class's constant uprootings, but he made fun of "women's libbers" who dared to presume that *wive*'s careers might influence where a family relocated. Moss Hart, screen-adapting Laura Z. Hobson's novel *Gentleman's Agreement,* spearheaded the fight against prejudice against minorities through the words of a character (the John Garfield–played Dave) who, while crusading against ethnic stereotyping, simultaneously lectured a dithering woman about how to be a more appealing "sidekick" to her fiancé. The Darien police may have noted some townspeople's condescension toward them and the residents' denial of crime the town harbored, but as late as the 1980s a high-ranking

Darien police official is said to have vowed that he'd be "dead and buried" before a female made detective.*

Of course, sexism existed everywhere before the 1970s; to ridicule it in retrospect is like shooting fish in a barrel. But while women elsewhere protested it, in wealthier towns the traditional family remained relatively uncomplained-about, in large part because it *worked* so well there. At the uppermost income levels, ambitious husband plus supportive wife was an economically thriving arrangement—for one thing, few other couples had the luxury of raising large families in such unqualified comfort.

"While the rest of America was out doing its thing and making social changes in the '60s and the '70s, the women in my mother's generation in Darien were Stepford Wives." So says a young woman who will here be called Julia West who now lives in another state—and who, when she was growing up in Darien, according to her account (detailed later in the book), narrowly averted a sexual assault by Alex Kelly. "They weren't being wonder moms. It's not that they were uncaring; it just wasn't in their chemical makeup. Our mothers were not very different from Melanie Kelly: very passive. The stereotypes were so strong in that town. The roles for males and females were so defined. The boys set the agenda and the girls just followed. The sexism was everywhere: That's why *I* couldn't speak out about what Alex did to me.

"And I really do think that's why it took Darien people ten years to figure out what Alex Kelly was doing."

---

*But Darien's original hero, Moses Mather, *was* a feminist. So strongly did the ardently anti-British clergyman support freethinking women that when one of his parishioners, angry that his wife had dared join the "enemy" Church of England, refused to allow her to ride the family horse to services, Dr. Mather gave the woman his own horse so she could worship independently, as she chose—at his very own congregation's nemesis.

CHAPTER 2

THE THING THAT THEIR NEIGHBORS SAY FIRST ABOUT Joe and Melanie Kelly is what makes the story poignant and complicates one's sympathies: "They were not your typical Darien parents." "He was a *plumber*, for God's sake." "They came from different backgrounds. I think her parents were . . . society. And he—well, he came from Southfield Village, a *very* poor place (now it's all black!)—the 'projects' of Stamford."

When you hear this, of course, you want to shout Good for them! However, although social class still exists as a handily first-grabbed-at descriptor in Darien, the family's dynamic appears to have had nothing to do with class but, rather, with rage, passivity, fear, humiliation, power, and denial. Some families run their course on these charged currents and smoldering accommodations, no matter how similar or dissimilar the parents' social backgrounds.

Joe Kelly is, indeed, a smart, ambitious, hardworking local-turned-prosperous property owner. He owns ten two- and three-family houses in town, which, an associate believes, "he bought in the seventies and eighties for $30,000 to $40,000 and turned them into $200,000 houses: that's how he scored." And he is a successful plumbing contractor who, though he favors herringbone tweeds and blue blazers in his nonworking hours, never stopped being a plumber—who *still* goes out on jobs himself. It is an attractive persona— Hollywood uses it a lot (think of Robert De Niro in his Armani suit and hard hat in *Falling in Love):* the blue-collar million-aire.

Today, at fifty-seven, Joe Kelly is a ruggedly handsome man with thick salt-and-pepper hair, deep-set eyes, and an intense, brooding expression that sometimes gives one the impression that he is about to explode. After you've observed him seated and he stands up, his medium-short height surprises; the seething energy in his face almost demands more inches.

One can imagine that forty years ago—when he graduated from Stamford High School, the son of a poor father who patronized the local pubs, on his way to trade school—his good looks were even more pronounced. He took some classes at the University of Pittsburgh and there, it is said, he met Melanie Lee Reisdorf, a delicately pretty, young blond Penn-sylvanian, a year his junior. Her parents, Jane and Russell Reisdorf, were wealthy. A neighbor remembers the "huge difference" between the two sets of family members that attended Alex's older brother Chris's funeral in October 1991—"Joe's family were loud and sort of wacky and wore big flower prints and big glasses and were talking to everybody, and Melanie's were staid, straitlaced and proper."

They married when they were in their early twenties. According to what a confidante of Melanie Kelly told a mutual friend, "Melanie fought her parents to marry him. I don't think they were ever happy about it." Interestingly, the couple, rather than remaining on her turf, moved to his, but to its far tonier side—to the very community a poor, ambitious boy from Stamford would both resent and aspire to: Darien. Joe Kelly might have thought he would take on the snobs on their own playing ground.

Their first child, a son they named Christopher, was born on May 12, 1965; a second son, whom they named Alex Andrew, followed on May 8, 1967. Both little boys were button-nosed, cherubic, with deep-set eyes and chiseled, even features.

A year after Alex was born, Joe Kelly, at twenty-seven, established Darien Heating and Plumbing. (The concern still bears that name.) It quickly became successful, by dint of his command of his trade, his shrewd business sense, and his personal service to his customers. "If you turned around and said, 'My faucet doesn't work,'" says a customer, "he'd come right over on Saturday night and fix it; the other plumbers wouldn't come 'til Monday." "Hardworking," "very helpful," "very charming" are the adjectives most people who have used his services use to describe Joe Kelly. He is spoken of enthusiastically—the "charming" invariably emphasized.

But some who worked for Joe attribute his success to a combination of good *and* less-good traits. "Joe is driven by money—that's what he lives for and breathes for, that's all he cares about," says an ex-employee. "He'd work hard all day and when he came home he'd do *more* work; he never had a secretary for his business. He never laid back with his kids." (Others corroborate this image of Joe as always working, almost never relaxed.) "It was Melanie who did everything with the boys," the man continues. "Took them on skiing trips to Vermont, alone. Joe didn't have patience with them."

Some feel that Joe Kelly harbored a chip on his shoulder in a town with its fair share of Princeton and Dartmouth alumni. "I think he had a hard time with the class thing," says an executive's son whose parents used his services. "He was from that whole macho background and he's going in and being a laborer for those guys who, if he had 'em in the ring, he'd probably kick their lights out. Those men whose houses he was plumbing were educated. And he wasn't. And he knew it. Was he insecure about it? No. I would say his stance was, 'Fuck em.'" But others recall him being less cavalier about this disparity—more reverential. "He used to say, 'I don't care how successful I get. If there's one thing I've always wished, it's that I had a college education—a *full* college education,'" says the daughter of a neighbor. "He definitely expressed that regret, more than once."

Like many self-made men with such feelings, he poured his own unmet ambitions and dreams into one son. Alex—the most charming, the brightest, the most brilliantly athletic of the three*—was the chosen vessel. "It was always Alex—'Alex will get a wrestling scholarship; Alex will go to Harvard'—it was never Chris. Chris he wrote off; Chris could never please him," Chris's friend Jay Bush says. Especially as he got older and suffered bad breaks (some self-inflicted), "Chris needed a hug from his dad, needed a 'good job!' and he never got it." Yet if Alex was the recipient of his father's expectations, something was off in the sending of the message. He never behaved like a boy who believed that his father believed in him.

Alex's mother, Melanie Lee Kelly, is the parent that Alex most resembles. Her face, framed today by dry silver-blond hair, is as fine-boned as faces get: the nearly ski-jump nose, the very thin lips, the eyes that are almost Slavic. Today, in her middle fifties, she seems drawn and tired. But those who knew her when she was a young mother in the unpretentious Holmes School neighborhood near the Darien-Stamford line where the family always lived, note with concern how much she has aged and remember her as a softer-looking, vivacious, and lovely woman.

Back then—in her regulation wardrobe of khaki slacks, argyle sweater over turtleneck, "and headband—*definitely* the headband—she was glamorous," a neighborhood young woman remembers. "Really, really preppy-looking and natural-looking, but *glamorous*. And cute and funny, affectionate

---

*A third son, Russell, would be born in 1974.

toward her husband and toward the boys. In fact, once when they were in junior high and high school, Chris and Alex had a party at the house and one of the boys almost came *on* to Mrs. Kelly—he couldn't believe she was their *mother!* She was fun and likable and he was really charming though hard to get to know. When you'd walk into their house he'd be sitting there smoking his pipe and he'd say, 'Well, hel*lo,* how *are* you?' in a tone of voice that I guess you'd call somberly flirtatious."

Others say (though not without affection) that Melanie Kelly was distracted, as if something—some preoccupation—kept impinging on her sense of punctuality. A friend remarks: "Melanie was a sweetheart but she was spacey—she was definitely out there, in her own zone. And she was *always* late—late getting the kids to school, late with dinner. That was just Melanie: If you were invited for dinner at six, you were lucky to eat by eight-thirty."

Still, "Joe and Melanie were a striking couple," another neighbor says. "People liked being around them."

They "moved up" in life, as couples are supposed to do: Their first home in Darien was a modest one on Hecker Avenue, near the police station; they sold that and moved to a large old house on Georgian Lane, regally situated at the end of a line of more ordinary development homes on small lots squeezed next to one another. Its living room was appointed in the rich dark woods and stained glass popular in the seventies. Well-placed touches of color brightened the traditional furnishings. "Melanie was definitely not a bohemian, but they did have an aesthetic—they were a little more granola than straight preppy Talbots," says a neighbor. Next, they moved up the block, to an elegant large yellow clapboard house on Christie Hill Road dramatically set, through a sprinkling of trees, far back from the road and in the center of several acres. The Kellys began acquiring a collection of early American paintings and antiques, of which Joe was particularly proud— boastful, some thought.

Although he was certainly not rich by Darien's own, extreme

standards, Joe Kelly had made it—and he was appropriately gratified. "Not bad for a plumber, huh?" he would say, of his shrewdly acquired properties and his increasingly elegant accommodations, to his wife's parents.

But the neighborhood he and Melanie chose to raise their children in was homey and friendly, even though it did boast several expensive private roads as well as Wee Burn. Here, the adults did not have affairs, as they did over in Tokeneke and Long Neck Point; kids with Popsicles in hands and feet dangling from bike pedals dotted the curbs. It was much more a typical middle-class neighborhood than the rest of Darien. Every Fourth of July, there was a block party. Families dressed up in Revolutionary War costumes—as drummer boys and militiamen. Melanie Kelly wrapped red, white, and blue crepe paper over the handlebars of all the kids' bicycles. The street party spilled into the home of Junius and Marcia Clark, whose four children—daughters Jennifer and Meg and, especially, sons Junius and Cyrus (Junie and Cy)—would remain close with the Kelly boys. Dixieland music blared from the Clarks' stereo loudspeakers. At a time—the 1970s—when much of the rest of wealthy America had flirted with antiestablishment politics and was enamored with "Me decade" blandishments, Christie Hill was a bastion of Andy Hardy America and unembarrassed patriotism.

The Kellys' next-door neighbors on Christie Hill were the Pinto family, who were even more uncharacteristic of Darien than they. Pool-cleaning-business magnate Dominic Pinto was, like Joe Kelly, a rough-hewn, self-made patriarch in a polished, inherited-money town. The Pintos were "characters": In an act that caused a neighborhood uproar, they briefly kept a tiger for a pet in the backyard.

As the Kelly and Pinto boys grew up, the Pinto house was always ringed by expensive cars, snowmobiles, and motorcycles. When they became teenagers, Russell Pinto, the son who was Alex's age, would drive Alex around in his prized Mazda RX-7, taking the winding country lanes at almost a hundred miles an hour. "Russ was known as a rich, spoiled kid, but he definitely was not a Buffy [country club boy]," a classmate says. "He was a hard partyer in high school—always one of the last ones to make it home at night." Russ and Alex were best friends. "Russ was gangly, bad-complexioned, and wore expensive clothes that fit him poorly, while Alex was catalogy-handsome," the classmate continues. Thus, Russ was an unintended foil for his friend's charisma.

"It wasn't a Darien Country Club or Wee Burn life that Joe Kelly lived," says Joe Kelly's old friend Frank Heral. "It was very down-to-earth. Every year Joe would get a table at the 'Honor Athlete of the Year' dinner some sports group held at a restaurant in Norwalk. He'd invite me and his friend Bob Clark, who owns the gas station in town, and we'd have a great time. Same with the West Point games. A big bunch of us had a potluck dinner. Everyone would bring something, we'd get into a rented RV—I made the arrangements; I had to stay sober to drive—and we'd drive down the Merritt. Get to the game. Grill the food. Drink. Throw the football around, watch the game, and drive home again. Joe Kelly was a great guy."

Heral pauses, then adds: "The only critical thing I can say about Joe is, sometimes when he had a few drinks, he needled me more than I wanted to be needled."

One young man also noticed that "Joe Kelly was definitely the heavy. Mrs. Kelly was sweet, soft, innocent, nice—the parent who tried to smooth things over." Up and down the hill, people whispered about Joe Kelly's temper. A neighbor's daughter says: "My impression is that she has always been tremendously dominated by him."

To those who observed her in the neighborhood during the 1970s and early 1980s, Melanie Kelly seemed at a perennial loss to handle her inordinately active young sons. "They were real physical kids, Chris and Alex, and just not very responsive to what people wanted them to do," one neighbor remembers.

"They didn't have any self-discipline. You'd go over to the Kelly house and the boys were always screaming, running, hitting each other. You know how Erma Bombeck did these little vignettes of the crazy family? Well, magnify that by about a hundred—that was the Kelly boys. It wasn't that the boys were evil or mean or plotting all the time; they just had *so* much adrenaline. Their mother couldn't control them. She just *couldn't* cope with it. We'd be at the house and the boys would be running amok and Melanie would come out of the kitchen with a plate of freshly made chocolate cookies. It was like she was blocking out what was happening."

As a Holmes School first and second grader, Chris Kelly was always getting into fights—"full-out, punching fights," a classmate remembers. He was such a handsome little boy—the sparkling blue eyes, dark hair, straight nose, and smattering of freckles; many thought him more classically handsome than Alex. Yet Chris lacked his younger brother's social facility, his ability to use his energy to make himself the center of things. Instead, Chris was insecure and hot-tempered—the class bully, the feared outcast. Chris's pugnaciousness instilled terror in other children—when he accidentally took home one child's baseball glove, the child preferred to go without the mitt the whole season rather than ask Chris to return it.

As the Kelly boys matured, the contrast between Chris and Alex heightened. A police officer who had encounters with both boys as teenagers expressed it this way: "Alex was smooth, charming, social. Chris—poor Chris: He was everything Alex wasn't: rough around the edges, a sweet guy but with a nasty streak—a headbutter."

But even as an adorable six year old, Alex's behavior contained moments that startled observers. He did things that other children would not dream of doing—and not merely because he was more of a risk-taker than they were, but, rather because, even at six, he seemed to have acquired a sadistic streak. One neighborhood child was at the Kelly house one day, playing with Alex and the family's pet dachshunds. All of a sudden, Alex picked up one of the dogs by its *tail* and, while the dog yelped in pain, he twirled the heavy little animal around and around as if it were a lasso and he were a cowboy.

The young guest was taken aback by this gratuitous cruelty, but remembers being even more stunned by "Mr. Kelly's response to Alex: He let out the most terrifying scream I'd ever heard. But then, I guess what Alex did merited that kind of screaming."

"I didn't know why at the time, but as long as I remember I felt pity for Melanie Kelly," says a female neighbor. "She was just always tired. Frazzled. Overwhelmed by her life." When Alex was seven and Chris nine, Melanie was expecting again; and this neighbor remembers a very pregnant Melanie Kelly sitting at the Fourth of July party among the other neighbor-hood mothers. "They were cooing, 'Isn't this exciting?' about the baby. But what was striking was that Melanie, after saying, 'Yes, it's exciting,' just kept repeating, 'I want it to be a girl; oh, I want it to be a girl, *so* badly.' It was odd that she'd come out and say that. Pregnant women usually say, 'I just want it to be healthy.'"

It was an awkward moment, for Melanie seemed to be expressing, far more bluntly than her tactful friends ever would, how unusually trying her boys were—how *stuck* she felt with them. "There was just this *desperation* in her face—it's stuck in my mind for years. You could just see her thinking, 'Oh God, *please* let it be a girl this time!' I felt so sorry for her."

Six weeks later, on August 15, 1974, Melanie Kelly gave birth to a third son. She and Joe named him Russell Thomas. He would turn into a blond, blue-eyed child, bearing a notable resemblance to his mother. A young man given to wearing dreadlocks, he lived for a number of years as a ski bum in Colorado and spent the winter of 1997 in Alex's old ski haunt, La Grave, France. "Russell and Chris were extremely genu-ine," a close family friend characterizes. "Alex always had a different personality. I would call it '*deceptively* charming.'"

* * *

Middlesex Swim Club—which featured paddle courts, tennis courts, and a pool—was a club anyone could join. A "starter club." People joked that it was "one step up from Weed Beach" in exclusivity. "Darien is so rich that you were thought of as poor if you belonged to Middlesex," recalls the daughter of an executive of a major beverage corporation. "You know a town has a problem when they separate people by country clubs, and Darien did just that." This young woman's family, like many others in town, belonged to Middlesex as well as another, "better" country club. But Middlesex was the only club Joe and Melanie Kelly belonged to.

At Middlesex, young Alex distinguished himself as a brilliant young swimmer. Still, the trophies he accumulated did little to turn him into a model country club boy, and the energy he expended in competitive events left him curiously unsated. He was a limit-pusher at Middlesex: always trying to sneak into the adult swim. Always being banished from the pool area for one prank or another.

By the middle 1970s, there was a teenage drug culture thriving in the suburbs surrounding New York City, especially the middle- and lower-middle-class hamlets of New Jersey, lower Westchester County, and Long Island. Connecticut townspeople thought themselves above the fray of the déclassé suburban infatuation with the recreational culture that was now holding forth in the discotheques, gay bathhouses, and downtown punk palaces of unsleeping Manhattan.

But in fact, drugs were all over Darien. They were being brought in from suppliers from New York and Bridgeport and were rounded up and redistributed by some of the residents of the Allen O'Neil Houses, the middle-income housing neighborhood near the Darien Fire Department in Noroton Heights. The O'Neil houses qualified as Darien's wrong side of the tracks. Allen O'Neil is where the kids who dealt cocaine, LSD, methamphetamines, and, of course, marijuana would go to meet their suppliers. Kids like Chris Kelly. The drugs were then sold to Darien High students as well as to some particularly precocious kids at Middlesex and Mather Junior High Schools.

After school, these kids would take a bag full of their newly purchased contraband, a book of matches, and either a "bat" (a small pipe) or a long glass water-pipe-styled "bong," and they'd tramp into the dense, scratchy woods, which conveniently shielded their mothers' eyes and noses from suspicion. Some daring junior high kids made forays into the woods *before* school.

It was, however, only the very, very rare *elementary* school student in Darien who did drugs. And Chris Kelly's little brother, nine-and-a-half-year-old fourth grader Alex Kelly, was one of them.

A couple of years later, according to several neighbors, Alex, together with his best friend and another neighborhood boy who was nicknamed "The Eskimo," began smoking marijuana regularly in a clearing called the Frog Pond, which was arrived at by trudging along a road called Bumpalong Path. (The woods near Christie Hill were rife with names that seemed to be straight out of *Winnie the Pooh.*)

Alex and "the Eskimo" later had another, more legitimate precociousness: They were the linebacker and running back, respectively, of the Holmes School Raiders. Most elementary schools do not have football teams; the right time for that sport's introduction, in terms of boys' physical ability to master the game and its physical risks, is thought by most athletic coaches to be junior high or high school. But Darien offered modified football to twelve-year-olds.

The two boys supposedly smoked marijuana before games. The result? "They were like *animals;* they were psychos; I mean that in a positive way—they were *great players!*" recalls neighbor Tom Kelly, who was a year younger and who was awed by them. But the parents were not so enthusiastic. Remembers another neighbor: "At the junior football league, the other parents were getting upset—the little kids were getting beat up by Alex. He couldn't control himself. He *wasn't* going to lose.

"Alex was always just a little too physical."

By the time Alex was thirteen and in eighth grade, he was brazen enough to smoke dope on the way to school. Neighbor Tom Kelly remembers "waiting for the school bus and Alex walks up to the *school bus,* smoking a joint! I thought, 'Wow, that kid's *crazy!'* Al Kelly was the kind of kid you could get intimidated by, but you wanted to be friends with him. He was a cool kid, a wild man." So Tom Kelly fell into the role of the admiring but sometimes taken-aback and wary younger buddy.

Eventually, the taken-aback side would outgrow the boyish admiration, and as Tom Kelly matured and gained an adult's conscience and sense of integrity, he would stop being silent about his friend Alex Kelly. And that principled position would inform Tom's testimony at Alex's retrial.

As a boy, however, Tom was game to be taken where Alex led him. One day Alex and a friend invited Tom and two other neighborhood kids to go into the woods with them. Tom remembers being handed the bong, putting the mouthpiece to his lips, inhaling, holding his breath, then keeling over and "coughing my brains out thinking, 'Never again, never again!'" while the older boys laughed and razzed him.

Tom Kelly is today the quintessential young Darien gentleman-homeboy: neatly ponytailed, in a band, a bartender at Back Street, and slyly funny.* Would there be an "again" for Tom Kelly and his friends in the Christie Hill crowd? Sure, but not until high school.

And it was during high school, when dope-smoking was part

---

*When Thomas Puccio, cross-examining Tom Kelly (known to friends as "T.K.") at the May-June 1997 retrial, sought to get the witness's rock 'n' roll image across to the jury by asking if he had recently purchased the suit he was wearing, Tom cheerfully shot back: "You looked so good in your suit, I thought I'd get one."

of many Darien kids' repertoire, that two good friends were with Alex in his basement one afternoon indulging when the sounds above made it suddenly clear that Mr. Kelly had come home early. Alex walked upstairs to greet his father as the other two boys waited in the basement. According to the less-close friend, the other jumped up and said, "Let's get out of here!" As the two walked tensely upstairs, they noticed that neither Alex nor his father were in the house any longer.

"Where is he?" the friend who knew the family's habits well was asked by the other.

"He's out behind the hedges, with his dad," the close friend answered. "And he's definitely getting swatted with the belt."

No wonder, the boy who heard this thought, that Alex had always seemed so afraid of his father.

It was "weakness" on Melanie Kelly's part, a sympathetic friend believes, that kept her from knowing quite how to intervene—to curb either her sons' increasingly disturbing behavior or her husbands' toughness with them. As time went on she appeared to become more defensive about the boys, and she carved out a world of activities for herself that provided a redeeming measure of control, sociability, and philanthropy. She loved having the girls in the neighborhood over—"she seemed starved for female companionship," says a woman who, with her friend, visited Melanie as a young teenager. They would visit and help her with her groceries; she made them popcorn and engaged them in talk about their lives. She was a concerned listener and she seemed to let her guard down with them. There was a sense that all was not right in her life, that there was sorrow.

Melanie was active in the Red Cross Blood Drive and in the Darien Junior League. But her most fulfilling activity was her political work as a member of Darien's Republican Town Committee. In Darien, "people who would anywhere else be Democrats are liberal Republicans," says an attorney and town leader, "and that's what Melanie was." She was quiet at meetings, voting against the conservatives in battles for First Selectman but not articulating her opinion in discussion. Yet simply *going* to those meetings seemed important to her. "I had heard that Joe was a strict disciplinarian—we had all heard that—and everything about Melanie's manner suggested someone who was more lenient," says the attorney. "So I sensed there was a tension there, with the childrearing. But we never met Joe. He never came to the meetings. I don't even know if he was a Republican."

A young woman who observed Alex growing up says, "He definitely had a sexuality to him, very early. Girls thought he was cute and in fifth grade, he declared that Rod Stewart song 'If You Want My Body (If You Think I'm Sexy . . .)' his favorite song—he played it a hundred times in a row and he sang along with it." By the time he was in seventh grade, a girl from across town was telling people she was sexually involved with him. However, whereas most young boys might boast of conquest, Alex was not only silent but, as one neighborhood friend attuned to the social gradations on Christie Hill puts it, "he probably would have denied it. He wanted a 'Muffie' [an upper-crust Darien girl] for a girlfriend. He was ashamed of her."

Alex's ascension as a star athlete, at both football and swimming, was hard on his older brother's ego. Chris had little *but* athleticism to succeed at, yet Alex was now outpacing him. Friends could see Chris casting about for an identity that would preserve his seniority and machismo. So when the opportunity struck to defend his brother's honor, he leaped at it.

One day in junior high, Alex had sprained his ankle during swim practice and was now in a cast and on crutches. Two neighborhood girls decided to tease Alex—and Chris—by pretending that one of them had also broken *her* ankle. The improvised plaster ankle cast and the borrowed crutches had the Kelly boys believing for a day or two that Alex had a compadre in the injury department. Then, Chris Kelly uncovered the ruse, while he and the girls were sitting outside one of the girls' houses. He blew his top and started swearing. The girls tried to explain: It was just a joke! They were *kidding!* The boys should be flattered that they had gone to such lengths for them!

But Chris was not placated. He picked up a full can of soda and, from a distance of several yards, hurled it straight at one girl's forehead. The girl ducked in time, avoiding serious injury. But she was left shaken, understanding how deeply Chris Kelly's pride could be wounded, and seeing the fury that their perceived humiliation could trigger in him.

But if Chris's reaction to humiliation was rage, Alex's was terror. And it was a second incident that took place while Alex was in the cast that reveals just how much terror Alex was vulnerable to. As recalled by the neighborhood worker:

Alex was idling with some friends outside a neighbor's house one afternoon at about 5 P.M. when Joe Kelly's red Corvette came screeching around the corner and ground to a halt in front of the spot on the lawn where his son and the son's friends were sitting. Joe Kelly's flashy car was itself a Darien anomaly; the screech of its tire rubber made it twice as intrusive. Next, Alex's father did what parents in this quiet neighborhood did not do—he screamed at the top of his lungs at his son:

"What the hell are you doing down here?! You're supposed to be home! Your mother and I are going out! You're supposed to be baby-sitting Russell!" Joe Kelly gunned his car up Christie Hill, shouting, "Get home *now!*" over his shoulder.

"Alex went into a *fit* of panic," the observer recalls. "He *panicked*. He was choked up. He was crying." The observer watched Alex raise himself up, push his crutches under his armpits, and agitatedly tell his concerned-seeming friends to stay where they were. But the friends insisted on helping him up the incline.

Alex was ahead of his able-bodied friends the whole time, and during the entire clomping, bumpy, awkward march, he was whimpering and crying. He crutched up his house's long driveway and entered the house through the sliding glass side door. Before walking in, Alex turned and whispered, "Go! Get out of here!" to the friends who were still trailing him.

The friends hid from view but remained on the property.

And then: "Mr. Kelly comes down the steps from the family room and *screams* at Alex, swearing at him. And he picks up an encyclopedia-sized book and he throws it—Alex is shrieking— at Alex's ankle: *right* at the cast, right at the injury."

The neighborhood kids ran off. Later, someone who knew the boys speculated: "If rape is about being angry at women, well, I think Alex became angry that his mother was never able or willing to protect him from the things his father did to him."

But the truth is, Melanie Kelly was never in a very good position to protect Alex. The preoccupation, the lateness, the vague sorrow, the retreat to political meetings—they all had a reason. Perhaps it was that she, like Alex and Chris, may also have been the victim of Joe Kelly's violence.

Jay Bush, one of Chris Kelly's best friends toward the end of Chris's life, and a former employee of Joe Kelly, used to be very troubled by signs that Chris was violent toward his girlfriends. Chris apparently tried to choke one woman and gave his last girlfriend black eyes. Bush says: "I'd say, 'Chris, how can you hit a girl?' And Chris would say, 'I know it's not right, but it's like a reflex. My dad used to do it all the time to my mom. It's a natural reaction. I get mad and the next thing I know I use my hands. I know it's wrong but I can't control it.'"

Chris's own acts of domestic violence were linked to alcohol consumption. "It was always when he was drinking that he lost control and hit women," Bush says. "A light would switch on Chris's temper, like a chemical thing in the brain. Same with Alex. A friend of ours' mother said she would see Alex"— as a teenager—"sitting in the kitchen drinking and then all of a sudden she'd notice the mood change; he'd become a completely different person. She said it was scary."

Bush witnessed, in the Kelly home, the violence that was only glimpsed by others. "Joe would come home from working hard, the three kids would be acting up, going off the wall— and he'd take off his belt. Or he'd slam Chris against the wall. I saw it. As kids, growing up, we used to see the kids getting beaten by Joe all the time. Belts were a popular way. Fists. Slamming them up against walls. In front of friends."

Thus, humiliation was part of the punishment. No wonder Chris responded to teasing by hurling soda cans; ridicule was a fraught issue. Later, Joe's humiliation of Chris in front of others would help trigger a chain of events leading Chris to a tragic, self-inflicted death. Whereas Alex, the more resourceful, less star-crossed son, would learn to humiliate others, especially girls and women.

When he was in junior high, Alex developed a nemesis at Middlesex Swim Club: the female lifeguard—a pretty, forthright, teenage girl several years his senior. The two had a pitched battle. The lifeguard's younger sister remembers her "coming home from work day after day, so angry from having had another rough day with Alex Kelly. Her boss at Middlesex was a big, strong guy—a football coach. He'd have to come in and help because she couldn't handle Alex all by herself."

"Alex did sexually harrassing things to the lifeguard," the beverage executive's daughter remembers. One day, after the lifeguard had been "riding Alex all summer—kicking him out of the club every day," Alex decided to get back at her. "With a handful of us kids watching," the young woman recalls, "Alex walked up to her and unsnapped the top of her bathing suit. It went *chooiing!*—and off it popped. She went, 'Oh, my God!' She was horrified and shocked for a second. She covered herself up. Then she looked like she didn't know what the hell to do—should she be pissed off, or laugh like the rest of us? We were all too surprised to do anything else *but* laugh. Anyway, it wasn't like she had big boobs—she was washboard-flat. So we treated it like no big deal. And Alex was *definitely* laughing."

Another young woman who observed Alex during these years believes "boys got a vicarious thrill from Alex because he would do things that they could never get away with doing." Later, a friend noticed Alex grabbing girls' breasts and snapping their suit tops at Weed Beach. Hey, what the heck—it was funny. And it was just part of being Alex.

One day, two of the young neighborhood girls who liked to visit Melanie Kelly had a surprise for her: They rode a pair of horses over. Mrs. Kelly seemed thrilled. She patted one of the horses on the nose, adjusted the stirrups, mounted, and seized the reins. Her body erect, her hair blond against the green trees and blue sky, she trotted a bit, then broke into a canter. "She had always had that worn-down look," one of the girls later remarked to a friend. "But now she got up on that horse and started riding around, and her whole body changed. She had so much control. She seemed totally liberated.

"It was the one time in my life I saw her truly happy."

By the time Alex graduated from Holmes School and entered Middlesex Middle School, which drew half the kids in Darien (Mather drew the other half, from the more consistently wealthy neighborhoods such as Tokeneke), he had an aura of magnetism about him. Within that stately red-brick Georgian building, encircled by a lawn of pines and evergreens, the boys thought him invincible and the girls found him adorable. And he was precocious. "He was starting to get the clout with the boys that would carry into high school," a female contemporary says, "because he could get any girl he wanted. He was definitely on the prowl."

One day, a new girl in town—the daughter of a corporate transferee from the Midwest, as so many in the town were—went over to the Kelly house with some friends. Her name was Jamie and she remembers, "Alex made this picnic lunch and we went out into the woods, behind where they had their tree house. We were really young—twelve, I think—and we were just fooling around and stuff, and I was still a virgin and I had never really fooled around, and he wanted to keep going. I told him no. But he didn't stop. For a second I was worried. So I told him, again, to stop. And he stopped right away, and everything was fine." Jamie's brother says, today, "My sister was always the one girl in town tough enough not to take crap from anyone."

In eighth grade, Alex acquired a ninth-grade girlfriend named Callie Cusack. Callie was from a "better" family than the crosstown girl who embarrassed him. She was, as a peer recalls, "a sweet, caring person," a classic "good girl."

Middlesex Middle School was divided between a blue-collar or druggy crowd—the "burnouts," who wore Led Zeppelin T-shirts and long hair—and the social crowd who were clean-cut and status-conscious. The boys from that crowd wore pink or blue Oxford pin-stripe shirts and wide-wale cords. "You had to be one or the other—it was black and white; there was no crossover," says an alumna.

Alex started out with the burnouts, but as one new boy in town, Jim Hunter, noticed, *"everyone* in the social crowd liked Alex, too, and soon he wanted to fit in with them so he started making an effort to dress nicer. Then he got this beautiful, blond, nice, rich, smart, A-student girlfriend—not his type at all." Her name was Paige Ginn, and if Callie Cusack was a good girl, Paige was more than that—a country club princess, the ultimate Muffie. When Alex started going with her, he dressed like he just walked off the set of *Beverly Hills 90210*."

Jim Hunter was intrigued by Alex's ability to look so clean-cut, acquire the prettiest, most straight-arrow girlfriend, and yet *still* flout the rules, *still* smoke dope every day. Alex seemed to make his own rules. One day he chucked his cords and shirt to come to school dressed in an American flag, like Abbie Hoffman! The two played ninth-grade football together—"Alex was aggressive though he talked a bigger line than what he'd do. He played only defense. Linebacker. He made a lot of tackles. He could hit pretty hard.

"He *liked* hitting people hard. That kind of thing would get him excited."

Jim was having a hard time fitting in in Darien. As another then-junior-high Midwestern émigré recalls: "Everyone went around acting like, 'If you aren't rich and from New England, you don't exist.'" For Jim, a lanky, laconic kid whose father had grown up as a farmboy and had worked himself up to executive status, "it was culture shock. Where we used to live, I never heard of a 'preppy.' I had never been to a school where everyone dressed the same: the Izod shirts, the Oxford pinstripes, the wide-wale cords, and all that junk. I got picked on because I parted my hair in the center. So I changed the part in my hair and I got the right clothes. I wanted to fit in and I wanted to have money."

Jim would hang out at Alex's house after school and talk to Mrs. Kelly. "His mom was pretty much one of the nicest people I ever met. She would do anything for Alex. She was totally good-natured—she would joke around. You could tell her anything. If she knew Alex was out drinking or something, I sensed it wasn't a big deal to her." As for Alex's father, "He wasn't around very much but when he was around he was stern and serious. He wasn't one to joke around with and I heard rumors that he had a temper."

Jim and Alex, and a lot of the Middlesex kids, spent weekends following a pattern that would continue—and escalate—as standard operating procedure all through their high-school years: calling around to see whose parents were going out of town for the weekend. "That was the big buzz—who's havin'

the party?" Jim remembers. There was *always* a party, sometimes several. And, like ants to a honey pot, all the kids flocked
to it. There were also other mellow places to chill with six-
packs and bongs: the Wee Burn golf course, the town graveyard.

And once kids got their licenses, they piled into cars and
went to the beach—Weed Beach—on the other side of town.
Beautiful, serene Weed Beach, whose flat vista gave off to
tranquil Long Island Sound, was Action Central for the kids
who drank and smoked cigarettes and pot—which was, it
often seemed, almost everybody. The kids would sit on The
Rocks and The Hill, crank tunes from their cars (turning the
radio up to maximum volume and leaving the doors and trunk
open), and party until the cops descended. And whenever the
town marching band played, the kids relished the opportunity
to taunt their favorite uniformed nemesis, hardliner Officer
Griffith, who was one of the band's horn players. (The Dead
would be cranked up in an attempt to drown out the John
Philip Sousa.) Such skirmishes were a staple of town life; with
a few sizzling exceptions (in the form of patrolman-Muffie
romances), The Cops versus The Kids was Darien's two-
hundred-ten-years-later restaging of the War of Indepen-
dence. The cops thought the kids were self-destructive spoiled
brats on overdrive, and the kids thought the cops were jealous
townies with nothing better to do than set up bogus speed
traps and maraud their parties. (Moses Mather was surely
turning in his grave at the woeful descent of the moral motives
for battle.)

By this time—the early 1980s—Darien, like most American
towns and suburbs, had suddenly cracked open like a split log,
yielding two types of families: intact and broken. The U.S.
divorce rate had hit an all-time high of about 50 percent in the
late 1970s—the years Alex and his classmates were becoming
teenagers. To a bedroom community so unreservedly based
on the traditional family unit, this social epidemic was like a

boulder hurled through a window. Women who had never prepared for careers as anything other than wife and mother were now scrambling to take jobs—any jobs: as nurses, secretaries, clerks, travel agents—so they wouldn't lose the large, lovely homes which, along with not much more, they'd been court-awarded. These mothers, who had always expected to be home after school, now distractedly handed out latch keys. Older siblings became their younger siblings' babysitters, therapists and—most importantly—liquor suppliers: journeying to the Beverage Barn or the Liquor Locker for a couple of kegs of beer and then some.

Thus stocked, suddenly fatherless and empty-by-day homes were thrown wide open, the host or hostess calculating that the cachet of providing a hot spot made up for the social status lost in their family's unraveling. Thus, the Darien teens—who did not have their own community center (this has since changed) because it was assumed that country clubs served that function—seized parental divorce as a party opportunity. And a sizable opportunity it was. A number of people who were in Darien High in the 1980s estimate that by the time they hit adolescence a third to a half of kids' parents were no longer married to each other.

Close friendships developed between a teenager of an intact family and a teenager of a divorced one. Through such dyads each teen could experience two lives: one in which parents and children remained in their unquestioned power hierarchy and another in which there was suddenly more democracy and parental vulnerability. Like pooling allowances and sharing clothes, such best friends split the difference on their fates: getting a reassuring dose of 1980s-style "Father Knows Best" at one house and a more bracingly untraditional—and conveniently unchaperoned—arrangement at the other.

Brad Lareau and Dave Spadacini exemplified this kind of best friendship. The Darien boys had been inseparable since first grade and when Dave's parents got divorced, "my mom kind of brought Dave into our family," Brad says. "The divorce wasn't easy for him so he was over at our house all the time for a lot of years, and it sort of went both ways: With his dad gone and his mom working, all of a sudden *his* house was a great place to hang out, because he had older brothers who were partying, so I spent whole weekends over there. So I was at his house half of the time, he was at my house half the time—we were *always* together. Everyone liked Dave. He was outgoing, a comedian and a musician and I was more reserved, but we played sports together. We just clicked. We were best friends. We knew we'd be friends for life."*

Dave Spadacini had another close friend, too, a mentor whom he looked up to for his charisma and musicianship: Rick Dawson. The son of a media executive, Rick was one of those kids who came from the Midwest but had found a way to fit into Darien. Although Rick was on the cutting edge of drug consumption and partying at Mather—"I was one of those kids who bought twenty dollars' worth of pot and turned around and sold forty dollars' worth of joints"—his rebelliousness was offset by talent. He was an ace guitarist, favoring the mellow upscale-white-boy sounds of an earlier generation, like Crosby, Stills, Nash and Young—and a natural comic. And, as one young woman recalls, "He was an unthreatening male. You could tell him anything and he wouldn't tell anyone else and he didn't put up a cool front."

"When I met Alex Kelly in eighth grade," Rick says, "he already had a kind of infamy about him. *I* partied, too, but *he* had a reputation of being really hard-core. He could consume *massive* amounts of drugs and alcohol. He wasn't at the point

---

*Four years later—on June 9, 1988—Brad Lareau was driving Dave Spadacini home from their celebration of Brad's twenty-first birthday. The pair had a lot to catch up on—Brad was in college in Colorado and Dave in Rhode Island. Adult life was just starting for them. They had topped off a keg party with a night at Jimmy's Seaside, and as Brad was nearing his block, he and Dave made an impulsive decision to go to a neighborhood party, so Brad turned sharply left instead of right. Brad misjudged the turn, the car ran up a curb, bounced two feet in the air, and hit a tree. Dave Spadacini died instantly.

yet where he was doing dope *in* school—that would come in high school—but he was doing it before and after. This stands out in my mind: I remember saying, 'How old are you?' And he said he didn't know. Then I asked, 'What's your middle name?' and he said he couldn't remember. I thought: This guy is *so* wasted . . .'"

Rick, whose parents joined Country Club of Darien, was fascinated by the hidden side of his new town. Billy Hughes was in his heyday as Darien's athlete outlaw and Rick got a kick out of watching the "awesome-at-everything powerhouse jock walk around town with a girl on his arm. When you heard a fight breaking out at a hockey game, you *knew* it was Billy Hughes." Billy was chased into the woods after he'd allegedly stolen a purse out of a car. Then there was that other champion athlete who, according to Rick, "probably spent more years at Darien High School than any kid in history" and incited jokes that "his coaches were paying off his parole officer."

But while hearing about these mythic bad guys was amusing, seeing examples of Darien machismo up close was unsettling. Rick witnessed an executive father engage his son in a backyard fistfight. "They were slamming each other in the face—it was brutal; it made me sick to my stomach." This same boy once spent a weekend night vandalizing Mather Middle School; when the police showed up, he pleaded hysterically to his accomplice, "Please take *all* the blame—or my father will *kill* me!"

There seemed, to Rick, to be a lot of boys in Darien who were terrified of their fathers but who nonetheless racked up police records. Which side of the inflammatory equation fed the other? Were the boys daring their dads to beat the shit out of them? Or were *they* beating the shit out of their dads by turning out to be hoodlums instead of budding executives? Corporal punishment was more prevalent here than most people imagined—some kids even got *paddled.* Yet these same parents would turn around and replace the cars their drunken kids had totaled: one kid had driven the family Saab into a lake, another had flipped and rolled his parents' BMW, and the next day each was driving around in another nifty vehicle.*

Did the parents not notice how much their kids were bombed out of their senses? As Julia West says, "Those *parties* we had! It horrifies me, thinking about them! How *did* our parents get to sleep at night? *What* did they *think* we were doing? Just going over to our friends' houses to watch TV? We would be in these huge houses with, like, a *hundred* kids there, totally running the place! Eventually the cops would get there but not until at least ten. By then we'd been drinking for hours. College seemed boring after those parties." (One To-keneke couple, dispelling the notion that country-club proper is the opposite of big and excessive, threw their thirty-five-room mansion open to wild parties for their adult friends—and only slightly less wild bashes for whichever of their eight children happened at the time to be teenagers.)

Joe Kelly disdained the rich-kid brattiness he saw around him and he didn't mind telling people so. When he found someone with similar values among his customers, simpatico conversations would spring up between the new-in-town housewife, startled by local custom, and the plumber-gentryman who, despite his wealth, viewed Darien with Stamford-projects disapproval.

"When we moved to Darien from Illinois and my twelve-year-old daughter asked for more allowance because 'all the other kids get fifty dollars a week,' I was shocked! And I told Joe so!" says a woman whose children are now grown. After Joe Kelly finished his work for the day, the two would often stand at her front door, talking about kids and values.

---

*Brad Lareau says: "Not all parents in Darien were like this. A lot of our parents made sure we had solid, work-for-your-allowance-and-get-a-summer-job upbringings. If there was an out-of-town rock concert all my friends were going to and I hadn't saved money for it, tough—I wasn't going. Tom Kelly's and the Clarks' parents also taught them those values."

"He was a hell of a nice guy: down-to-earth, very personable with his customers, didn't put on any kind of airs. I had no idea he and his wife were that well-fixed; he always came over in work clothes. I was worried about raising my kids in Darien. We'd talk about some of the spoiled kids in town who'd drink and drive and wreck their parents' cars. He'd say, 'I never got away with things like that when I was young! Why do these kids have to do all this when there's plenty of money?' He talked about being raised very poor, not with money or comfort but with love."

Yet that vision of his childhood may have been a function of selective memory. A Darienette whose father was raised across the street from Joe Kelly has said that her father remembered seeing Joe Kelly, on many occasions, being hit by his own father.

But the Illinois woman recalls: "We'd talk about the fear we had of our kids being killed in drunk driving accidents and getting into trouble and he'd say things like, 'By the grace of God . . .' that hadn't happened to his boys. He *seemed* like a very good parent."

By the time Chris Kelly was in high school, Joe Kelly must have been resigned to having, in his oldest son, a resolutely downscale scion. Chris was a handsome teenager—some think he resembled the actor Keanu Reeves—but "he never got beyond hanging out with the Italian Holmes School kids: the guys in shop, the motorheads," a friend says. Another calls this as much choice as limitation: "Chris *wanted* to be blue collar. That was his *thing.*" Certainly, though, when a parent has written you off, the least-competitive road seems the safest.

Chris, alone among the members of his family, spoke in "ain't's" and double negatives. He was in Darien High's Alternate Learning Program (ALP), which centered on trade-school courses such as power mechanics. He wore Ozzy Osbourne T-shirts and tattooed his body. (When he broke up with one girl whose name he had so emblazoned, he had the tattoo artist fuse her name's first two letters, ingeniously transforming "LISA" to "USA.")

One night in 1981, when he was sixteen, Chris Kelly pulled out of his friend Jim Kenyon's Brookside Road driveway on his moped and made an impetuous left at a blind corner. A car driven by a clergyman swung around the corner the other way and hit him. Chris was tossed in the air and came down hard. A Darien police officer recalls: "He fought with the ambulance crew and he wouldn't let them do things they needed to do; he fought with his father—he was totally out of control." Partly as a result of his initial resistance to treatment, this officer believes, Chris Kelly sustained a spinal cord injury.

Chris was in a rehabilitative hospital for months; the hospital was too far away for his friends to visit. His life in the hospital became insular and frightening. "His mother was really good about it—very cool in crisis," a friend of Chris's says. "She organized a caravan of about twelve kids to go up there with a cake for his birthday. Mr. Kelly didn't say two words at the party. When things go bad, he seems to keep his mouth shut and not really express himself—except with rage, I guess."

Chris was in traction for about four months, in a wheelchair for several months, and ensconced in a body cast for a number of months after that. "It was so tough on Chris and so sad," says the friend who had the job of driving him around and getting him in and out of his wheelchair. "I think the whole experience made him into a very lonely person."

Chris was left with a permanent limp and chronic pain that threatened to move his already extant drug dependency into deeper channels, especially now that his activities—and his opportunity to shine brighter than his younger brother Alex—were so severely limited. "Before the accident," that same friend says, "Chris had been a great skier and a really good athlete; now he was left with not a lot of things to excel at. He fell into a scary group of bad people.

"At this point, I think Mr. Kelly started *really* giving up on Chris and pinning all his hopes to Alex." Joe's talk of Alex going to Harvard, Alex getting a wrestling scholarship, Alex becoming a lawyer began in earnest—and, perhaps, in desperation.

But some believe that being so summarily written off relieved Chris Kelly. He was off the hook. His acceptance of his social, intellectual and now physical limits left him somehow more at peace with himself. "You'd see him at a party and he was always *so* bombed, but he'd become comical," says a friend who used to be terrified of him when he was the Holmes School bully. "He'd give you a big hug. He was, finally, harmless. Looking back on it now, that's when the brothers began changing places: Chris was getting more mellow and Alex was developing a dark side."

One night Jim Hunter had a group of kids over when his folks were out of town. Alex was one of the crew. The next day, Jim's father approached him with an I-want-to-get-to-the-bottom-of-this look. His silver pen set had vanished from his office. At the time, Jim didn't make any connections.

Jim's parents had become close with another wealthy executive's family—the McGarrys. The McGarrys had a daughter named Mavis, who was Jim's age and in school across town at Mather. Mavis cultivated a fetchingly haphazard look: stringy blond hair, big T-shirts. In a milieu where girls strove to look polished and perfect, she had the audacity to thumb her nose at the rules. In addition, Jim recalled, she didn't pay that much attention to schoolwork. "She was loud, kind of obnoxious, really energetic, talking all the time, and had a lot of charisma," he says. Alex, who was dating Paige and other A-student Muffies, met Mavis through Jim—and disliked her.

The Grateful Dead—the long-ago Palo Alto–based house band for Ken Kesey's Merry Pranksters which had, along with the Jefferson Airplane and Big Brother and the Holding Company, been the preeminent San Francisco psychedelic band during the 1967 Summer of Love—had defied their gelled-in-aspic origins and acquired a second life as a rallying point in the lives of white suburban 1980s teenagers. "Hanging out at the mall didn't answer this new generation's need for human contact and meaning," explains Steve Silberman, coauthor of *Skeleton Key: A Dictionary For Deadheads* and authority on the group and the culture it spawned. "So you had the emergence of what Deadheads call 'trustafarians'—children of affluence who took off their preppy clothes to dress like homeless rastas; who followed the Dead to its shows and got community, spirituality (and, if you were goodlooking, lots of relationships) without anyone asking about their family tree or their trust funds."

The parking-lot scene at the Dead shows—kids drinking beer, smoking joints, and dropping acid; dancing on top of their cars, playing the footbag game hackysack; buying and selling everything from drugs to jewelry to dancing-bear-logoed T-shirts—was, during most of the 1980s, a rite shared primarily among college students. In 1987, however, MTV aired a daylong *Day of the Dead,* and high school students started joining the older hordes driving four and five hours a weekend to Dead shows. But the Darien High kids were ahead of their time. They were regularly driving to Dead shows in the early 1980s.

"The mellow, not-too-extreme music, the casual partying: it just fit in with our lives," says Brad Lareau. "I suppose today we'd be listening to Phish. Back then, it was the Dead." Rick Dawson says: " 'Scarlet Begonias,' 'Fire On The Mountain,' 'Terrapin Station,' 'Friend of the Devil'—we loved those songs! What spoke to us about the Dead? It was music from Woodstock; there was something trippy about it, especially when we were getting exposed to pot and psychedelics." Yet it was the form, not the substance, of sixties values that appealed to the Darien kids. Says one of Alex's cohorts: "Acid was not a spiritual thing; it was not about changing the world for us. It was just another buzz, another goof." Rick Dawson agrees: "Peace and love had nothing to do with it. Dropping out and the counterculture had nothing to do with it. The kids in Darien knew they would grow up to be like their fathers—trading stocks and bonds, marrying the right people, making big money—but they wanted a little time to be separate from their parents, to be rebels."

Rick played rhythm guitar in Darien's first Dead-style band. One day during a practice break the band was hanging out at a pond in Tokeneke and haggling over what to call themselves when one of the group threw a bottle cap in the water to hit a fish. "Hey, did you get it?" he was asked. "Nah, I just nicked the fin," came the answer. The band had its name: Nick The Fin.

Rick gave lessons to Dave Spadacini, who took over Rick's position in the band after Rick went on to college. Under first Rick, then Dave, the band played at Darien's annual "Weedstock" at Weed Beach, at the senior prom, at all the parties. "Nick The Fin was the backdrop for all our crazy melodramas," says one of the main female members of Alex's crowd.

One of the biggest events in town was Nick The Fin's bashlike nightly band practice (complete with groupie "Finheads"). It was held at the large Tokeneke estate of a bandmate, a hard-core Deadhead whose wealthy parents could not have been more preppy—the Wee Burn membership, the penchant for lime-green apparel—*and* who were also "the nicest, most quality people," Rick says. "They had great values; the kids all excelled in school; the family didn't possess any of the crap that usually goes with the Darien stereotype. We'd have the music going with eighty kids downstairs, and [the bandmate]'s mom would be pleasantly chatting"—impeccable manners were a great shield for wild-partying teens—"like, '*What* elephant in the basement?'

"Alex," Rick recalls, "was an infamous Deadhead." He and Jim Hunter silk-screened T-shirts with pictures of Jerry Garcia's face on them. One Saturday Jim, Alex, and Rick Dawson got in Rick's car and drove up to Saratoga Springs for a Dead show. They drove to the show in the same way many Darien kids were driving those days: with abject recklessness. Rick recalls: "I had no speedometer, I had no gas gauge. It should have taken us four and a half hours to get there but instead it took us ten. By the time we get to the campsite the three of us were *really* hallucinating. [Jim] was fine but Alex was weird. He had this weird grin on his face. I was getting a little creeped out by him.

"The concert hadn't started yet. We were at a campsite at the edge of the woods. We pitched a tent. We were hanging out, partying with the other Deadheads. We stayed up all night. But, within that time, Alex would . . . *disappear* for big chunks of time: an hour and a half. Two hours. And all of a sudden he would be back. With that stupid smirk on his face. If you asked him where he went, he wouldn't respond, he wouldn't say anything. He had funny silences, come to think of it. Like, all the other guys would talk about sex. Alex never did."

But Rick's strongest memory of that weekend is of something that happened before the threesome drove to Saratoga. "We went to Alex's house—I think for the drugs that he had there. We get to the house. Alex and I go in. His mother is there and she seems kind of quietly upset about something. Alex goes into the other room and all of a sudden his father starts saying something—and Alex is *really* scared. He goes, 'No, Dad!' like he's defending himself against something.

"I wasn't supposed to be watching, but I was. His father did one of these open-handed *smacks* on the side of Alex's head. It wasn't a little slap on the cheek—his dad *clubbed* him on the side of his head! His mother was in the other room, listening—doing the dishes or something and pretending nothing was going on, but you could tell she was thinking about what was happening.

"But she didn't say or do anything to stop it. And afterward

Alex went in his room and came out again and we left for Saratoga and it was like nothing had happened."

In the fall of 1981, right about the time that Chris Kelly had his accident, a thirteen-year-old girl named Margaret, new to town and a Middlesex ninth grader, was hanging around the house while her older sister was having a keg party. She was slightly built and so physically immature she had not even started menstruating. Except for one game of spin the bottle, she had never kissed a boy. She did not dress with special care that day, but the circumstances that developed would leave her remembering, years later, exactly what she was wearing: a pair of beige corduroy pants and a blue sweater.

A boy at the party was standing near Margaret. He pulled a bag of pot out of his pocket. He was good-looking, dark-haired, and he had a bandaged splint on one finger—apparently from a sports injury.

Today, Margaret has a substantial profession and is living in another part of the country, married to a man from a family very prominent there. She told this story to only three people— her sister and two friends—before February 1986. After that time, she remained silent, telling only her husband. This is her exact remembrance of the events that evening: "It was cold, it was dark, the party was going on, the music blasting. He said, 'Do you want to go smoke a little pot?' And I'm like, 'Oh, I'll try some!' I was trying to act cool, because there was an older crowd there."

The boy led Margaret out of the party, across the street, behind a neighbor's house—into the woods. "We were going to sit down and smoke some pot. But we never got to the pot. He slammed me down—pushed me. And then he started kissing me. I was: 'No! I thought we were gonna smoke some pot!'

The next thing Margaret knew, the boy pulled his pants down and put his penis into her mouth. "I was like: No! No! I was choking! I was in shock. I couldn't do anything with it in

61

my mouth. I tried pushing him off me. He said, 'Don't say anything.'"

"He ripped his pants down and then my underwear down. He held me down and covered my mouth so I wouldn't scream." The boy forcibly penetrated Margaret. He raped her. "Then he got up and ran away."

Margaret was left alone in the woods behind the neighbor's house. As to how long she lay there, "I couldn't even tell you. I know it was longer than five minutes." She was so dazed that when she did manage to stand up she did not have the presence of mind to reassemble her clothes. She says: "It was cold but I didn't even notice." She hobbled from the woods to the street like a sleepwalker. "I was walking down the street and people from the party were just pointing at me and laughing. And then I realized: Oh my God, what am I doing? My pants and my underwear were still down around my ankles!" Blood was running down her legs.

Margaret quickly pulled her underwear and her pants up and walked back to her house, where the party was in full swing. She went around to the back door, found her sister, and, while the other kids were still downstairs in the family room and the kitchen, the two dashed upstairs to Margaret's bedroom. Once the door was shut behind them, Margaret burst into tears.

"I remember pulling my pants down and showing my sister all the blood on my legs. My sister said, 'My God!' Then she said, 'Everything will be all right,' and 'I'll find out who did this.'" When Margaret's sister asked her what the boy looked like, Margaret replied: "He had a broken finger."

The sisters vowed not to tell their parents, among other reasons—Margaret smiles ruefully at the lopsided priorities of young adolescents—"because we didn't want to not be able to have any more parties."

The next morning, Margaret ran over to her best friend Louise's house. Louise was a fellow Middlesex ninth grader, also thirteen. Today Louise is a professional woman who lives far away from Darien; whenever news of the Kelly trial makes its way to her local paper she thinks back to that long-ago Saturday morning with her dazed-looking best friend walking in her back door. This is what she remembers: "[Margaret] wasn't crying. She looked stupefied. She told me what happened, but she didn't use the word 'rape'—we didn't *know* the word. She stammered, 'I . . . I . . . think . . . we had sex.' Then she told me the whole story and I knew it was wrong—it *wasn't* what sex was supposed to be, being pushed down in the woods and forced! She said, 'I think I'm pregnant. We have to find a place to get an abortion!'"

Margaret recalls Louise then leaping up and saying, "'I'll get the phone book!' She went in the other room and came back—we were in her den. We locked the door behind us and we put a chair in front of the door to make sure no one would come in." Louise says: "I don't even know *what* we looked up in the yellow pages—'A' for 'Abortion'? 'B' for 'Baby'? *We* were babies!"

Margaret remembers that they turned to "P" for "Pregnancy." She remembers finding several agencies listed, including the local Planned Parenthood. As she picked up the receiver and started to dial, she whispered nervously to Louise: "We can't use our real names! I'll make up a fake one!"

Margaret called Planned Parenthood, but as she started to tell her story in her high little voice, she panicked. "'I think I'm pregnant; what can you do?' I said, and then before they could say anything back, I hung up." She did the same thing with the next clinic listed. The next one. And the next.

Then she set down the phone for the last time. She realized she could not bring herself to finish a conversation with a clinic counselor any more than she could tell her parents what had happened. And, although she had bled, she would not go to a doctor. She and her sister had vowed they would tell no one and now Margaret also swore Louise to secrecy. The two girls did not even know enough about reproduction to understand that since Margaret had not yet started menstruating, it was extremely unlikely that she could be pregnant. Nor did it occur to them that Margaret could get the boy who had done this to her—the mysterious boy with the broken finger—in trouble, big trouble, by reporting him. No. They felt the burden was *all* on them.

On Monday Margaret's sister came home from Darien High School and said, "The boy with the broken finger? His name is Alex Kelly."

Margaret had nightmares in the weeks after the rape. "I would wake up all sweaty." For some reason, she held onto her mud-caked blue sweater—for years preserving it, in exactly the condition it was in that night, in a plastic bag under a pile of other clothes in the bottom drawer of her white bureau, which was inside her closet. "Once in a while I'd check to see if my mother had taken it out of the drawer. She never did. It always stayed where it was."

Margaret is not sure why she saved the sweater. Was it to give her mother an opportunity to find it, question her about it and coax the story out of her? Perhaps. Or did she keep the sweater in order to *avoid* being found out—because sending it to the dry cleaners would have caused her mother to wonder how it got so dirty? (At thirteen, you do not send your own clothes to the cleaners—your mother does. *Nor* do you "lose"—destroy—your clothing without your parents noticing what is missing.) Did she keep it in the drawer as potential evidence against Alex Kelly—and, as such, as a symbol of her power and control over him, which otherwise never *felt* like power and control—especially when she'd run into him at a party? (At which times she would—nervously—ignore him.)

It might have been a little of all of these things—even the contradictory ones, Margaret has come to conclude. The reason did not matter. The sweater *was* the rape. As long as it was lying in her drawer in her closet just feet away from where she slept, then it was in her soul.

One day, when she left Darien for college, Margaret threw the sweater away.

Today Margaret is happily married, but she says she spent years, in prior relationships, feeling worthless—like used goods; and for a long time she nursed a nagging fear that the rape had somehow destroyed her reproductive capability. When Margaret heard about Alex Kelly's arrest for the rapes of Adrienne Bak and Valerie Barnett, "I felt a little guilty. I thought maybe I should have done something back then. But how was I supposed to know what to do? When I look back on it now, it's amazing I could even put it behind me as much as I did."

Initially, Margaret's husband—appalled at what he termed the prospect of Alex Kelly getting away with any more rapes—thought she should go to the prosecution with her story. But Margaret decided not to, for the reason so many rape victims do not come forward: the very realistic fear of being excoriated on the witness stand by a ruthless defense attorney whose primary task is to destroy your credibility in front of a jury. Whenever she thought over the possibility of becoming a prosecution witness, "I thought, 'Oh God! They'll tear me to shreds!'" She could just hear the defense lawyer sneering, in open court: "'Oh, so you slept with this person, did you?'"

After a great deal of initial reluctance, Margaret finally agreed to be interviewed for this book, with the use of a pseudonym, because she wanted to help set the record on Alex Kelly straight and because she wanted to offer her story as a gesture of support for other women who, as girls, may have gone through what she did.

Rape is the ultimate "unrespectable" crime, for the victim as well as the culprit. It might be argued that a young sex offender is *more* protected—more unapprehendable—when he is a son in a corporate town than when he has any other kind of relationship to any other kind of American community. The more insular, gossip-prone, and image-valuing the com-munity—*and* the more accepted and enmeshed within it the perpetrator (thus inviting the widespread presumption that the encounter was consensual)—the greater the risk coming forward entails. The greater the pressure the victims feel to *never* break their silence.

Still, even greater than the fear of being found out is Margaret's fear of her attacker, all these sixteen years later. "Please tell me he will finally be convicted," she said as the case went to the jury in June 1997, in a voice tense with sixteen years of nervousness. "Because if he isn't, I *know* he will do it again."

When told, on July 25, that Alex Kelly had been sentenced to a sixteen-year prison term, Margaret—and her husband—seemed enormously relieved.

The sexual problems that people have often manifest themselves in childhood. If a problem is discovered early enough, it can be treated, sometimes even cured.

Margaret's story is not the earliest. Alex's problems may go back to just before he reached adolescence. One peer of Alex's gives the following account: When Alex was about twelve years old, he and an even younger neighborhood girl ended up in a bedroom at a local party. Alex's friend walked into the room, only to find Alex performing what looked like oral sex on the girl. When Alex saw the accidental intruder noticing him with shock, Alex laughed.

Whether Alex and the girl were engaged in sex or just horseplay, the friend left the room, shaken. That person says today: "I knew what I saw was wrong and I wanted it not to have happened. I wanted to tell someone who would do something to stop it. But I didn't. I just brushed it off. I let it go."

CHAPTER  3

DARIEN HIGH SCHOOL—WITH ITS SPRAWLING WINGS OF low-slung, tan brick buildings that cantilever down a sloping glen to acres of playing fields—sends 84 percent of its graduates to four-year colleges. Some go to Dartmouth, Harvard, and Princeton, and many to small colleges with homogeneous populations (one alumna calls them "mini-Dariens") like Middlebury, Kenyon, and Dennison. A disproportionate share of Darien High graduates end up at Colorado schools, where studies share priority with skiing. Academics are important here, insofar as the parents demand the best and expect their children to go on to leadership-class careers but, despite the fact that a number of the faculty are Ph.D.s, learning for learning's sake is not necessarily valued by the parents or the students. One former teacher says, "The teachers used to complain that there was a level of affluence but not a level of intellectualism." An administrator: "I would not call most of the students intellectuals, but they're skilled. The vast majority break 1,000, 1,100, 1,200 on their college boards."

What *is* important—what is *very* important—at Darien High is athletics. When Alex Kelly was a student there, between

1981 and 1986, two thirds of the eleven hundred students participated in extracurricular athletics. "Sports are almost *primary*," says then assistant principal Gerard Coulombe. "Right behind sports"—but not before it—"is getting a good education."

Another former teacher and administrator is blunter. Referring to the school in the eighties: "It was definitely a community in which sports ruled and boys were worshipped. You had a lot of spoiled young males in Darien. See, when you have blue-collar kids playing blue-collar sports, like track and basketball, there's a humility that cuts against some of the jock-coddling. But in Darien, there was no humility. Athlete-worship and class entitlement got melded. The boys who played football and lacrosse at Darien High—they were Roman gods. They were little kings."

Alex Kelly's athleticism had a decided out-of-school component, and it was his combination of sports and drugs, which had begun when he was a child, on the Holmes School Raiders, that garnered him the awe of the boys. "He was great at 'shrooming: doing [psychedelic] mushrooms and waterskiing," recalls a female peer. "He loved to snow-ski after inhaling whippets [nitrous oxide pellets]—and he inhaled more whippets at one stretch than other kids thought *they* could tolerate." He was an ace skier.

His reputation for being an "animal" on the football field escalated. "He was a one-hundred-sixty-pound kid going up against *two*-hundred-forty-pound linemen and *succeeding!*" a younger classman recalls. "He used to spit on people during games. He used to growl. When he'd get in a set position in football, he'd start laughing. *Laughing.* Yeah. He was crazy."

Sometimes that "crazy" physicality could spill over to encounters with girls. The father of a football player picked his son up after practice one day and saw "Alex walking around in front of the school almost naked. He had his shirt off. He had his practice pants off. I *think* he had on a jock strap (I saw him from the back)—I'm not sure. He was goofing off. There were girls there. I personally got along well with Alex—he was a nice kid. But he was out of control. You wanted to go up to him, grab him and say, *'What* are you doing?'"

If, in football, Alex growled and went after players eighty pounds heavier than he was, his modus operandi in the paramount sport that he mastered—wrestling—contained more elements uncomfortably closer to sadism. Alex had two trademark moves: the split scissors, where the wrestler yanks his opponent's legs apart, and the guillotine, in which the wrestler has the opponent pinned at opposite extremities and is stretching him in both directions. "Alex," one wrestling fan recalls, "would put submission holds on his opponents to the point that they would give up." But *he* would not quite give up. "And he'd just look into the stands and be smiling at the stands while these kids were yelling in agony."

The early to middle 1980s were a precarious time for American teenagers. Adolescent drug use increased, with some drug-treatment authorities believing it had *doubled* from the 1970s. (It would decrease substantially in the late 1980s.) Drinking had always existed as a central part of Darien High School life. Now drug-taking had moved up—from being the province of the burnouts to being the province of the jocks. "Drugs weren't for the losers," one young woman recalls. "They were for the cool kids, the top athletes."

During Alex's years at Darien High, the first day of school always started off with a bang—a morning at Weed Beach getting sloshed on mimosas before classes. Once in school, pot was sold—by Alex, among others—in the smoking area, which consisted of a couple of picnic tables on a blacktop outside the senior cafeteria. (The seniors had a separate lunchroom from the lower classmen. Further segregation was provided by social class. "On one side of the cafeteria," an alumna recalls, "were the Chris Kelly types, the ALP kids who wouldn't go to college; on the other side were the pretty kids, the Wee Burns.")

Kids had "wake 'n' bake" hits of dope upon rising, bong hits en route to school in their B'Mers and Saabs (the girls) or (the boys) their Camaros, GTOs, and Chevelles. (Certified hot rods with "big block" engines were the vehicle of choice.) Some kids pulled out baby bats in math class, slunk behind their books for a hit, then walked to the open window in the back of the room, stuck their heads out and released the pungent vapors into the air while the math teacher chalked formulas for the surface measurements of cubes on the blackboard. The girls' bathroom in the art wing was another favored site for cannabis breaks.

Wednesday was X-Day—school let out early so that clubs could convene: the Green Thumb Club, the International Club, the Debate Team, the Future Problem Solvers. A group of kids who wouldn't be caught dead in any of those organizations came up with a club of their own: the Keg Club. On X-Day they'd zoom out of school, shoot over to the Beverage Barn or the Liquor Locker, roll the purchased kegs of beer into the designated parent-free house, where all the other Keg Club members—bonged and batted and sometimes coked up—would assemble to play drinking games: sink the sub, slammers, anchorman, Herman the German—Darien High teens had names for drinking games the way Eskimos have names for snow and Italians have names for pasta.

But the premier Darien High drinking game was quarters. In quarters a player takes one quarter between thumb and forefinger and snaps it down on a table, in an effort to bounce it right into the glass of beer that's positioned in front of it. If you got the quarter *in* the beer, you chose a person to drink all the beer in the glass. Prodigious quarters players got other players loaded.

Athletics, drinking, drug-taking, wealth, everyone's families knowing each other—some teachers and administrators at Darien High thought this combination bred what they gingerly termed "respect problems." First of all, there was the basic entitled-teen respect-for-workers problem (kids treating the school custodians like servants). Then there were the respect-for-school property problems (kids burying cars on the lawn, hoisting cars onto the roof, flooding the hall on Senior Prank Day). Finally, there were boy-girl respect problems. Principal Velma Saire and assistant principals Ed Higgins and (after Higgins left for another job) Bruce Hall and Gerard Coulombe were constantly tearing sports posters off the walls because they'd been defaced with boys' double-entendred remarks about girls' sexuality. The history teacher (and later vice-principal) Anthony Pavia was *such* a stickler on respect issues that girls who were insulted or taunted by boys and who did *not* complain were sometimes treated by Mr. Pavia to an instructive playing of Aretha Franklin's "Respect," which literally spelled the concept out.

A number of teachers privately lamented the lack of strong females at the school—surprising since the girls *seemed* so self-confident. These were girls much like Carolyn Bessette, from Greenwich, who grew up to marry John Kennedy Jr. One girl fashioned herself a feminist yet got drunk at the prom and let boys paw her. As one male teacher recalls, "You had so many girls at that school who were beautiful, talented, intelligent, athletic, and affluent—they were five for five! Yet they let the boys treat them like garbage!"

Sometimes it seemed that if you were a girl in Darien, you had to laugh to keep on top of things. At least that's what four best friends in Alex's crowd named Kathy Bishop, Cory Johnson, Jillian Henderson, and Emily Meehan thought. They'd laugh in an all-for-one-and-one-for-all fashion: with packs of cigarettes and two gallons of vodka or scotch, and a stack of seventies CDs (Cream, Pink Floyd, the Rolling Stones, the

Doobie Brothers) playing because they *wished* they could have been in *that* generation. But mainly they'd listen to the hot new alternative groups: R.E.M. Depeche Mode. The Cure. The Violent Femmes. And they'd drink to drown out whatever-it-was—nobody quite had a name for the emotional pain they were feeling. They'd drink until they passed out cold. And then three of them would carry the one who passed out into the shower and douse her with cold water to revive her.

The Four Girls wore throwback-sixties clothes: their older brothers' faded jeans with ripped-out knees and butt-patches, long flowing dresses from Manhattan's Antique Boutique and baggy T-shirts and sweaters. They were anti-Muffie clothes: "The point," Kathy says, "was to look like we just rolled out of bed. And we were always barefoot." They huddled around their scotch bottle and told each other funny, self-deprecating stories about boys they'd "boinked," forgetting what little education in contraception they did receive at school (says Jillian: "They didn't teach us birth control at Darien High, because for parents to accept birth control being taught, they have to accept the fact that their children were engaging in sex, and our clueless-ass parents would rather remain ignorant"), and relying, instead, on the "pull-out-and-pray" method like turn-of-the-century farm girls. They were the Muffiebusters: They disdained the girls who were fake and stuck-up and insulated from the risks and the pain of life— who weren't *real*, like they were. They prided themselves on having friends from all the crowds: the ALP kids, the science nerds. They'd toss out brilliant theories about why this town was so fucked up and they promised they'd pool their diary entries and write a movie about it.

And then they'd drink some more: sneaking out of the house to play slammers at the graveyard, or going to the Rocks at Weed Beach with six-packs and cigarettes. The cops would beam their flashlights over the mass of long blond hair and shout, "You girls! Whataya doing here?!" And the Four Girls would dash to the car, drive drunkenly home, and sneak in the back door at three A.M.

Looking back on their sophomore and junior years: "We'd hold onto each other so we wouldn't fall down," says Jillian. Kathy: "We were each other's life support." Jillian: "We thought we knew a lot more about life than we did and thought we had a lot more control than we did." Kathy: "It's amazing we all didn't get beaten up, raped, or killed. We lived like there were no consequences—walking through minefields without hesitation." Emily: "If it wasn't for having each other, I don't think we'd be here today."

The Four Girls ranged from pretty to ravishing; all were rich—or rich-enough; yet each one felt like a misfit. "The image of Darien was so huge," Kathy says, "that kids just couldn't live up to it." Certainly Kathy didn't think she could. Curvy, full of fun, wickedly funny, everyone's confidante, big-hearted Kathy was sometimes too reckless for her own good. There were her four major car crashes, for example—one of which almost killed Jillian. There was her inability to shake her older, druggie boyfriend whom the other girls thought was psycho.

Kathy was adopted—as was Cory; and the sense of not quite knowing who you really were that came from that fact "was the thing," Kathy says, "we both lamented over when we were drunk."

Emily Meehan was tiny, artistic, ethereal. She *seemed* delicate and vulnerable—Kathy talked of that "deer-in-the-headlights" quality that always made the others want to protect her—but no one could play a meaner game of slammers at the graveyard or hosted better X-Day parties. Emily's mother was a divorced mom; every morning, Mrs. Meehan would moped off to her nursing job—even in snowfall. Having a plucky breadwinner as a role model saved Emily, she says today. She couldn't have turned out spoiled and vapid, even if she'd wanted to—especially since she worked her way through college—not the Fairfield County Princess way of obtaining a higher education.

Jillian was the sultriest, the most sarcastic, the zaniest. She'd dance on tables at parties. She was a beauty, but her older sister was a raving beauty, and Jillian was often struggling with her weight. Jillian's mother was still modeling—at age *fifty*. And her advertising-executive father was one of *the* best-looking men in a town where more than a few dads were Robert Redford–handsome. In Darien, those who would anywhere else have been prom queens battled inferiority complexes—not just in their schools but in their living rooms. Being a pretty, blond girl in Darien was like being a pretty smart kid at Harvard.

Jillian's parents, like Emily's, were split up, yet they couldn't make up their minds about *staying* split up. Once, when they were on a (unsuccessful, it turns out) reconciliation trip to Europe, Jillian chucked school for Weed Beach for two weeks, getting incompletes in her classes.

Cory Johnson was the elegant, wholesome-looking beauty— the crowd's Grace Kelly. (She later became a Ford model, as did one of Jillian's sisters.) "We all would have settled for looking like Cory for just one hour," sighs Jillian. Cory was also the idealist, the social critic. Coming to Darien as a "hick from the Midwest, I was blown away by how insulting kids were to everyone," she remembers. "I couldn't believe how rampant slang against other races was. Hearing a girl in school say 'Jews smell' and that all Italians were 'Mafiosi'; seeing blacks stopped for walking down the street: I wanted to get out of there *fast.*"

Cory was "the ear, the stabilizer," Jillian says, "the one who was normal enough to comfort and advise the rest of us." One of the reasons she was normal may have been that her mother, to the astonishment and anger of many of the other parents, had adopted a militantly pay-the-consequences ethic. If Cory and her friends ditched school and left wet towels and liquor bottles all over the house, the police were called. The only other parent in town aside from Cory's mom who'd had their own kid arrested was one of the police detectives. Stuck with a narc for a mother, Cory was always seeking refuge in Jillian's house, or Kathy's house—that is, when Kathy wasn't hiding out at Emily's. Once, in a gesture of bonhomie prefiguring *Thelma and Louise,* Cory and Kathy leaped off the sixty-foot-high cliff Castle Rock, holding hands, hitting the icy water so hard their backs were purple for a week.

It sometimes seems to the Four Girls that their life together was, as one puts it now, *"Clueless* Amid the Colonials."

None of the Four Girls was a straight-and-narrow Muffie like Alex Kelly's girlfriend Paige Ginn was. Yet they were in Alex's crowd—the wild crowd—and Paige wasn't. Some of Alex's friends thought Paige was a trophy—even more than a trophy, perhaps, an *amulet,* a means of dispelling demons.

Some kids bought coke from Alex at Weed Beach and at parties. He wasn't the only kid who sold drugs, of course. But he was way up there with the group who did. That was the funny thing about Alex: He was so smooth, so manipulative that he covered himself with another layer of himself. "I remember being so blown away by the ability of his craft—he was an expert charmer and manipulator; he sort of seduced you in that sense," says Cory. Kathy agrees, and adds, "But sometimes you'd look in his eyes, and you knew there was something wrong. You'd see a twistedness there. You could see he could snap."

In the spring of 1982, shortly after Alex and Paige had broken up, a typical Darien High party was underway at a big house with a pool in Tokeneke. Beer was flowing from the keg taps. The cops burst in at 10:30, shook things up; then, as soon as the pot was ditched and the music dimmed, they left.

A fellow sophomore girl in Alex's social circle, a former

Mather student, Julia West, had arranged through a friend of a friend to try to get Alex to the party. "It was typical high school shenanigans—girls trying to get boys to come over." Julia had had a little crush on Alex all year, although she knew it wasn't a realistic one: Alex dated the blond knockouts. Julia was more the sensible, favorite-sister type, the kind of girl who becomes class secretary and then college sorority president but who doesn't expect boys to fall all over her. She had social authority at Darien High and had older friends who were among the school's elite.

Today Julia says, "My experience with Alex was probably the link between him being a boy dealing with sex in a seminormal way . . . and him being totally off his rocker."

Here is what she says happened:

Alex hadn't said a word to Julia all evening. He seemed to be keeping his distance, not just from her but from most of the kids at the party. This didn't surprise Julia—she and her friends had noticed that although Alex was always very enmeshed with one girl, and he was very loud and aggressive, he wasn't sociable. "He was kind of aloof. He would bond with his girlfriend, but that was it. Alex was essentially a loner."

Once the party thinned out, Julia, Alex and some others sat around playing quarters. And playing. And playing. Julia passed out cold. "Next thing I know, I wake up. Now, Alex had barely spoken to me." Which is why Julia was so stunned when "Alex—perfectly coherent, *not* drunk—was standing over me. He'd gotten my sweatshirt over my head. He was holding his penis in my face! I bolted up. 'Alex, *what* are you doing?!'"

"He began trying to, in some feeble way, say something like 'I want to make love to you.'" Yeah, right! Julia thought. Alex Kelly may have been one of the cutest guys in school, but she knew the difference between a boy who was genuinely interested in her and one who was making a gross, rote advance on a seemingly opportune target. "I said: 'Go away! You didn't even talk to me all night—you think I'm going to be all psyched-up for *this?*'"

Apparently thrown off balance by her forthrightness, Alex continued to "urgently plead" for sex. When she grabbed her car keys and said, "Come on! I'm driving you home!" (because there was no other way for him to *get* home), his surprise turned into humiliation. She was slightly older than he and had her license while he did not; the snappish offer of the ride might have seemed like dismissal of his machismo—rank-pulling—to him.

"He was *really* mad. He started stomping around the house. There was almost no one left in the house; it was getting close to midnight; I got nervous. He called me a bitch. He said, 'I can't believe you're such a prude!'" Julia retorted: "Yeah, sure! I'm gonna lose my virginity in a one-night stand like this!"

Alex and Julia got into Julia's car and, despite the fact that she had been drunk enough to have passed out, she proceeded to drive him home. "Once we got into the car he wouldn't speak to me. Then, as we got to Leeuwarden, near his house"—and, ironically, near where the rapes of Adrienne Bak and Valerie Barnett would later occur—"he says, 'Stop here! Let me out!' I said, 'You know Alex, you don't have to be such a jerk about this.' But he couldn't communicate. Didn't want to discuss it. Just got out of the car, slammed the door, disappeared."

Monday at school, Alex wouldn't talk to Julia, even when they were in a group of mutual friends. Tuesday at school, the same deep freeze. "Alex's normal persona in school was that of the easygoing stoner, so it was weird and out of character for people to see him walking past me like I didn't exist." Wasn't Alex overdoing this wounded-male-ego business?, Julia wondered. Especially since the popular heartthrob hadn't really wanted her—and *they both* knew that. Okay, Julia thought, maybe he was just too embarrassed to be normal around her. They had been friends before the incident and she wanted to assure him she bore him no ill. A phone call might alleviate the awkwardness. Julia called Alex's house and left a message. He did not call back.

The next day—Wednesday, X-Day—a group of kids skipped school for a special, early-starting keg party at another sopho- more's house. The boys especially thought it was a goof to be getting sloshed and watching cartoons at nine A.M., while all their classmates were stuck analyzing *Hamlet* with Mr. Bou- vier or discussing the causes of World War I with Mr. Pavia.

Then Alex showed up. He walked right up to Julia and cheerfully greeted her as if nothing awkward had happened. Julia flashed a "weird, huh?" look to her best friend, who'd known of Julia's three-day effort to ease Alex out of his angry funk. Then—weirder—Alex ignored Julia throughout the par- ty. "By now," Julia says, "I had definitely dropped my little crush."

But, to Alex, there was suddenly unfinished business. "Three o'clock comes along and all of a sudden, Alex says, 'Julia, we have to talk.' If I'd had half a brain I wouldn't have gone anywhere with him 'cause he'd shown me he was untrustworthy. But I was stupid. And I never imagined that *he* would ever be any more stupid than he'd been the other night. Besides, I *knew* he wasn't attracted to me. I always thought sex was motivated by attraction. I never thought it could be motivated by violence."

So Julia said, "All right. Fine."

And Alex said, "Follow me."

And Julia, who was wearing a one-piece bathing suit with a towel wrapped over it, asked, "Follow you . . . where?"

He walked across the street and started into the woods.

"Alex, why . . . are we going . . . *here?*" Julia asked, reluc- tantly picking her way through the trees.

She recalls him replying, "I want us to be away so we can hash this out. I don't want people to know about this."

Julia thinks back to her decision to go with Alex into the

woods and she says, "I'd been drinking, so I wasn't on top of my judgment. But, still, going into the woods with a boy from your crowd wasn't the type of thing a girl would be worried about.

"He trudges. I follow him. 'For God's sake, where are we *going?'* I ask him. He finally sits down. We're in the woods, a distance from the road." There was a silence. Then Julia plunged in with girlish, conciliatory words: "Okay, I know you were drunk the other night and I was drunk and it was a stupid thing that happened but we don't have to make a big deal out of it and—"

Julia stopped talking when she saw Alex looking at her strangely. "I swear to *God*, this *mask* came over his face. This *mask!* It was like his eyes—it was so scary! It was *not him.* It was Jekyll and Hyde. He wasn't hearing anything I was saying."

According to Julia: "He grabbed me by the shoulders, pinned me down, into the sticks. Ripped my bathing suit. Violently! *Off!* He ripped it so the boning popped off (which is a pretty horrifying thing for a sixteen-year-old girl) and it peeled right down.

"I was so taken aback, I started screaming: *'What* are you *doing?!'* He said, 'Shut up!' He was not attempting to kiss me or anything. He was pinning me down, he was groping me, he was trying to pull my bathing suit all the way off. And then— don't ask me what possessed me but—I punched him in the face!

"I'm sure it didn't hurt him, but it stunned him. Just totally stunned him. He sat back. Physically, he could have continued to do what he'd started to do, but my nerve in having punched him and the fact that I had big-clout friends among the upperclassmen must have made him stop. I had just enough over him that he couldn't continue. He said—in a voice so possessed, it was scary—'Why am I doing this to you? I can't believe I'm doing this to you. I've known you for so long.'"

Wrapping her wrists, which had been scratched and bloodied, with her towel, Julia retorted: "'No kidding, why are you doing this?! You are totally crazy! You're fucking nuts!'

"He was steamed up. His eyes were almost misting. He said, 'I'm sorry; I'm sorry; I shouldn't be doing this to you.'"

"I remember thinking: 'Why does he keep saying *'to you'*? Then I immediately knew. I just *knew* it: He had done this to other girls. And it was totally premeditated: the approach at the party, the walk into the woods."

In retelling the story, Julia pauses for a deep breath. Then she says: "I was *mindblown.*"*

Just like Margaret, Julia was terrified that others would find out what had happened. And just like Margaret, "It never occurred to me," Julia says, "that Alex had done something that *I* could get *him* in trouble for." But if Margaret's insistence on silence came from fear of pregnancy, punishment, and Alex himself, Julia's was rooted in another fear: the fear of ridicule. As they left the woods Alex, according to Julia, said harshly, "'Nothing happened and I don't want anyone to think it did.' Which was the meanest thing I think he could have said. I was so afraid that if I told what happened, Alex, in denying it, would say something to the other boys that would humiliate me even further. I was *so* insecure."

Fortunately, it was only a week before school was out so

---

*Two friends of Julia's encountered her just as she was walking back to the party. One, a male, first mentioned (in the course of his own interview for this book) a day where "I remember it was three o'clock because somebody said, 'If we were at school we'd be getting out now.' All of a sudden [Julia West] comes climbing out of the woods, crying. She was cut up. Scratched up. She's crying. She's hysterical. We immediately brought her over and said, 'What's wrong?! What happened?!' She said: 'Alex Kelly just attacked me. In the woods.'" The second friend, a woman (the "we" the man was referring to), was located, telephoned, and told that the man had mentioned the day, the girl, Alex Kelly, and some kind of incident. Whereupon she recalled: "Yes, I remember it. It certainly sounded like Alex had attempted to do something [Julia] did not want him to do. It was definitely more than a boy putting an unwanted move on a girl. It scared her. It seemed serious." Neither source had spoken to Julia West (or to each other) in years. After hearing these stories, the author made an independent effort to find Julia West. The story that appears in the text is Ms. West's account.

Julia didn't have to endure the awkwardness of running into Alex every day for too much longer. "It was really weird. I could never sort it out. I didn't know how to handle it.

"'Cause everyone thought Alex Kelly was the greatest guy."

What if Julia and Margaret had not been frozen into silence? What if the girls had told their parents what Alex Kelly had done and their parents had called Joe and Melanie Kelly? And what if Joe and Melanie Kelly had taken their son for treatment?

"At fifteen years old, a sex offender is easily treatable," asserts clinical and forensic psychologist William Samek, Ph.D., director of the Florida Sexual Abuse Treatment Program, who has treated or evaluated about 4,000 sexual offenders in eighteen years, including hundreds of fifteen year olds. "Especially one who is showing remorse and showing guilt, both of which this boy displayed when he apologized [to Julia]." On the basis of the incidents with Margaret and Julia, Dr. Samek says: "This is someone who could have been worked with.

"A fifteen year old can do a whole lot of changing in a year: twice as much as a twenty year old and three times as much as a thirty year old [Alex Kelly's age now]. And for that fifteen-year-old sexual offender, the permanency of the cure is dependent on the progress made by the parents." If the Kellys had come to someone like Dr. Samek in 1982, the treatment would have been three-pronged: Alex in individual therapy, Alex in a treatment group, and Joe and Melanie in a parents' group, where their marriage, and any abuse within it, would be explored.

"Parents," Samek says, "are an essential part of the treatment because they are an essential part of the illness."

Since rape is the ultimate boundary problem, what teenage sex offenders often have in common is families with boundary schizophrenia, "families in which there are too many secrets *and* too few secrets—the parents don't tell the kid he's adopted but they do leave the bathroom doors open; or they've hidden the fact that the father has an arrest record, but they let the kids overhear adult lovemaking. Or"—as seems the case— "there is extreme inconsistency of discipline. One parent overcontrols and overdominates, the other *under*does everything. One parent is too punitive, the other spoils the kid rotten. Or, the father is harsh and the mother slips around secretly afterward and tries to undo the harshness; dad says, 'Go to bed without dinner' and mom sneaks in at eleven with a bowl of ice cream." Dr. Samek pauses, then notes: "That's a very good way to raise a sociopath."

The individual therapy for a young sexual offender is "heavily confrontive," Dr. Samek says. This is why most sexual offenders will submit to treatment only if the alternative is prison. "It's not like the rest of us, where we go to a shrink and come out feeling better. If I'm doing my job right, when someone comes out of a session with me he feels *worse*. The treatment is so combative, it makes him want to run—and that's the point: Rape is an illness where the afflicted man tries to avoid feeling pain by running to excitement. I have to break that run.

"I teach him that rape is a metaphor for abuse of power; that any insensitivity is a rape; I'm constantly applying the word 'rape' to other things he has done and keeps doing. 'Rape, rape, rape': I'm always using the word, constantly challenging him for lies he tells himself." The young man is also taught *impulse control,* through techniques like "thought-stopping," leaving a scene, writing—anything that will delay the urge to rape; and he is taught *fantasy suppression.* "It's the opposite of what Freud said. With rapists, you don't have an unconscious thought *instead* of acting; rapists have fantasies and *do* act on them. So we teach them which fantasies they must learn to suppress, namely, any that have to do with violence or using someone else."

It would have been a grueling, time-consuming two-year

process, Dr. Samek says, but Alex Kelly could have been effectively cured in his teens. He need not have victimized any more girls. And his sixteen-year prison term could have been avoided.

Not long after her unnerving encounter with Alex, Julia learned from friends that two other girls she knew had had experiences with Alex as well and were terrified of anyone finding out. Both girls had something else in common. "They were a little overweight and insecure," Julia says, who herself had felt painfully insecure—not pretty enough to have rated Alex's interest under ordinary circumstances. "Alex knew who to get. He obviously went straight to the vulnerable ones."

After these stories were surreptitiously shared, Julia and two of her friends invented a nickname for the handsome, charismatic sophomore. It was so secret a nickname, it was rendered in initials: "Alex Kelly, M.R."—as in "Marcus Welby, M.D."

M.R. stood for Mad Rapist.

Nobody else had that nickname, and no other boy in school seemed to be a rapist. Still, there was a continuum of behavior—and a *milieu* for that behavior. The Four Girls knew of at least two incidents with other boys. Once, a girl they knew of passed out, came to, and found a boy was standing over her, unzipped. Another time, a girl had awakened to find that her vagina had been smeared with dog food by a group of boys who had left a dog in the room. Good, proper Darien boys, all of them.

Indeed, the mid-1980s through the early 1990s was still a time (perhaps the last time) when such behavior among upper-middle-class boys was tolerated, at least by some, as fraternity-boy-prank funny. In 1989, in affluent Glen Ridge, New Jersey, three star athletes allegedly raped a mildly retarded seventeen-year-old girl (among other things, penetrating her with a baseball bat and a broomstick) while nine other boys watched.* In 1992 five white male students at New York's St. John's University were charged with raping a black female student.**

Today, things are radically different. Darien High, like many other high schools, now has two faculty members in charge of gathering and documenting sexual harassment complaints. There are about ten to fifteen student-on-student harassment complaints a year at Darien High (as there might be at any similar school where sexual harassment and date rape are talked-about issues). Says a local administrator: "We're dealing with this issue all the time. I take boys into my office and say: 'We don't give men the benefit of the doubt anymore. Things people thought were funny twenty years ago? They're not funny anymore. You'll *fry* for them.' When the boys say, 'But the girls *like* to be talked dirty to,' I say, 'Maybe some do. But the *minute* you say something that's unwanted (the key word is *unwanted)* that's legally, morally, absolutely when you have to stop.'

"We've learned that we must jump in, and we *do.* When it comes to our attention that a girl may have been harassed or mistreated, we tell her parents, the boy's parents; we do an investigation, get written statements, make an immediate suspension and an overly steep referral for counseling."

None of this was in place between 1981 and 1986. The terms "sexual harassment" and "date rape" were unknown to the kids. No one would *dream* of reporting such incidents. Girls desperately wished to remain popular. The Four Girls (two of whom are now stockbrokers; two full-time mothers of young children) look back on their time at Darien High and believe

---

*The three defendants (two others originally charged had charges dropped against them) were convicted in March 1993—one defendant for second-degree conspiracy and attempted aggravated sexual assault (carrying a seven-year maximum sentence), the two others for aggravated sexual assault against a mentally defective person (carrying a fifteen-year maximum sentence). Free pending appeal for four years, they were finally sentenced on June 30, 1997.
**One guilty plea, three acquittals, and a reduced-to-misdemeanor charge resulted.

they had the worst of it: the drugs-drink-and-disrespect culture was both the most in vogue *and* the least warned against.
"We were the test-case kids," Kathy says. "After we passed
through the eye of that storm, the rules changed and girls were
more protected."

If you were a girl back then, it was hard to keep pretending
the rules applied equally to both sexes. Girls were "slutty"; boys
were "players." At least boys paid for girls' abortions. And went
with the girls when they obtained those procedures.

But that did not necessarily mean that their motives for
going were sterling.

Once Kathy's boyfriend and Cory accompanied Kathy to
Medical Options in Stamford, the place where all the Darien
girls dealt with their unwanted pregnancies. It was not her
first occasion. As she sat on the plastic, attached-bucket-seat
chair—afraid, and guilty (what if her own birth-mother had
aborted *her* instead of putting her up for adoption?) in her
opened-at-the-back paper gown and her feet on the cold
linoleum—she heard the vague sound of disembodied good
cheer from behind the room divider: her boyfriend, cracking
jokes. Then *louder* jokes.

It dawned on Kathy that her boyfriend was acting extremely
inappropriately. Cory, observing him uncomfortably at closer
range, had already come to that conclusion. The room was full
of distressed girls about to get abortions, yet, as it turns out,
Kathy's boyfriend saw the assembled company as something
of an opportunity. He turned to Cory and opined, "Hey, this is a
great place to pick up chicks!"

Getting a drift of his M.O., Kathy flew out to the crowded
waiting room. Pinching her paper gown closed in the back
with both sets of fingers, she bawled him out like a Bridgeport
warehouse foreman. People were looking at her funny. Everyone else was dressed and she was nearly naked. Still, she told
him to leave—just *leave!* Then, hands clamping the back of the
gown, cheeks flushed, Kathy shuffled back in to her plastic
seat to take care of their little problem.

After the abortion, the two stranded girls (Kathy's boyfriend had driven himself home) were forced to call a taxi.

One night Cory and Kathy and Emily went down to a local liquor store and sweet-talked the clerks into selling them vodka without IDs. (Cute girls could always do that.) They ran into a bunch of kids who were going to a Dead show at the Brendan Byrne Arena in New Jersey. It was a school night but—hey! what the hell! Mescaline was passed around like it was 1967.

After the concert, Emily and Cory lost their rides home and wound up spending the night all alone in the cavernous space on the wet-paper-towel-strewn tile floor of a public bathroom. Kathy, meanwhile, had ridden home in a car where tabs of acid were dispensed. She came home from the concert *flying*.

That was enough for Kathy's parents. They packed her off to a Westchester County rehabilitative clinic, Arms Acres. The first person Kathy saw when she walked in the door was another pretty Darien High girl who had a drug problem and also used to vomit out the contents of her school lunches every day into the toilet of the girls' bathroom. Kathy and her friend fell upon each other: giggly, conspiratorial—two hip outlaw chicks stashed into this pricey dry-out bin by their parents.

They giggled and talked and whispered and dished the staff and personnel up and down and sideways. Then Kathy started weeping—almost uncontrollably. The tears washed down her face in streams. In sheets. In buckets. They felt so good—like a burst dam of relief, of gratitude.

At last—thank God—her mom and dad had stepped in and stopped her from destroying herself.

But not all the parents did this.

By the beginning of junior year, Alex Kelly and Mavis McGarry, the girl he had disliked on sight when he'd met her through Jim Hunter, were involved. Perhaps Alex's initial aversion to Mavis came from his sense of how vulnerable he would become with a girl as strong-willed, rebellious, and high-volume as he was. The girls like his mother—the Paige Ginns, the Callie Cusacks, the adaptive, reactive, passive "good" girls—were probably therapeutic for Alex. They validated his preppy side. No matter what he may have been secretly impelled to do—taking girls into the woods—as long as he was with the Paiges of the world, such pathological aggression was tamped down and hidden.

But Mavis was feistier. She was a headbutter, a button-pusher. To the Four Girls, she was as cool as they came—"an icon," Kathy Bishop recalls. "She'd sort of float all over town in her big sweater, a little like a Cheshire cat. Very laid back. In control of what was going on. Not gonna be any boy's armpiece. I wanted to be like her."

Some at Darien High thought Mavis was as beautiful as they came—"drop-dead gorgeous" is one description. Others saw her more critically. "Mavis probably could have been attractive," says Rick Dawson, "but she chose to be trashy looking. Unshowered, sweaty, no bra, bleached blond, worn-out T-shirt." If a wealthy Darien executive's daughter can be said to have acquired an outlaw mystique, well, Mavis McGarry had one.

Soon Alex was seen driving Mavis around in Mavis's mother's sports car. And Alex was "publicly playing the bad boy," as Jillian Henderson says, "and getting cocky about it. They had tons of fights—loud, across-the-parking-lot screaming matches: 'Fuck you, Alex!' 'Fuck you, Mavis!' But you didn't feel she was being dragged around. You felt that they were equals." But equal as it may have been at first, such a relationship is too volatile to be healthy. "I wouldn't say they were a cute couple," one friend of Alex's recalls. "I would say they were two psychos going out together." Kathy Bishop sums it up: "Mavis and Alex were a movie. They were Darien High's Bonnie and Clyde. They were our Sid and Nancy."

Students spent free periods in the cafeteria, where the radio was on, between classes, and sometimes Alex and Mavis exploded into fights there. Cory Johnson remembers "being scared seeing Alex screaming, swearing at Mavis—they're both running around the cafeteria, and he's literally picking up chairs and throwing them across the cafeteria at her. Fifteen people were watching. There were no teachers around. They were like cat and mouse; they *liked* it."

Tom Kelly witnessed that same or a similar scene (the chair throwing in the cafeteria seems to have occurred at least twice), as did Jillian Henderson. Jillian remembers this as the point at which she ceased thinking that Alex's relationship with Mavis was equal—or entertaining. "He was going ballistic. You could just see it in his eyes—it's almost like something snaps. I had seen it when I watched him wrestle. He prided himself on being psycho. He was always, like, 'Yeahhh!' after matches. And everyone, all the boys, would be, like, 'Yeah, big Al!' The meaner, the bigger, the cooler, the more sadistic and satanic—the more he got off on it." Jillian pauses. "I saw that that day in the cafeteria." According to Jillian, the assistant principal at the time, Ed Higgins, intervened to calm Alex down.

One day shortly after Alex's chair throwing, Carl Smith, who eventually became Darien Student Body President, was looking out of the classroom window during English class. That window gave off to an open walkway. "I saw Alex outside, with Mavis up against the wall," Carl Smith recalls. "He had his arm or his hand around her throat and he was choking her.

"We all saw it—the whole class. Everybody looked out. Everybody was alarmed. There was some sense that this was serious." A female teacher also saw the incident. "She walked outside and, verbally, tried to stop it." And what did Alex Kelly do? "Alex yelled at her to walk away."

So much for school authority figures.

Carl Smith later learned that Alex and Mavis "had been having an argument over the fact that she said she was moving away and did not tell him she was leaving."

This reason for his emotional violence seems to comport with what Alex's former high school classmates and the journalists covering his trial both noticed about Alex (the latter through his behavior with Amy Molitor during every break in testimony): his extreme, almost physical, dependence on a girlfriend.

Mavis did move away to North Carolina for a period of months (she supposedly came back to Darien with a southern accent). At some point after she returned, a freshman girl was walking through the empty halls when everyone else was in class, on her way to a meeting with a teacher. This young woman recalls:

"I heard a female voice screaming. The sound was coming closer to me, so I ducked into the closest empty classroom. The classroom doors were solid with a small window area. I peered through that. I saw Alex chasing Mavis at top speed—she was probably a good ten feet in front of him—and she was screaming as she was running, like she was trying to get away from him.

"And right about when they got even to where I was, he caught the back of her hair and yanked her off her feet. Then they just started fighting. Fists were flying—both parties. It was at least ten minutes that they sat on the hall floor, beating each other. They were both making noise. Everybody knew Mavis and Alex as the type who would fight and then make up—they were always together but it always seemed something was wrong. I was a freshman and they were juniors, this strange unknown couple.

"But seeing this, at close range, was very traumatic for me. Alex Kelly scared me to death, ever since I saw that."

According to then assistant principal Coulombe, the school did not let this behavior go unnoticed. "This is a young man who had been monitored for some time," Coulombe recalls. "There had been numerous conferences with his parents."

But the behavior did not change. One day after school, after the school buses had left, Coulombe recalls Mavis "going out toward the school's front parking lot." Alex was with her "and they were having a very violent argument: name calling, expletives flying all over the place—from both of them."

The high school entrance is marked by a large circular driveway that, resort-hotel-style, takes the driver right up to two buildings: the main entrance (its roof ivy-hugged in summer) and the auditorium, whose outer wall consists of stainless-steel-separated panels of plate glass windows. It was here, in front of the auditorium, that Alex was standing.

"Mavis was walking away," Coulombe continues. "Alex was calling her to come back. It was a violent callback and she wouldn't come." Mavis got in the car. "I was watching his reaction to her leaving. I was asking him to cool down, to calm down. I wanted to restrain him."

But, as with Dr. Higgins, and as with the female teacher, Assistant Principal Coulombe's efforts were ultimately ineffectual. The prospect of his girlfriend getting into her car and driving off inordinately upset and frustrated Alex. As Gerard Coulombe vividly recalls, "Alex was so angry, he put his fist right through the plate glass window."

The glass shattered; Alex's flesh was ripped; blood flowed. It was horrifyingly clear to Coulombe that the volatile student had sustained a serious injury. He says, "I thought he was going to bleed to death. He was lucky—he didn't. I covered up his hand and brought him inside to the health office. He started to calm down the minute I was able to move him inside. I had a school nurse go there and take care of him. I called the parents. They came right down. I believe his dad took him to the hospital."

Alex's volatile relationship with Mavis was the object of secret envy and fascination by a freshman girl who was as worshipfully infatuated with him as if he were a rock star. Her name was Amy Molitor, and, like many Darien girls, she had everything: blond beauty, athleticism, popularity, and the material indulgence of her extremely wealthy parents. "Amy's mother wouldn't hesitate spending thousands in a day, shopping for new clothes for herself and Amy," says a former close friend. "Even in ninth grade, Amy wore only Joan & David shoes and only Ralph Lauren clothes. She had always gotten everything she wanted."

But what she wanted more than anything else in the world was Alex Kelly—who, of course, was all wrapped up in Mavis and who didn't even know that Amy Molitor existed. "Alex was *the* coolest guy in town and Amy had this utter fascination with him," Amy's friend says. "It's as if he were Tom Cruise."

Indeed, the words that Amy penned (in that fat-lettered lower-case printing that is de rigeur for teenage girls) around the picture of Alex in yet another friend's yearbook shows the extent of her sycophantic feelings for him (and proves that boys who mistreat girls often, sadly, garner grandly undeserved adulation). "This man to the right of this page is my idol . . . ," she writes. "My goal, which will never be, is to kiss him, even if its [sic] on his pinkie toe. . . . I'll go crazy if I talk about him . . . I'm head over heels in true love with Alex Kelly . . ." After signing her initials and a happy face, she adds, "P.S. One of these days I'll get him if it's the last thing I'll ever do."*

Amy Molitor did not have the kind of family that would render the choice of a racy boy an act of rebellion. Rather, such a boyfriend might seem normal to her. "Amy's was not your typical Darien family," the close friend says, "any more than the Kellys, in their different way, were a typical Darien

---

*A friend of Amy's who has seen this inscription and who heard Amy speak in these adoring terms for a year says, "People keep asking why Amy's still with him, but that yearbook quote in itself is the explanation: She made up her mind thirteen years ago that she just *had* to have him. That obsession with Alex was deep in her soul. There was just no question about it."

family." But if Alex's family was atypical because his father was a plumber, Amy's was atypical, the friend says, because both her mother and father (who divorced when Amy and her little brother Tyler were very young) were jazzier than most proper Darienites. Amy's father, whose last name was Arnold—"a tall, good-looking man with a mustache who lived at the Jersey shore—was," the friend says, "a free spirit. And Amy's mother, Bobbie Dee, didn't mind walking around the house wearing thong bikinis in front of the kids. You wouldn't find that in most other Darien households."

Amy claimed to adore her natural father, the friend says, while she did *not* get along well with Ed Molitor, the Fieldcrest Towels executive whom Bobbie Dee married about the time that Amy entered grade school. (The family then moved from Darien to Surrey, England, for Ed Molitor's work with Field-crest, from Amy's second- through seventh-grade years.) "Amy despised Ed. She had a terrible relationship with him. In junior high and high school, Amy would say: 'My real father understands me and Ed doesn't.'

"It might have been an escape for her, imagining that her real father understood her so well, even though she rarely saw him. It may have helped get her past the confusion of the conflicts between her and Ed. Maybe she thought she could relate to her real father because he was partying and so was she." (Amy also wrote in the yearbook: "Ninth grade is the pits! . . . But partying is awesome!") Whatever the reason, Amy developed a longing for the natural father whose name she had dropped. And the friend says, Amy seemed to resent her mother for leaving this preferred father for the trouble-some replacement. "Maybe this is where Amy's stand-by-your-man attitude came from—her anger that her mother didn't stand by *her* man, causing pain to Amy."

One day in the cafeteria, Alex told Jim Hunter that he wanted to write a book about his life. He even had a title chosen: *Living on the Edge.* Now, not a few wealthy suburban teenage boys would have loved to apply that romantic cliché to their lives. (Shrewdly, the rock group Aerosmith eventually named a song for the sentiment.) But Alex Kelly was one of the very few for whom that term was *not* hyperbolic—and not merely because of the violence with Mavis, the drugs, the alcohol, his extreme approach to sports, or his sexual violence against other women.

For by this time Alex Kelly had—secretly—become a burglar.

According to later news accounts, right before the start of the school year, on August 31, 1983, Alex had walked into two homes on Top O'Hill Road and made off with jewelry, silverware, and foreign currency. Then, a month later, he entered and stole from three houses in two days—two, very near him, on Leeuwarden Road; the third on nearby Hickory Lane. He waited two months, until November 17, to hit a home on exclusive Delafield Island. Shortly after New Year's—on January 5—he moved closer in: burgling the home of a neighbor, on Christie Hill Road. A month later he hit a Stephanie Lane residence. Alex chose the houses shrewdly: Most were located on the choice blocks west of Wee Burn Country Club and north of the Connecticut Turnpike; thus, they could be counted on for expensive yields.

Nobody knew any of this, of course—but Jim Hunter did notice that "all of a sudden Alex seemed to have all this money." Enough to buy expensive sport and leisure clothes and equipment: a brand-new slalom waterski that he was so excited to use on his parents' boat; Gore-Tex jackets and Patagonia clothes he was suddenly wearing on ski trips. And Mavis had acquired the expensive Vuarnet sunglasses she had propped atop her head.

Alex kept his new avocation to himself. But, according to what Jim Hunter says today, he did tell Jim about an ancillary gig he had by now claimed to have developed: credit card theft. One day early in the second semester of their junior year, as Alex and Jim were walking down the Post Road after school, Alex let on to Jim how "he was getting this big kick out of trying to steal credit cards from people. He would steal every opportunity he saw. He'd say, 'Let's walk by that car and see if something's in it.' He said he once stole from a teacher at Darien High—he walked by her room and her purse was on her desk." It was Jim's understanding that Alex would use the cards to charge merchandise at various stores.

To Jim, it seemed glamorous.

Jim had a weekend job pumping gas at the Exxon station on the Post Road, across the street from the movie theater. He got Alex a job there as well. One day, after both boys had been working together for a couple of weeks, "Alex said to me, 'This is what I've been doing . . .' Basically, he would fill the tanks up with eighteen dollars' worth of gas, but run the credit card through for twenty-one or twenty-two dollars. The customers would never look at the pump. They didn't care. And he'd take the money—the difference—out of the drawer for himself."

Jim says he didn't think much about what Alex was doing ("I obviously didn't think about too much in those days") until, a couple of weeks after Alex detailed his scam, "I ended up getting fired. All of a sudden my boss was, 'Well, the cash register came up short.'" Apparently, Jim believes, Alex had broadened his gambit and was now ripping off the gas station rather than, or along with, the customers. Jim was "fairly angry," but his anger melted somewhat when Alex also got fired a week later. The boys remained buddies, and Alex began telling Jim of the burglaries—he seemed particularly proud of having burgled the home of the Nielsens, who owned the town's gardening store.

On March 23, 1985, Alex and Jim were walking home from school and Alex pointed to a house on Holly Lane. "Nobody's home," he said. (By this point he had become good at stake-outs.) "You want to go into it?"

Jim thought about it a second, shrugged, and said, "Sure." Alex was still the leader and he the follower.

The two boys walked around the back of the house. "The

windows were open. Alex busted out the screen." (Actually, the resident later reported that the screen had been slit.) "My heart was racing. Alex was pretty calm."

They climbed in the window and padded around surroundings that could have been either boy's living room. Plush sofas with needlepoint throw pillows. Gleaming Georgian mahogany end tables and breakfront. Framed English hunt pictures. They walked carefully around. Jim could feel his heart bang against his rib cage. He recalls: "Alex said, 'What we really want is the silver—that's the first thing you want to get.' So we looked around, but there really wasn't any silver. So then he keyed in on the stereo equipment."

Alex and Jim unplugged and disassembled the stereo system: "receiver, tape deck, a couple of other things. Then we went out the back door—and straight into the woods."

Today, Jim Hunter is a sales representative with a wife and young child, living in another American city. He speaks, with long pauses, in short and often pronounless sentences. He looks back in dread amazement not just at the criminality but the sheer stupidity of the enterprise. "Carrying all this clunky stereo equipment, in the middle of the afternoon, of all things!" Yet, however amateur the gambit, Alex had clearly been getting away with it for half a year now. "So we set it in the woods. Continued on to his house. Got his mom's station wagon. Drove back to the woods, picked up the stereo equipment, took it over closer to my house, and stuffed it in garbage bags and then hid it in the woods near my house."

Jim made himself a present of the tape deck, and as he slid a Dead cassette into it that night and realized it gave off a much better quality sound than the tape deck he and his brother had, he thought, Hey, not bad. Jim's father didn't give him an allowance—he expected his son to work for his luxuries and he bought him necessities, as needed. The other Darien kids hemorrhaged new clothes and sports and musical equipment. Bang and Olafson speakers. Timberland boots. Guys like Alex always seemed to have things. Guys like Alex's best friend

Russ Pinto, with his black Mazda RX-7, *really* seemed to have things. "So that," Jim says, "is when it all started for me."

Since being fired from the Exxon station job, Jim had picked up an after-school job raking leaves for an older couple on Nolen Lane. One day, shortly after Jim's initial burglary with Alex, the older couple told Jim they would be out of town the following week. "I noticed they had a bunch of the silver Alex was talking about—plates and cups and stuff. So, being the bright kid I was, once they were gone I went back in the middle of the night and, sure enough, they had left the windows in the back of their house open. There was just a screen.

"So I removed the screen and I went in and took all this silver." Indeed, eventually the police would estimate its value at $25,000. "Filled up a duffel bag full of it. Took it. Went and hid it. And the next day told Alex about it. And he's all excited." Excited on Jim's behalf, presumably—because this was *Jim's* robbery; Alex wouldn't be entitled to a share of the proceeds. But Alex was going to be generous with his know-how. "He's like, 'Well, I've got to take you down to the city and I'll show you how to get money for it.'"

Jim was gratified. He'd been the novitiate, the understudy. Now he had pulled a heist of his own, and Alex, the master of the game, was sufficiently impressed to advance him up the next rung of the ladder: fencing the merchandise. (It is unclear just how Alex had learned to do this.)

"The next day after school, we get in the car. I'm driving. We stop off at my house for the duffel full of silverware. Drive into the city. Took the I-95"—the Connecticut Turnpike, the faster of the two routes (the Merritt Parkway is the more genteel and scenic) from Darien to Manhattan.

There are a number of quarters of Manhattan in which two Fairfield County teenage boys might be said to be fish out of water, and the Diamond District, the block of West 47th Street, between Fifth and Sixth Avenues, is one of them. A teeming, other-centurylike world unto itself plunked whole into the midst of the hotel and shopping district near Rockefeller Center, the street is filled with bearded Hasidic Jews who ply the same craft their great-great-grandfathers first plied in the ghettos of Europe because diamonds were valuable, portable, and hideable: If the Cossacks descended, if the next Inquisition erupted, you could try to bribe a captor not to harm your children.

Alex had come here before with the booty from his previous heists. He and Jim snaked through the black-hatted, black-coated, Yiddish-speaking throngs, carrying the clanking duffel bag full of silverware, as casually as they could manage.

"There's the place," Alex said, pointing to a cluttered storefront with a WE BUY/SELL GOLD AND SILVER sign.

A swarthy, unsmiling man of unclear ethnicity stood behind a glass display case. "Alex starts talking to the guy, says we have all this silver we want to sell. It was definitely a shady deal." Did the merchant have any idea how it was obtained? "Oh, I'm sure. Two seventeen-year-olds with a bag full of silver?

"The guy ends up buying it. Giving us five hundred dollars. All of a sudden *I* had five hundred dollars!" (Neither Jim nor Alex had any idea that the silver was valued at fifty times that.) Jim's part-time job at the gas station had brought him less than a hundred a week. "I had never even had *two* hundred dollars at one time! This was like—*Jesus!*"

Jim was dumbstruck as they started back to Connecticut. Stars were in his eyes as he clutched the steering wheel. As the car alighted from the West Side Highway to hop the Cross Bronx Expressway for the Turnpike, Alex turned toward Jim and coolly said: "I can get you a quarter ounce of cocaine for that."

Jim had partaken of cocaine, but knew nothing of costs and quantities. "A quarter of an ounce? How much is that?" he asked. A couple of weeks ago he was pumping gas, going to school, and doing a little pot; tonight he was a certified profiteering house burglar invited to become a serious dealer. And he *still* had to get home in time for dinner.

"Seven grams," Alex answered.

Jim fumbled to lower the volume on Pink Floyd so he could get a handle on what was coming down here. "What am I gonna *do* with all that?" he almost pleaded.

Alex had an answer. "Well, you can always sell half and get, like, three or four hundred dollars for it. And keep half. And then you'll be all set."

Jim started mulling it over out loud.

Alex said, "If you give me the money I can get it from this guy I know."

After dropping Alex off, Jim walked into his house seeing stars, breathing hard: five hundred-dollar bills weighing down his pants pockets and a giant guilt hangover weighing down his eyebrows. He walked around for a couple of days nursing Alex's proposition. The world of larceny was new to him. He felt like twice the farmboy he'd been when he first came to Darien. Dare-ye-in. I dare ya to be in with the in crowd in this ye-olde-New-England burg. *Bare*ly in: if you were a nerd, a herb, a hayseed, a loser, a bonehead, an asshole, a wimp, a wuss, or a rube.

In the smoking area outside the cafeteria, during a free period between science and history, Jim handed Alex the cash. All five hundred dollars of it. Then he walked into Mr. Pavia's U.S. History class, shaking: He was now one half of the Darien High Class of '85's version of the Cali Drug Cartel, yet, he realized, he didn't even know what a quarter ounce of cocaine *looked* like.

As it turned out, he never would.

Several days passed, during which Alex continued to assure Jim, "It should happen tomorrow." "Tomorrow." And, again, "Tomorrow." Then one day Alex came up to Jim in the cafeteria with a man-we-gotta-*talk* look on his face. Jim recalls: "He's like, 'Well, I got it last night and I came home and went into my room and had it in my pants pocket, and it was really late and I took off all my clothes and got into bed. And then my dad came in and picked up my pants and he's, like, 'Where have you been?!'

Alex looked so upset as he continued: " 'He went through my pockets. He found it. He flushed it down the toilet.' "

Jim's stomach sank and he flushed with anger. "I said: 'You've *got* to be fucking *kid*ding me! I cannot believe what you're telling me!' " But Alex shook his head helplessly.

Jim was reeling. He suspected that Alex was lying, that he'd pocketed the money. "I just went home and stewed. Things kept turning around in my mind: Do I believe him? Then I thought: Does it even matter what Alex did? Shit, I *robbed* a house! I robbed these nice old people I was *working* for! Why did I even *do* it?" Eventually, after a few days he concluded Alex *had* been lying. Alex had taken his five hundred dollars.

Jim had gotten into other trouble with Alex, less than a month earlier. The two boys had attended the Darien High hockey game against its big rival, Cheshire High. After the game (which Darien won), Alex and Jim were involved in a brawl on the ice against the opposite team's fans. Shoving, spitting and hockey-stick-banging erupted; the ice had to be cleared by police several times, yet the brawling persisted, with more and more kids joining the melee. Jim and Alex were among the youths arrested.

Purse-snatching, drug-taking, brilliant athleticism, especially in football and wrestling, the use of the area's woods for criminal activity—and now all-out melees at hockey games: Alex Kelly's high school career was, indeed, beginning to resemble the local legend Billy Hughes's. Some wondered if Alex was not consciously imitating him. Or attempting to outdo him.

During this same period of time that Alex had become a house burglar, Chris Kelly was veering out of control. Police were stopping him for speeding on his motorcycle with alarming regularity. Yet Melanie Kelly reacted by redoubling her involvement in the town's Republican Committee. One of the group's leaders would "see her at meetings three or four nights a week, during the time that the boys were getting in trouble. It always amazed me that she would be out at these meetings—behaving as if nothing else was going on in her life."

Perhaps there was no other way for Melanie to emotionally survive *but* to imagine that. Perhaps Joe's temper, with the boys' misdeeds, had become too extreme to deal with. Or perhaps she really was the thing that people would end up calling her during Alex's eight years in Europe—the *last* thing in the world she ever wanted to be: a bad mother.

One night, a Darien police officer, Rebecca Hahn, was doing radar scans on the Post Road— "and," as she recalls it, "here comes a motorcycle at ninety-five miles an hour." Hahn pulled out in her car and radioed in: "In pursuit—motorcycle—I can't catch it!" More and more, the Darien cops spent their evenings in these Keystone Kops pursuits, trying to save kids before they wrapped their legs, brains, and vehicles around lampposts. This harrowing chase of Chris Kelly was nothing unusual for the patrolmen.

Rebecca Hahn (now Rebecca Nathanson, professor of criminal justice at a local community college) recalls: "I chase him all the way down to the Stamford line. He almost hit one of our police cars that tried to block him. Goes around, gets on the highway. We put it on the hotline, not knowing where he's going."

Like Christie Hill Road's own Evel Knievel, Chris "gets down to where the cops are working the Mianus Bridge detail. [The bridge was being repaired after it had collapsed.] Those cops have heard it on the radio. *They* take off after him. Chris gets off Indian Field Road in Greenwich—by now he's also got a state trooper after him. The state trooper radios in that the motorcyclist is going too fast to even *try* to chase him. Then he ends up running his bike up a dirt embankment and crashing.

"We go to Greenwich Hospital, 'cause they want me to identify him as the person I chased. And he's in the hospital raising a freaking ruckus the likes of which you have *never* seen. He got banged up pretty good: broke a leg, head injury."

Jay Bush says Chris told him how his father had reacted to the injury. "The doctor called up Joe in the middle of the night and said, 'Look, we've got your son here. Don't be alarmed— he's going to make it—but he needs an operation.' Joe just said, 'Put Humpty Dumpty back together again; put him in a cab and send him home.' Then he went back to sleep. So Melanie went down there and sat with Chris and held his hand."

But if Joe Kelly was glibly matter-of-fact about his oldest son's injuries, he was anything but matter-of-fact about the police coming into his home to arrest the boy.

After Chris was released from the hospital, Officer Hahn, a young woman with masses of curly red hair who does not suffer fools gladly, went to the Kelly home on Christie Hill Road, armed with a warrant to arrest Chris for reckless driving.

Officer Hahn was the first and lone woman in the Darien Police Department (and eventually the force's first female detective)—Darien's own bona fide feminist heroine. Her pet issues were domestic violence, which she deplored as a police officer and as a woman (cop boyfriends, she'd noted sadly, were often potential batterers), and rape. Rape was not about sex—it was about power: *She* knew that, but sometimes it seemed the courts didn't. Officer Hahn had finally helped effect the conviction in May 1983 of a twenty-seven-year-old Stamford auto mechanic, on a rape charge. The mechanic had met a young woman at a Stamford bar, the Rocket Cafe, then took her to the Darien graveyard (the Four Girls' favorite drinking site), whereupon he attempted to strangle her and he raped her. The mechanic had been arrested in the past for rape, then acquitted; arrested again for a second alleged rape and, again, acquitted. After this third arrest, Becky Hahn felt that if he walked again, every woman in town, from the waitresses at the Sugar Bowl to the Muffie moms at Wee Burn, would be in danger.*

But the bigger, more amorphous danger, Becky knew, was The Attitude. Male cops, God love 'em—they had The Attitude bigtime. They were supermen, conquistadors. Becky was always trying to convince her colleagues that their highly physical, "win-at-all-cost, no-one-gets-the-better-of-me," approach sometimes only dug them in deeper. "They go in with the big *S* on their chest and, the first thing, they have to lay hands on everybody. They use strength and force before they use reason. *My* attitude was: We don't have to get into this big fight with these people! When someone's not cooperating, if a cop gets in his face, he'll just *escalate* it."

But if it was "me against thirty guys" in the squad room, it was her against hundreds of peers at Weed Beach and at the keg parties. For Becky Hahn, like the young people she policed, was an executive's daughter from the neighboring town of Trumbull, by way of St. Louis. She'd discovered police work serendipitously: As a horse-obsessed teenager, she'd taken a part-time job in the high-school-level Police Cadets corps solely in order to earn money for the upkeep of her prized steed. That job led her to go on to a criminal justice major at a local college. She discovered she liked police work almost as much as she liked jumping and riding and trekking to horse shows.

Her police uniform signaled to Darien parents that she was a member of the working class; as such, she got a glimpse of them in ways that might have been hidden if she'd socialized

---

*The auto mechanic was sentenced to twenty years in prison. He served eight and is now out of prison.

with, rather than apprehended, their children. ("Do you *know* what you pulled me away from?" they'd dismissively snap at her when they arrived at the station, at her behest, to pick up their drunk and unchaperoned fourteen year olds.)

So, as the sole woman on the police force and as a business-man's kid in a blue-collar job, Officer Hahn was used to watching Darien people of all classes and genders behave in ways that made her roll her eyes heavenward. She thought the town held no more surprises. Still, when she went to the Kelly house she was taken aback by what Alex's friends had already been struck by: the father's great rage and mother's passive silence.

She recalls: "I go in the back door and Chris is sitting in the family room, watching TV. My partner and I knock on the door. I say, 'We have a warrant for your arrest.' He says, 'Okay'—lets us in. Stands up to get his jacket to come with us."

The Kellys had already been called and informed of the impending arrest. Still: "Joe comes out of the kitchen like somebody lit him on fire. 'Who the *hell* do you think you are!'" he yells at me and my partner. "'You have *no* right to be in my house!' He proceeds to go up one side of me and down the other—berating, berating, berating: loud, aggressive *scream-ing!*"

Didn't this man know his kids had real problems? That rampaging against the messenger at this advanced stage of his sons' predicaments was not just the ultimate kamikaze version of The Attitude but a pathetic attempt to hide in clear sight? Hahn had turned up Alex or Chris Kelly at every party she ever busted; Chris and his vehicles were the bête noire of the department; every Darien cop who was working the night of the hockey melee, plus Troop G of the state police, had to be called to the rink because of the chaos Alex instigated.

"You have no right to be in my house!"?

Joe Kelly had to be dreaming!

Yet the mother's behavior seemed even stranger. While her

husband was screaming at the two uniformed officers, "Melanie Kelly just stood there," Rebecca Hahn Nathanson recalls today. "She just stood there and didn't say or do anything."

It is hard to know what to make of the Kellys' behavior at such moments. But beneath their different forms of defensiveness—Joe Kelly's outsize fury, Melanie Kelly's passive stoicism—there surely was pain. That pain was suggested years later. After Chris had died from an overdose and Alex, charged with the rapes, was hiding in Europe, the Kellys attended a Darien social event and made a remark to someone present. In those rueful—and likely exaggerated—words resided a lifetime of disappointment and heartache.

They said: "Don't ever have children."

CHAPTER 4

AFTER LUNCH PERIOD ON MAY 31, 1984, AT THE END OF Alex's and Jim Hunter's junior year—and about three weeks after Alex took the five hundred dollars from Jim—Darien High was abuzz: Mavis and Alex had been arrested! At school! And they had put up one hell of a fight!

The Darien police had come upon them sitting in the Kellys' car during lunch hour. When it was found that Alex's driver's license had been suspended, Detective Ronald Bussell—who would eventually become Alex's chief nemesis—approached the car and saw Alex (not one to take responsibility if he did not have to) pass a bag full of pot to Mavis. As the Darien *News-Review* would later report, "When Officer Bussell tried to seize the evidence, McGarry allegedly tossed the baggie back to Kelly"—the two *were* well-matched—"who then ran towards the high school scattering the contents of the bag on the pavement. The detective, however, managed to detain McGarry and retrieve the bag containing marijuana 'residue.'"

The newspaper's account continues: "Kelly emerged from the high school a few minutes later and submitted to arrest."

It is not clear if Alex was on his way to, or from, committing another burglary at the time of the arrest, or if the police were just acting on an educated hunch that the spate of very recent burglaries in the Kelly neighborhood might be something that this known troublemaker had some knowledge of. Whatever the reason, something that Alex said at the station apparently led the police to question him about the ten houses that had been burglarized since August 31. Did they happen to know anything about any of these incidents?

Alex apparently had something to tell the police—at least with respect to somebody else.

Jim Hunter (who had somehow missed hearing about the day's dramatic events) was waiting around after early-football practice for his mother to pick him up. And waiting. And *waiting*. When she finally got there he asked, "What took you so long?"

The reply was not one he'd expected. "The police were just over," Mrs. Hunter replied as evenly as possible. "They searched your room and the basement and found a stolen tape deck."

"At this point," Jim recalls, "I'm just *spinning*. I'm: Oh my God, I can't *believe* this!"

What eventually followed was Jim's tearful confession to both his parents. In direct contrast to Joe Kelly's attitude when Chris had been arrested, Jim Hunter's father informed his son: "You're going to go to the police station and turn yourself in."

The next day, Jim, accompanied by his mother and father, did just that. He sat down with Detectives Bussell and Hugh McManus (who is presently police chief). "Oh, I was *shitting*— I was *very* scared," Jim remembers. "They started talking about Alex and all the things they thought he was involved in. They thought he had burglarized all these houses. And they brought up the gas station. They said, 'You're in a lot of trouble. You better come clean.' So—to hell with Alex—I told them everything."

Telling wasn't good enough. The detectives demanded to be led to the silverware fence. So Jim took a ride into Manhattan with the two and pointed out the storefront. "The detectives really put the screws to the guy and got some of it back." Some, but not most: The silverware stolen by Jim that the fence hadn't yet gotten rid of was valued at only $2,000—apparently he had resold the other $23,000 worth.

Now came the arrests.

Jim was charged with one count of second-degree burglary and one count of first-degree larceny.

On June 15, 1984, Alex was arrested. He was arraigned on June 25, in Stamford Criminal Court, on nine counts of burglary and nine counts of larceny. In addition, he was charged with aiding and abetting Jim in his pawning of the silver from Jim's burglary. The Kellys began what would eventually become a pattern of rescuing their son from criminal situations: They raised the $10,000 posted for his bail, and then sat down with the police and determined the worth of everything Alex had stolen.

Mavis turned herself in in early July. She was faced with charges of third-degree burglary and sixth-degree larceny and was released on $2,500 bond. Her parents hired Stamford criminal defense lawyer Michael "Mickey" Sherman. Sherman had successfully defended the recently convicted Stamford auto mechanic who Becky Hahn had arrested for rape on his two earlier rape charges. (He had declined to represent him the third time.) Though he grew up in Greenwich, Mickey Sherman is not your typical Fairfield County type—he's more Long Island or L.A.: a perenially bronzed, ever-jesting, middle-age man who favors Leroy Neiman prints and who can't resist going on Geraldo Rivera's cable TV show, even when Rivera (genially) insults him, or dropping the name of his self-described best friend, singer Michael Bolton. But the

starstruck quality is dropped at the courtroom door; arguing a
case, Sherman is shrewd—one local legal observor said "brilliant"; and he is a consummately realistic dealmaker. (Says
Senior Assistant State's Attorney David Cohen, "Mickey is
gifted in the art of getting the attainable.")

All three*—Alex, Mavis, and Jim—had "youthful offender"
status (all were sixteen when they'd committed the crimes) yet
only Mavis was spared: The charges against her were
dropped. "The judge," Sherman says, "did his best to give her
a very stern lecture about what could have happened if she'd
been sent to jail, and impressed her with the seriousness of the
offense." Shortly after her case was dropped, Mavis's parents
whisked her away from Darien; she was never seen there
by the Keg Club crowd again.**

During Mavis's proceedings, however, Sherman met Alex
and his parents. The meeting between Sherman and the Kellys
would, a year and a half later, prove significant.

Kingk! Kingk! Kingk! Kingk! Kingk! Kingk! Kingk!: the sound
of dozens of steel cell doors, including his own, snapping
automatically closed, one right after another, was the part of
being incarcerated that most stayed in Jim Hunter's mind
every night as he fell asleep in the John R. Manson Youth
Institute, next door to the Cheshire Correctional Facility in
upstate Connecticut. *Kingk! Kingk! Kingk! Kingk! Kingk!:* At
least he had his own cell now. The first night they'd put him in
the mental wing, where the other young prisoners were

---

*A fourth defendant—a girl—was also arrested on conspiracy to commit
burglary and larceny; her case was disposed of.
**Some of the old crowd in Darien did see a woman they thought was Mavis,
in disguise, being interviewed on a tabloid TV show shortly after Alex was
brought back to Connecticut from his eight years as a fugitive. This author's
calls to the producer of the show brought denials that Mavis McGarry had
ever appeared on it. Repeated calls to Mavis's last known place of employment, in Los Angeles, failed to turn up any leads on her current whereabouts.

screaming and making noise all night. Jim had "bawled and bawled and just couldn't believe it!" *Thirty* days! But his parents had insisted he serve the sentence immediately. They wanted the experience of prison to be burned into his consciousness so he would never do anything like *that* again. Two burglaries was *not* something to be let off the hook for—that's the way Jim's parents saw it.

Not so Joe and Melanie Kelly. In contrast to the Hunters, the Kellys were not rushing Alex (who had committed nine burglaries to Jim's two) into punishment so that he might learn a hard but useful lesson. Instead, they hired an estimable criminal attorney, John Vallerie, to find the best deal for Alex, and they were giving Alex the summer off. As for therapy or counseling—an educator in the area authoritatively speculates: "Did the family seek intervention in a serious or ongoing way from the time he was arrested for the thefts? Probably not."

One thing Alex did do that summer, Jim says, "was go around telling everybody I'd narc'd on him." Worse, "My dad said someone drove down our road and threw a rock through our window. He couldn't see who it was but he saw a black sports car drive up." Jim was convinced it was Russ Pinto's RX-7. "I'm sure Alex got him to drive it and Alex hurled the rock. My dad said, 'Yeah, I think it was Alex'. I said, 'I *know* it was!'"*

Whether or not the rock had been thrown by Alex, he was apparently not grounded during that summer of 1984. While Jim sweated it out at Manson, Alex went to a party given by

---

*During Jim's first year at college, he was dancing at a Dead concert and "I feel this tap on my shoulder and I turn around and it's Alex, saying, 'Ah, look at this freak!' like nothing had happened. I gave him a look and walked away." Years after that, when Alex had fled to Europe, FBI agents visited Jim in his new home state and asked them if he knew where his old friend was— there was a $100,000 reward. Jim snorted out a laugh and replied, "Believe me, if I knew where Alex was I'd have that money right now; I would love that to be the case." He says: "I always thought if I ever saw Alex after that, I would beat the shit out of him and then drag his ass down to the nearest police station."

two brothers. The large colonial-with-pool burst with kids drinking beer as the music of the Police, Bob Marley and the Wailers, and, of course, the Dead boomed from the stereo speakers. One brother—here called Nick—was walking around checking on things, making sure no one was where they shouldn't be. He remembers Steel Pulse was playing as he walked up the bedroom landing. "My bedroom door was closed—not a normal thing. So I opened the door." Alex Kelly and Nick's friend Darcy were on Nick's bed, both fully clothed. "The second the door opened, Alex just let go of her. All I remember is . . . [Darcy's] look of fear. She yelled my name— like, 'Nicky!'—and jumped—*ran*—right over to me. I instantly knew something was wrong. I was, '[Darcy], *what's wrong?*' She didn't answer. She was dying to get out of there, I could tell it in her eyes. She just *bolted.* She just literally ran *straight* downstairs."

A few minutes later, Nick's older brother, Reed, came upon Darcy sitting with a friend in another room. Reed says: "She was crying. She was totally, physically upset, just *freaked* out. Obviously, something had happened that was traumatic for her. I was thinking: What's *this* all about? Why is she so shaken?

"She said, 'Please make Alex Kelly leave.'*

"So I did. I asked him to please leave. He was calm and good about it. He left the party."

Nick says, "I saw [Darcy] not too long ago and she said—this is how she's always described it and how she describes it to this day: '*Alex Kelly was not letting me leave.*'" He had been physically restraining her in some way.

The arrests of Alex, Mavis, and Jim; Jim's incarceration; Mavis's disappearance off the face of the earth—all of this shook up the Darien kids. Alex's being able to hang out and

---

*The author wrote to Darcy (a pseudonym), requesting an interview. She did not reply.

party all summer as if he'd done nothing wrong—*that* shook up the Darien kids. It was proof that some kids could keep sliding by on luck. But for every kid like Alex, there was another who paid with his or her life, simply for being at the wrong place at the wrong post-party moment.

A girl the whole crowd loved was killed that summer when a pickup truck, driven by an inebriated friend, crashed and rolled on a highway. At the girl's funeral, the Four Girls, who had been close to her, were almost inconsolable. Why her? Why so young? What had she done to deserve this? They cried for their lost friend and for the end of their own innocence. Every year, it seemed—sometimes twice a year—another Darien teenager was killed in a car accident. If life in this town was perfect, then why did these things happen? The answer, of course, was not to drink while driving—maybe not to drink at all. That's how all the bad things started.

At summer's end, on September 14, 1984, Alex Kelly stood before Judge Martin Nigro in his fake-mahogany-backed courtroom in the shabby brick Superior Court building (it has all the judicial grandeur of your average DMV) that's plunked in the middle of the parking lot adjacent to the Stamford police station. Alex and his parents had emptied their pockets and taken off their jewelry and buckled belts before passing through the metal detector in the cramped lobby. As they waited for the elevator to the second floor, they probably heard fellow arraignees, sprawled on the phone booth seats with the accordian doors open, screaming through the receivers to their bail-paying girlfriends.

It is the task of a jurist in Nigro's position to talk tough to those juvenile offenders whose futures are not necessarily destined to be linked to this building. So when the sweet-faced young man in the blue blazer stood before him with his nine robbery counts, Judge Nigro might have scared him, as he had Mavis. Or barked, as he had to Jim: "I *never* want to see you back here!"

But Judge Nigro's words from the bench to Alex Kelly reflect something more than the standard tough warning. They suggest genuine disgust with the young man *and* acknowledgment that Alex was being coddled by the system. Alex's parents, through a deal Alex's attorney John Vallerie had worked out, would now make restitution to their son's robbery victims in the form of payments totaling about $100,000. In exchange for this, part of Alex's thirty-five-month sentence at the Manson Youth Institute would be suspended. Judge Nigro affirmed, disapprovingly, that the parents' cash-for-early-release was part of the deal.

"You're getting every consideration possible," the judge told Alex. "You're a thief, a burglar, and of no use to society, as far as I can see. You're buying your way out of a jail sentence." Nigro then grumbled that he had approved the cash-restitution-for-plea deal only "because I think that the victims shouldn't suffer anymore."

Judge Nigro read a portion of a letter from one of the burglary victims, who said she would never feel safe in her house since Alex's break-in. Yet she was the exception. "The attitude of the victims," the judge said, "is an attitude in almost every instance of extreme generosity that *I* would not have entertained if I were a victim in this case. I would have wanted to see this punk put in jail for fifty years. Now your family is going to have to suffer for your conduct. You're going to jail, but not for as long as I think you should be."

Immediately after his sentencing by Judge Nigro, Alex was transferred to the John R. Manson Youth Institute, where he was an inmate for slightly more than two months—until November 21, 1984. Alex's sanction for the burglaries is invariably referred to today as "rehab" (which the post–Manson Youth Institute part of it was), thus deemphasizing the crime. But the first part of Alex's punishment was *not* rehab.

Says Manson's warden, Robert Ronne, rather bluntly: "We are a prison."

Clearly, there is no mistaking the facility for anything else. The compound of sprawling wings of cells is ringed by six rows of razor ribbon, controlled by computerized fence alarms, and guarded by an armed perimeter vehicle—an officer with a weapon who drives around the compound twenty-four hours a day, seven days a week. Alex Kelly must have swallowed hard when he entered his six-by-eight-foot cell, with its six-by-eight-inch window, learned that there was one shower for every two dozen inmates, and realized that for the indefinite weeks to come all his daily movements would be made at the pleasure of the 300 guards. "The guards tell you when to take a shower and when you can make a phone call," Warden Ronne says. "All phone calls are recorded— there is *no* privacy. I never had an inmate who *wanted* to stay."

Very few of the 359 other inmates were boys with backgrounds like Alex's. "To quote the former [Connecticut Corrections] Commissioner Manson, 'You're innocent until proven broke,'" says Ronne. (Indeed, that Alex ultimately served only one sixteenth of his sentence attests to the fact that, in part thanks to his parents' ability to make the $100,000 restitution for the stolen goods, he was fifteen-sixteenths "innocent.") Fights broke out a lot, and inmates made weapons "out of everything you can imagine," Warden Ronne says, "from Bic pens to mop handles," though the worst of the boys were locked away in the chronic discipline unit. Wake-up was seven, lock-down at ten.

But between those hours, the young inmates at Manson were run through a gauntlet of activities that were both diagnostic and productive. For the first of his two months at Manson, Alex was either at high school classes or going through "needs assessment" (tests and interviews to determine his medical, mental health, educational, vocational, drug and alcohol needs) and "risk assessment": his potential danger in various areas, including the area of sexual offenses. The assessments are made on a scale of one to five—from least to most needy and at-risk. The assessments, once finalized, are forwarded to treatment providers within the facility—but in Alex's case he was not at Manson long enough to get treatment there.

Dr. William Samek, the sexual disorder specialist, when told of the program at Manson, wearily opined that it sounded like standard insufficient juvenile treatment. He believes that juvenile facilities often teach the young offender "that the system is lying when it says there will be consequences for his action, that all the consequences he will get are another slap on the wrist."

Samek may have been right. At some point after his release from Manson in November 1984, Alex went into drug rehab for four months—and almost immediately after his release from that program, a football teammate remembers going to a Fourth of July pig roast, "and there was Alex—it was the first time anybody had seen him in a while—doing lines of cocaine in the car and going, 'Hey, what's up, man?'"

In the fall, Alex returned to Darien High not as a pariah but as the object of admiring fascination. Reentering in what would have been the second semester of his senior year,* "he was, like, a legend," says then-freshman Ed O'Neill. "I remember all kinds of people saying, 'He's a bad, bad man,' in an awed sense. And, 'Wow, that kid went to jail for robbing houses.'"

His recent incarceration may have also added to his luster in the eyes of his biggest secret admirer, Amy Molitor. With Mavis gone from the scene, the beautiful Amy, now a sophomore, moved in to claim her self-admitted idol. Says Amy's

---

*Having lost the year, this effectively became his junior year; he became part of the class of '86 instead of the class of '85.

then close friend, "It was the most exhilarating moment of her life to get what she always wanted."

If Amy's parents were concerned that she had taken up with a boy who had just gotten out of juvenile prison, they certainly didn't show it. "Amy's [real] father liked Alex a lot," the close friend says. "And Amy's mother was, I think, fascinated by him."

Within their social group, Alex-and-Amy were about the hippest thing going. Today, she is remembered by numerous high school peers as, almost unquestionably, "the most beautiful girl in the class" (no small honor, of course, given the embarrassment-of-riches to choose from). She and Alex went through stages—for a while, they dressed like hippies (especially for Dead concerts) in matching fringed suede jackets. "Then they went through a very racy stage, where they were both hiphopping out of their parents' sports cars," a friend remembers.

"Everyone was in awe of Alex-and-Amy," says a young man, a year younger than Amy, who was an actor in high school and is now a media rep in Manhattan. "They were the best-looking couple—she was beautiful, absolutely beautiful. But, at the same time, they were very distant from other kids. A lot of people didn't know them."

What people *did* know—could not help but know—was how sexually charged their relationship was. If Alex and Mavis had fought grandiosely and compulsively, he and his new girlfriend showed affection with that same lack of restraint and apparent exhibitionism. "Initially it was gross," says a younger classman. "They were so touchy with each other: during free periods, in front of a hundred people. They were commonly spotted like, literally, going at it, in the cafeteria. People would say, 'They're so horny . . .' and 'God, they should get a room!' But, mostly, people didn't comment on it. People just took it for granted." This young man adds: "Looking back on it, he was *always* involved in a serious relationship, which was weird. Few other kids were—not *all* the time. It was like he was a dependent-type person—he needed the affection of someone at all times."

What most people did not know, but might have guessed, is how heavily the components of risk and limit-pushing figured into Alex and Amy's intimacy. One of Amy's friends knew that one of the things Alex did was tie Amy up—just her hands. "It wasn't your typical high school sexual experience," says Amy's friend. "I remember her specifically telling me it was *the* best, but I was stunned when she told me some of the things they did—things you're not prepared for when you're fifteen." The friend was worried. But "they were having fun. A lot of it took place in her own house with her parents home. At any moment they could have gotten caught—they liked the risk."

It is possible, in retrospect, to speculate that Alex's mistake (from the standpoint of his own self-interest) was in taking this risk-intimacy from a consensual to a nonconsensual situation. ("If you tell anybody, I'll kill you" may be a suburban teenage boy's idea of haute-eighties noir sexplay—or it may be a literal threat; it depends on whom you say it *to*.)

But, however willingly Amy may have participated, her boyfriend was also able to behave in ways that were frightening. "He really had a temper and he was jealous of any guys she got close to or had past relationships with," the friend says. "They got into an argument once—drunk. She had to run from him. She told me, afterward, 'I was scared of him.'"

Shortly before the end of the school year, Jillian Henderson and another girl very close to the Four Girls, Kimberly Marengo, were at a party. So was Alex. Jillian was running late—she'd been in trouble with her mother and had a strict curfew—and Kimberly had already taken off. Alex offered Jillian a ride home in his parents' wood-paneled station wagon. From their childhoods at Middlesex Swim Club all through their crazed drink-and-dope Weed Beach and Keg

Club days, Jillian had known Alex as someone who was "never *not* in trouble." But then, she was not exactly Miss Prep herself. "Ever since that night," Jillian says today, "I've spent a lot of time wondering: *Why* did I accept the ride with him? But hindsight's twenty-twenty. And I think I figured that since Alex was going out with Amy—she was pretty straight-and-narrow; a sweet and bright girl—it looked like he was turning everything around."

Once in the car, Alex turned down a street very close to his home: Nolen Lane (coincidentally, the location of Jim Hunter's solo burglary foray). "It was right across from Wee Burn Country Club—a circular road, so I knew there was no exit." Jillian was a little nervous—what were they doing *here* in this cul-de-sac?; he was supposed to be taking her *home*—but then she realized that "Alex had a good friend, J. R. McDermott, who lived there and maybe he was stopping there for some reason."

But Alex did not mention visiting J.R. He just pulled up to the curb and turned off the engine. Jillian went from being a little nervous to *a lot* nervous. And annoyed: She had been going out with a friend of Alex's "forever." And she was friends with Amy. And it was late. Jillian was rarely at a loss for a tart riposte, but now she was almost pleading. "I said, 'I'm in so much shit with my mother right now, I need to go home!'"

Alex's reaction? "He put his hands on me and told me to 'shut the fuck up.'

"I had a skirt on—not a miniskirt but a skirt above my knees—and he put his hand between my legs and it wasn't a nice touch—it was a grab." When Jillian told him, again, that she had to get home, "He started grabbing me and getting *real* angry.

"And he basically pulled my arm and opened the back door and put down the seat [of the station wagon, converting it into a flattened back area]. And the whole time I'm thinking, 'Oh my God! Is he watching too much TV or something?'"

Jillian says what Margaret said, and what Julia said in their interviews: "We didn't really know about date rape back in 1985. And I was just fifteen years old."

So Jillian did as she was told. "I shut up. I was scared. I just shut up and got in the back with him. There was no kissing—he just had a goal and there it was." Not only did the act have nothing to do with romance, but, she believes, "It didn't have anything to do with sex, either. He had one hand around my throat and my head was hitting against the station wagon door—he was really trying to jam my head into it. And he kind of thrust. It was real forceful and real quick and real vulgar. Then I started crying, and he told me to get the hell out of the car.

"And he made me walk home. It was about two miles from my home." (It was a block from Alex's.) "My underwear was in his car, but I wasn't going to plead, 'Could you please let me back into your car so I can get my underwear?'

"I walked all the way home, alone, in the middle of the night, crying."

Things were escalating for Alex. Whereas his post-alleged-attack behavior with the earlier girls had been nonverbal (running out of the woods and leaving Margaret there, dazed) or verbally cutting but not angry (telling Julia he didn't want anyone to think he'd done anything with her), now, with Jillian, there was verbal anger ("Shut the fuck up!"). And now there was not a description of just a sexual attack but one also of a physical threat: the hand around Jillian's neck.

The next day Jillian ran over to Kimberly's. She had bruises on her thighs from the attack and she showed them to Kimberly. Jillian told Kimberly: "He *pinned* me *down!* I don't know what the deal was. I don't know what I did to make him so angry."

Dr. Samek, the sexual disorder specialist, thinks he understands. "The disorder progresses," he explains. "Increasing anger is one symptom. As the perpetrator gets angrier at himself—he now knows he's a slimeball—he has to dump that anger elsewhere. He does so by being more vicious with his victims. He gets angrier at women in general as a displacement of his anger with himself."

But, just as Alex's alleged attacks were growing more vicious, the girls' responses were getting gutsier: Margaret had been terrified and totally passive; Julia had punched Alex (but had snapped into silence right after that). Jillian took things one step further: She and Kimberly decided to be vocal and aggressive about Jillian's attack. But even that approach could not get past the byzantine power relations of 1980s high-school sexism. For if Margaret was muffled by fear related to propriety (to this day she's afraid that her socially prominent in-laws will know she was raped at thirteen) and Julia by painful insecurity (to have a boy tell others that he would never choose to have sex with you was unbearable), then Jillian fell victim to an old technique: Let the girls fight it out between themselves.

According to Jillian: At Weed Beach the next day, Kimberly laced into Alex: "You scumbag! How could you do this to my friend! And, by the way, nice to cheat on Amy after just a couple of months . . ." Alex then told Amy that Jillian had had a crush on him ever since their childhoods at Middlesex and that *she'd* come on to *him* in the car the other night—the incident was all *her* doing. Fueled by Alex's version, Amy bawled Jillian out in decidedly girl-gang epithets ("You fucking bitch . . . !") for trying to take away her boyfriend. She also vowed to tell *Jillian*'s boyfriend on her.

Jillian says she begged Amy: "Please do not say anything to [her boyfriend]. Whatever you do—I don't care if you hate me; I don't care if you think I'm a liar—but understand: *Alex* is the one who is sick." Amy stormed off and Jillian thought: Shit . . . I *liked* Amy! And now our friendship is history.

The Four Girls sat that night wondering how it had come to this: Two girls, both of them wronged by the same boy, forced into fighting *against* each other.

It was so damn unfair! Why did boys have so much power,

anyway? (Maybe Mr. Pavia was right when he sat girls down and said: "If the boys don't come and watch your field hockey games, then why are you out there cheering for them at their football games? *I* wouldn't!") What did it take for a girl in this town to be believed about a sexual matter? If you were a girl like Jillian—a cut-up, a smart mouth; not some goody-two-shoes—did you lose your right to any dignity, credibility, or feelings? Were you just flat-out not taken seriously? Was it just assumed that you always went around "asking for it," even when "it" was an attack? That any cool boy could do anything he wanted with you? And, once he did, *you'd* be blamed? *You'd* get in trouble?

The Four Girls wondered why life was so deceptive. Turn on MTV and there was Madonna strolling around, singing "Borderline," and there were Deborah Harry and Pat Benatar: *so* knowing, they never had to have any facial expression—they just looked hiply blank, vaguely imperious, and *incredibly* cool. The Four Girls were game to play by these rules—they were pretty sharp babes. But, in real life, the rules hadn't changed to keep up with those images. When the shit hit the fan and a girl in a car with a boy was made to have sex when she didn't want to—well, forget all those MTV images: It was back to the way your mothers had grown up—you were either a virgin or a whore, and if you weren't a virgin, then *no one* would listen to you.

Kathy Bishop says, "[Jillian] told everybody what had happened with Alex, but no one believed her."

Jillian recalls: "After that night, Alex would brush by me real close in the halls at school and say, 'Slut . . .', like he enjoyed intimidating me."

Nine months later, when Alex was arrested for the two rapes, Jillian learned the motifs of the attacks—the ordering of the girls into the open hatchbacks of the vehicles, the hand around the neck—and, with great frustration, thought, "Those things, they were his *signature!*" If only she could have been heard and respected when it happened to her, she might have provided a warning, a censure. She might have prevented those rapes.

Months after that, when Alex had fled to Europe, Jillian ran into Amy at a party. "Amy was drunk," Jillian says, "and as she walked up to me I thought, 'Oh my God, she's gonna let loose or hit me!' But she just said, real softly, 'You weren't lying when you said those things at the beach, were you?'

"And I just said, 'Amy, it doesn't matter anymore. Don't beat yourself up about it.'"

The incident with Alex affected Jillian greatly. "You say to yourself, 'I guess this is all I'm worth, after all.' Before what happened with Alex, I had only had one boyfriend. After that, I became promiscuous. You spend your time looking for that one person who will pop out of the woods and tell you you matter, but you go about it the wrong way. At least I did."

After graduating from Darien High, Jillian went to a university near Washington D.C.; while there, the aftereffects of the incident with Alex, combined with a college friend's abusive relationship, led Jillian to do volunteer work at a women's crisis center. She took hotline calls from victims of rape and domestic violence, and she worked with their children. The experience, she says, "helped me—one, because I saw how much worse it was for a lot of other people, and, two, because talking to those women helped me work through what I was going through. And it helped them to hear that they weren't alone." Shortly after that, Jillian met the young man who would become her husband—a military academy graduate. "At a time when I needed stability, he was that base." They married and have two children.

Jillian was interviewed by the prosecution prior to Alex's trial. But she ultimately—reluctantly—decided not to offer to testify for fear of hurting the career of her military-officer husband through her association with something that might be considered a sex scandal. As it turned out, Jillian's testimony would not have been admissible; no other alleged victims' testimony was allowed into the prosecution case in *State*

v. *Alex Kelly* by either Judge Martin Nigro in October or Judge Kevin Tierney in the May retrial.

Human behavior is complex and paradoxical. Despite the escalating trajectory of Alex's problem, he had become what he had never been before: an earnest and hardworking student. One classmate remembers him handing the algebra teacher, Miss Hannon, "extra work that he'd done, and looking so boyish, like a little kid who wanted to do good."

"I don't know what actually focused me," Alex told ABC's *Turning Point* in April 1996. "Doesn't everybody have ambitions? I was trying my best to get there." He was on his way to making the honor roll.

Alex started his senior year promisingly. As English teacher and wrestling coach Jeff Bouvier would write in a praiseful article published prominently in the Darien *News-Review*, "He was honorably mentioned by the Bridgeport *Post* for his efforts at noseguard on DHS's football team. . . . Mike Sangster, Kelly's football coach, said that he (Kelly) 'returned to football after a year layoff and was very coachable. He tried to do everything just the way we told him and, because of an intense psychological approach to the game, he was a dominating force in the middle of the defensive line.'"

But the upbeat picture that Sangster gave to Bouvier for publication did not tell the full story. One of Alex's football teammates that year remembers Alex on the football field *this* way: "He was always going nuts: jumping up and down, yelling, screaming, getting real fanatic. It was constant: at practice, at games. He was always a little more keyed up than other people. He knew how to behave in a social setting, but when he gets his adrenaline going, I don't think he can control himself that well.

"Alex went after me one time during a practice, a live scrimmage. He was on the defense, I was on the offense. He was holding a blocking dummy. He didn't see me coming.

You're still supposed to flow to the play like a normal defensive team would, but he just didn't see me. I accidentally knocked him over, and his helmet flew off." Alex's reaction? "He *ran* at me. With his helmet off. He was just . . . running *at* me. It was like he was going crazy over having been knocked down." The young man laughs nervously, remembering. "I stepped to the side and he fell right over. I was scared. I thought, 'What the heck triggered *that?* It was a perfectly clean play.' I went, 'Whoa, settle down.' And he did settle down, a few minutes later.

"But that was Alex. He snaps at certain moments. The guys who were watching weren't shocked. They knew he had that side to him. It was almost like you had to slap him out of it or something."

Jeff Bouvier's article went on to showcase Alex's brilliance as a wrestler. Alex had had a perfect 11–0 win record for the season and he was the rags-to-riches team's "odds-on MVP." But what the article failed to say about Alex's wrestling, many others have said.

A fellow team member told a friend: "Alex used to get all coked up before meets and pace up and down on the sidelines, like a madman, just waiting to go on."*

One wrestling spectator recalls, "You'd be in a crowd and someone would say, 'Alex is really goin' off there.'" A second says: "You get a wrestling opponent in some kind of awkward position where you're forcing some kind of pain to the point where he'll go, 'Stop!' and the other person will win the match: that's generally how Alex ended his matches. I remember watching and thinking, 'Wow, the other kid's *yelling.'*"

The most-repeated Alex Kelly wrestling story involves Alex's match against a large African-American wrestler from another school who was in the same weight class as Alex but appeared

---

*Jeff Bouvier did not respond to requests for an interview. As to whether any of the coaches may have known of Alex's alleged premeet cocaine use, one former student opined, "I doubt it."

much stronger. This wrestler was so self-confident, he'd shaved his number of wins into his hair. He arrived at the meet with his father and they regarded the Darien team as something they might have for breakfast.

Alex psyched out the player by looking at him while banging his own head against the padded wall. "Alex was really getting into it," a spectator recalls. "Staring the kid down. The kid and his father were laughing at Alex—like, 'You chump . . .'

"Within thirty seconds, Alex had the kid on the stretcher."

Finally, the mother of a wrestling teammate recalls another injured opponent. "The kid was tall and thin. I know he was hurt. The EMS crew was called in. They had to take him off the floor. It was very shocking."

Yet none of the coaches, teachers, or administrators put the excessive aggressiveness and hints of sadism together with aspects of his known history (the physically volatile relationship with Mavis, the burglaries) and thought Alex's behavior was cause for intervention. An administrator explains, "In a situation like that, where the kid's made progress, everybody is tripping over themselves to not have them slip back. There was a degree of wishful thinking."

During Christmas vacation 1985, Alex went skiing in Vermont. One night, he and two brothers named Mike and Dave went to a bar in Ludlow called the Pot Belly Pub. According to a friend to whom one of these young men spoke, two girls were at the pub—one seventeen, the other eighteen. Alex and his friends left with the girls and went to the house where one of the girls was staying. One of the girls, here called Diane Sales, went into a room with Alex.

What happened later in the evening is described in the investigative file on Kelly. According to someone who perused the file, when things became affectionate, Diane Sales (who had never had intercourse before) at first felt in control. But when she asked Alex to stop, he refused. He pinned her arms down and raped her.

Very soon after the incident, Diane Sales went to a local

hospital emergency room and had a "rape kit" (the standard test for rape) administered. Rape was indicated.

According to a source close to the prosecution, Diane Sales reported the incident to authorities in March 1995, shortly after hearing of Alex's return to this country for prosecution.

Contacted by this author in July 1997, Diane Sales confirmed that she had been a victim of Alex Kelly and that the experience had "most definitely" been traumatic. She said she had considered pursuing prosecution but that an attorney had told her it would be costly to build up a case "and even then it would be more of a heartache and headache on myself and my family than anything." But she told her story to an FBI agent on the case. Prosecutor Bruce Hudock tried to introduce Diane's testimony at Alex's rape trial, but Judges Nigro and Tierney disallowed testimony about Alex's alleged prior sexual assaults. Hudock scheduled Diane to make a statement at Alex's July 24 sentencing, and Diane flew to Connecticut from her home in a Western state to do so. But the judge (who did not even allow Adrienne Bak's mother, sisters, and husband to read their own statements) did not allow Diane Sales's testimony.

It was barely a month after this incident that Jeff Bouvier's glowing article on his star wrestler appeared in the hometown paper. The whole second half of the fifteen-paragraph piece praises Alex as having been "rejuvenated" and "rehabilitated" after his year out of school. Kelly, Bouvier writes, "is also impressing people in the classroom. He is currently earning A− grades and broke the magic 1,000 mark on the SATs. Kelly is applying to Colorado colleges and doesn't have to go begging for recommendations from his teachers."

Bouvier quotes a social studies teacher as calling Alex "talkative, verbal, and very conservative . . . actively involved and he cared about his work." He also quotes two female fellow students who spoke praisingly of Alex—one calling Alex a "model student-athlete."

While acknowledging that they were serious crimes, Bouvier treats Alex's premeditated burglaries mainly as the helpless byproduct of a courageously overcome drug problem—and Bouvier concludes his article with these optimistic words: "He is open about his 'problem' and speaks candidly to groups of freshmen about drugs and their potential to ruin a life. Or, in Kelly's case, to postpone the attainment of successes."

In fact, his friends from the time say, if Alex was off drugs it was not for a very long time.

According to the sexual disorder specialist Dr. Samek, it should not be surprising that Alex Kelly appeared, to Bouvier, to be so clearly on the road to success. "One of the keys" to the rapist's mentality, the doctor says, "is conning. They lie and manipulate skillfully. Especially the highly intelligent ones. The brighter the rapist you are treating," Samek says, "the greater is the possibility of thinking you've done a better job of treatment than you have. When a young man with this disorder has an I.Q. of over 120—which means he is in the top 10 percent, intellectually—it's riskier."

Alex Kelly was now living up to his intellectual capability: He received all A's and B's in his senior year.

Whenever a young person flamboyantly self-destructs just at the point that he has been showing great promise, it is tempting to speculate that the burden of living up to a parent's expressed (but never-believed) expectation is too great to bear. *Or* that that young person's anger at the parent is so great, he becomes destructive in order to hurt and humiliate the parent who has hurt and humiliated him. Either or both of these suppositions helps explain what happened next in Alex Kelly's life. But other factors were probably also building up to an inevitable crescendo that only Alex could foresee. "As the disorder that is rape progresses, the threshold increases," Dr. Samek explains. On the basis of his experience, the doctor speculates: "At this point Alex was probably doing a lot of masturbatory fantasy and finding that it took greater stimulation than it used to to get the same amount of excitement and pleasure. To get that greater stimulation, more violence in the fantasies was required."

Jeff Bouvier's article appeared in the Darien *News-Review,* accompanied by a photograph of a happy and wholesome-looking Alex, on Thursday, February 6. The next day, Amy Molitor left with her family for a winter semester-break trip to Florida. Alex was to stay in town—the Fairfield County Interscholastic Athletic Conference Championships were coming up in one week and he was expected to win handily in his weight class. Very few kids were staying in town during break week—most were off to Florida for sunshine, like Amy was, or to Vermont or New Hampshire for skiing. Alex did not want Amy to go away—and not just because so few kids would be left to hang out with. He seemed to know he needed her to rein him in in a very real and very serious way. Weeks later, Amy Molitor would confide this to a friend: "Alex begged me not to go away. He said, 'Please don't go away! Please don't go away! I think something bad is going to happen.' I *know* something bad is going to happen.'"

CHAPTER 5

SOPHOMORE DAN ANDERSON WAS HAVING SOME KIDS over on Monday, February 10, the night of the varsity basketball game, so the word got out among those who hadn't gone away for winter break: "Hey, party at Anderson's, seventhirty."

The Anderson house is a very large white two-story modified ranch with dark green shutters and a basketball hoop out front. It and its neighboring homes on Driftway Lane—right on the Tokeneke line (clear across town from Christie Hill Road, Leeuwarden Road, and Wee Burn Country Club)—are set far back on rolling acreage, so secure in this most exclusive part of Darien that they are neither fenced from the road nor from one another.

Early in the evening a group of kids started assembling there. "We were definitely the cool sophomores," is how one of the young men describes the crowd. Still, it was a small—one might say a scraggly—group (so few kids were left in town), and, though they may have been "cool," they were not the heirs to the Weed Beach crowd. Dan Anderson himself is, today, a clean-cut young man who exudes an almost old-fashioned rectitude. Kristen Stanley, another partygoer, was so conscientious a student, she went from Darien High to Princeton University. Though Andy Winebrenner—today a wide-smiling young man full of cool-dude panache and enthusiasm—was a diehard Dead fan, he was first and foremost a "prep" and his older brother Dewey was senior class president. These were *not* the outlaws.

In fact, when Tom Kelly got to the party at 10:30 P.M., "I remember thinking how lame it was. Ten kids sitting around a table, playing quarters. I remember wishing there were more girls there. All the girls were two years younger. I don't even remember hearing music. It was just a horrible, boring party."

Tom was there with Alex Kelly, who had picked him up earlier in the evening in Amy Molitor's Jeep Wagoneer. Then they'd gone to buy a case of beer. "We drank a few beers and I'm sure we smoked pot, then we went to the basketball game." Tom's friends Josh Edwards and John Houchin were on the basketball team; afterward, Alex, Tom, Josh, and John went over to Josh's house, so the two players could shower. The four boys then drove to Dan Anderson's, arriving at around 10:30.

And that's just the time that Adrienne Bak started getting desperate about securing a ride home in time to make her curfew.

Adrienne, who had just turned sixteen, was one of four children of Bill and Georgina Bak (pronounced "Back"). Bill was a corporate executive, Georgina a homemaker. Jeff was the oldest child; then came Kristen, a senior at Darien High, Adrienne, a sophomore at St. Mary's Academy in Greenwich, and finally Kimberly, who was at Middlesex Middle School. The Baks had moved to Darien from Illinois when Adrienne was in fourth grade and had recently moved to 1 Leeuwarden Road, into a very large white Colonial with a picket fence, on the corner of Christie Hill—and just doors from the Kellys' house.

The Baks belonged to the Country Club of Darien. "They were an all-American country club family," says a young man who played tennis with Adrienne. "Mr. Bak was a big corporate hitter, a CEO. Mrs. Bak was always playing golf and catching rays, living the good life. All the kids were jocks." Jeff Bak, a hefty young man, was playing center on the Clemson football team and recently had a tryout with the Tampa Bay Buccaneers. (A country club friend of Bill Bak's and Bill had talked, over golf, of how Jeff had grown and bulked up in one year, in preparation for college football, "from six-foot, one hundred eighty-five pounds," the man says, "to six-three, *two* hundred eighty-five pounds—he became a behemoth.") Adrienne was on the country club junior tennis team and on school soccer, basketball, and softball teams. Kristen and Kim were also athletes. And Georgina Bak taught aerobics at the First Congregational Church on the Post Road and Brookside Road.

The Baks' weekends might have been spent at the country club, but their values were grounded, not superficial. Bill Bak—a tall, very thin, dark-haired man who wore glasses and who one fellow clubman described as having "Ichabod Crane-ish looks"—was a definite family man, despite his dry wit, his enjoyment of golf, and what the fellow clubman describes as his "pretty typical business executive suburban guy" ways. "Some guys," the man observed, "would hang around after golf, others went home to their families. Bill Bak was one who went home after. And he always came to events with his wife. He was a family guy."

The Baks watched their kids closely. All had curfews. Bill and Georgina waited up for the girls when they returned home from parties, as they had waited up for Jeff, when he was in high school. If you didn't call from a party to say you'd be late coming home, you were grounded. If you called to say you'd miss curfew and did miss curfew, time was shaved off your *next* curfew. "Grounded" was a word not only heard but applied. "They were a normal family in a town where too many people only *looked* normal," a friend says. "The kids didn't screw up."

In fact, Adrienne's transfer from Darien High to St. Mary's, a private coed Catholic high school, had been made because her grades had not been quite up to par and her parents wanted her to have the benefit of smaller class size and more personalized academic attention. Accordingly, Adrienne's days were longer than her sisters'. She had to be ready for the school bus at seven A.M. and, what with after-school sports practice, she didn't get home until dinnertime. Then it was homework and bed and another long day. Having just turned sixteen, she had never had a steady boyfriend, and she had never had a sexual relationship.

Adrienne's friend Rob Jazwinski, a football teammate of Alex Kelly's whose parents were friends with the Baks, had told her about Dan Anderson's party. Rob was a Darien High senior, and he offerred to drive her over. Adrienne was excited to be going; since her days at St. Mary's were so long, it was only during school breaks that she had a chance to catch up with old friends from Darien High—girls like Sarah Marden, who had been a neighbor and friend of Dan Anderson's all her life and so was certain to be at Dan's party. Besides, in two days the Baks would be leaving for a family ski trip in Vermont, so this would be one of Adrienne's few nights available for socializing.

Adrienne dressed in her sister Kris's purple, ankle-zippered jeans, a button-down shirt, and a white V-necked cotton-knit sweater. She ran out the door when Rob arrived—her curfew four long hours away.

The case of beer Rob had picked up was on the floor as they took the thirteen-minute drive through the windy roads—lined by now-bare and spindly-seeming trees—across town. From Leeuwarden Road, they wound their way down High School Lane, past the buildings and snowed-over playing fields of Darien High. They swung over to Middlesex Road, then onto Leroy; from Leroy to Sedgwick, right onto Mansfield and down that hill of modest homes and into the center of town. At the Post Road, Rob drove under the railroad tracks (Darien News Store to the left; Black Goose Grille, Sugar Bowl, Darien Sport Shop, police station all to the right) and took Tokeneke Road straight out. He stopped at the light at Old Farm Road, drove past Rainbow Circle, past the woods abutting Tokeneke Elementary School. Where Tokeneke Road makes a T with Driftway Lane, he took a right to Dan Anderson's house.

The two walked into the party and Adrienne greeted her friends. It was about 7:30—three hours before Alex Kelly would arrive, with his friends Tom, Josh, and John.

Adrienne socialized with her friends; she and Rob made plans to see the Darien High basketball game later; she played quarters around Dan Anderson's kitchen table—she was picked to drink the juice glass full of beer about four times. During her testimony at the May–June 1997 retrial she said she had taken care not to get drunk because she knew that at the basketball game, "I would see friends of my parents" and "I couldn't show up at the game looking [drunk]." (Six other partygoers also took the stand at the trial, for the prosecution, and testified that Adrienne had not been drunk.) At 9:30, she and Rob went to the basketball game. Although Darien High was very close to her house, she opted, after the game ended at about 10:45, to go back to Dan's party with Rob "so I could spend more time with my friends."*

Once back at the Anderson house, "at around eleven," Adrienne recalled at the trial, "I asked Rob if he still wanted to take me home. He said, 'I'm not ready to leave yet.' I figured maybe he'd want to leave in a little while. I just waited." After

*All quotes of Adrienne's come from her testimony, under oath, on May 15 and 16 at the retrial of the rape case against Alex. The quotes are from notes taken by the author, who attended this and other portions of the retrial.

asking Rob one more time if he was ready to leave, and after he said no again, and with her 11:30 curfew looming, Adrienne called her father, somewhere between 11:00 and 11:30, and told him she was looking for a ride. He offered to pick her up at the party, but that would have been "humiliating," as Adrienne recalled feeling. "It seemed that I was the only one who *had* a curfew. When you're sixteen, you want people to think you're self-sufficient." So she told her father, "Please don't come! I'm sure I can get a ride." (Bill Bak testified in court, on May 21, that "the impression I was left with" from the phone call "was that [his picking her up at the party] was the last thing she wanted."

Adrienne continued, with increasing urgency, to try to secure a ride home from those kids who had driven to the party. She asked her friend Sarah Marden; Sarah said she was not ready to leave. (The ensuing events of the evening made Sarah regret, with pain, that she had not taken Adrienne home.) She asked others. Andy Winebrenner recalls, "She said, 'I really need a ride home; I don't want to be grounded!' But no one would give her a ride."

By now Alex was at the party. "He was off in the corner," Andy Winebrenner remembers. "He wasn't socializing, yet at the same time you knew he was there 'cause he was loud."

Tom Kelly, who had arrived with Alex, remembers Adrienne "wasn't even sitting at the table playing quarters. She was up and around and on the phone, and I remember her saying, 'Is there anyone who can drive me home?' And everyone was like, 'Forget it,' 'cause it was totally across town."

Adrienne had never met Alex Kelly, but what she had heard about him—the house burglaries, the "rehab"—made her wary of him. Yet he was the only one at the party who was driving that night who lived near her. Tom Kelly recalls, "She's saying [to the group], 'Come on, please. I'm gonna get in trouble! I just talked to my parents!' So basically when she asked one more time, Alex was, like, 'Aaaagh, I'll drive ya home.' Like: I *guess* I can drive you home." (As indicated by a remark that Tom would make to Alex the next day, this reluctance of Alex's must have seemed feigned at the time— part of a pose of Alex's.)

Leaving the party with Alex Kelly, Adrienne ran into another friend, Mike Gedney, who was entering the house. They exchanged pleasantries. Adrienne testified in court that, as Gedney was walking into the Anderson house, "I turned to [Alex] and said I could probably get a ride from Mike Gedney. He said, 'No, I'll give you a ride.' [He] said five times, 'I'll give you a ride.'" So, by the time they approached the Jeep Wagoneer, Alex's stance had changed from the appearance (according to Tom Kelly's account) of doing Adrienne a favor by agreeing to give her the ride—to *wanting* her to get in the car with him.

Tom Kelly stayed at the party. He, Josh Edwards, and John Houchin, "were expecting Alex to come back after he drove Adrienne home. But he didn't. Alex never came back to the party." Then, ironically, the girl who would later so regret saying no to Adrienne said yes to the boys: "So," Tom Kelly continues: "Sarah Marden gave us a ride home a half hour later."

As Alex took the left from Driftway onto Tokeneke Road— past the nature preserve and the grade school—Adrienne did not want to talk. Adrienne was uncomfortable being with Alex Kelly because of what she knew of him. But Alex's own silence seemed tense—almost eerie. "He seemed preoccupied," Adrienne recalled. "He didn't look at me. He didn't talk to me. He didn't turn the radio on. It was very strange. I thought it was odd."

Alex drove across the Post Road, up Mansfield, left on Sedgwick, right onto Leroy Avenue, with Partridge Lane on the right. Then, passing the Darien United Methodist Church on the left, he drove through the high school and made a left onto Hollow Tree Ridge Road. He stopped at the sign at the

corner of Hansen Lane. "He came over on top of me and tried
to kiss me," Adrienne recalled on the witness stand. "I told
him to stop. It seemed weird—he told me he had a girlfriend.
He didn't talk at all. He tried to kiss me again. I told him to
stop.

"He started driving toward my house. I was almost
home. . . . He asked me if I wanted to smoke pot with him. I
said, 'No! I want to go home!'" Adrienne was alarmed. "He
kept driving. I said, 'Stop! This is my house!'

"He turned down the street, a hundred feet from my house.
He turned around in a circle"—a cul-de-sac ringed by three
houses and a wooded area, through which you could enter the
Kelly property—"and stopped the car. It was pitch-black. He
turned off the car and came over on me and he tried to kiss me
again and I tried to push him away. And he grabbed my throat.
He tried to choke me."

So far, this description includes aspects described by others
allegedly attacked by Alex: the offer to smoke pot (Margaret),
the silent, dissociative demeanor (Julia, Jillian), the hatchback
vehicle (Jillian), and the hand on the neck (Jillian). Now,
however, Alex went farther than he had with Jillian, who,
unlike Adrienne, had not protested (Jillian had felt she *could
not* protest): Alex *squeezed* Adrienne's neck. And the angry
command (to Jillian: "Shut the fuck up!") became a deliberately rendered threat:

"He said," Adrienne continued, "I was going to make love to
him or he was going to kill me."

Alex the unbeaten wrestler now pinned Adrienne
("wedged" is the way she recalled it) between his body and the
seat. "I couldn't lean forward because he was on me and he
was choking me and I was trying to lift my body so the
pressure of my neck wouldn't be so much." As he had allegedly done when he was with Jillian, Alex, momentarily taking
his hand off Adrienne's neck, used both hands to release the

backseat of the vehicle so its hatch was flat.* Then: "He grabbed my throat and said, 'Get to the back of the car.' He was on top of me and he grabbed my right arm and started . . . pushing me backward into the back of the car.

"He got into the back. He was still in front of me and kind of on top of me and I couldn't go any further. He got up and I started to pick myself up and he told me to get undressed. He started"—here the increasing anger at the victim that Dr. Samek says is part of the disorder's progression surfaces— "screaming at me to take my clothes off."

Adrienne refused to take her clothes off.

Then Alex did what Margaret says he did with her and what Julia says he tried to do with her before she punched him: "He ripped off my jeans. He unbuttoned them and pulled them down. I tried to [resist] but he was too strong. . . . He took off my shirt and sweater. I knew he was going to rape me. . . . I started to scream."

For the rapist, Dr. Samek says, the stimulating "foreplay" is often the victim's fear and resistance. And the challenge—the thrill—lies in completing the act despite the escalating threat of apprehension. By their own accounts, neither Margaret, Julia, nor Jillian had done what Adrienne was now doing: attempting to alert neighbors or police through screaming. Given the rapist's need to continually raise the threshold of excitement by increasing the risk level, the scream for help is a peak.

Alex reacted to Adrienne's incipient scream this way: "He choked me harder and harder. . . . He told me this could be easy or this could be hard. He wouldn't have to hurt me." *"This can be easy or this can be hard . . .":* It sounds like "Living On

---

*Whether or not Alex ever took one hand off her neck to release the seat was one of the reasons the first trial ended in a hung jury: Adrienne had said, in her police statement, that Alex had momentarily taken one hand off her neck to lower the hatchback but during the October 1996 trial had mistakenly said he had kept both hands on her neck the whole time. At the retrial she testified that he had released one momentarily, telling Thomas Puccio that in the first trial "I made a mistake."

the Edge" (or, for that matter, "Saint of Circumstance"): a teen-suburban-boy-tailored cliché, a bit of macho melodrama pulled from a mid-1980s MTV video. (Jillian had wondered if Alex was watching too much television, but then Jillian was worldier than Adrienne.)

"He jammed himself inside me," Adrienne continued. "He was pushing himself inside me so hard my head was banging against the door. He screamed at me to keep [my legs] open and every time I tried to close them he would just choke me harder."

The ordeal seemed to have lasted—as Adrienne declared in court—*"Forever."*

Adrienne "couldn't even close my legs because [I] hurt so much. I rolled over to my side. I saw the blood underneath me. It was on the rug and on my legs." It was also on the carpet of the Jeep. "I covered up [that] blood with a scarf—I thought he would punish me if I bled."

Alex permitted Adrienne to get dressed, which she did in a quick, scattershot manner. While dressing, "I asked him why he did this to me. He said he didn't know. I asked him again and he just said he couldn't control himself. . . . He just put on his pants. He told me if I told anyone he would do it again 'and I'll kill you.'" As he drove her the short distance home, "He just kept saying it over and over: 'If you tell anybody, I'll do it again, and I'll kill you.'"

Adrienne got to the front door—it was locked, so that her parents would know, by having to let her in, exactly how many minutes after her curfew she'd arrived home. "I knocked," Adrienne testified—(her father remembered that she "banged" on the door)—"and my father came to the door. I didn't know if [Alex] was still behind me."

Bill Bak could see that his daughter was "very, very upset." "My father asked me if I was okay and I said I just had a fight with a friend."

"I made an effort to stop her," Bill Bak recalled, "and I asked her what was the matter [but] she was gone—she was just gone."

Adrienne: "I went up to my room and fell on the floor and just started crying."

Kristen Bak had heard her sister "running up the stairs, past my room and then banging the door" of her own bedroom, Kristen testified on May 22, 1997. She was alarmed. "I went to her room to see what was going on," Kristen continued. "I opened the door and that's when I saw her, and she was on the floor . . . in a fetal position, in a ball on her bedroom floor. She was shaking uncontrollably and she was sobbing and she kept saying, 'Oh my God, oh my God!'"

Bill Bak then told Kristen to go back to her own room. Kristen did so—only until her father had gone back to his bedroom. Then she reentered her sister's room. "When I went back in there she is still on the floor in the same position, and she is still shaking and still sobbing. She started hyperventilating like she couldn't breathe. I got down next to her and I said . . . 'What's wrong? Tell me what's wrong!'"

But Adrienne wouldn't tell. (She had taken Alex Kelly's threat seriously—that he'd kill her if she told anyone.) Kristen then took Adrienne by the shoulders and could see that "her neck and chest were bright red." She also noticed, with alarm, how haphazardly Adrienne was dressed: Her blouse was inside out and partly unbuttoned beneath her V-necked sweater, her socks were stuffed in the front pocket of her jeans—and her bra crammed in the back pocket. More alarmed, Kristen continued to implore and finally Adrienne made Kristen (in Kristen's words) "promise that whatever she told me I could not tell anyone—*ever.*"

Kristen recalled, "I promised. And that's when she looked at me and said, 'Alex Kelly just raped me.' She started to cry very hard and I just grabbed her and held her and rocked her. . . ."

Adrienne described the attack to her sister in detail.

The natural instinct for rape victims is to want to cleanse themselves, both literally and figuratively (unfortunately, evidence of the rape is often lost this way). So Kristen took Adrienne into the bathroom and ran a bath for her. Kristen recalls, "I took her by the shoulder and I could see that her neck and chest were bright red. There were white marks that looked like a hand print." More alarmingly, "when I took off her pants, her pants were covered in blood and her underpants were all bloody and her legs were all bloody."

Kristen was stunned. Hearing the ordeal described in Adrienne's words was one thing; seeing the physical impact was quite another. She said she was going to the kitchen to get Adrienne warm milk—but what Kristen Bak really did was go to the basement. There, she called their older brother Jeff, at his Clemson University dormitory.

Adrienne recalls running "downstairs and [Kristen] was on the phone with my brother." It was clear that they were talking about her. Adrienne then got on the phone with Jeff and told him what happened. "He told me I'd have to tell my parents. I said I was too scared. He said if *I* didn't tell them, he will [sic]." (Jeff Bak was enraged at what had happened to his little sister: so much so that, as various sources have said, he wanted to come right home and physically have at Alex Kelly.)

Adrienne started upstairs to tell her mother—"She *burst* into the room," Georgina Bak recalled, in her May 22 testimony, while Bill Bak was summoned to the phone with Jeff, whereupon Jeff told their father what Adrienne and Kristen had told him.

As Bill Bak was hearing the news from his son, Georgina was alone with her daughter. "She didn't look like herself," Georgina Bak recalled, on the stand. "She was very, very upset. Her face was red. She was sobbing. She was shaking. I tried to ask her . . . what was wrong. She said, 'I can't talk about it.' She was terrified of something."

"I hugged Adrienne," Georgina Bak continued, "and she got into my bed . . . and I just held her and just tried to comfort her."

Meanwhile, Bill Bak was reeling from what he'd been told. "I was in shock, I was angry. I was amazed at what my son had told me," Bill Bak recalled feeling.

Upstairs, the story was coming out more haltingly. Georgina Bak did not pressure her daughter. "She held me," Adrienne recalled. "She didn't ask me anything."

Sufficiently calmed, Adrienne told her mother what had happened. Mother and daughter cried together. At some point Bill Bak approached the pair. "My wife was cradling Adrienne and [Adrienne] is trembling and crying and sort of horror-stricken, and my wife is holding her in my bedroom and I talked to Adrienne. She was pulling away from me."

Georgina stayed in Adrienne's bed that night so Adrienne would feel safe enough to fall asleep.

But Bill Bak could not sleep—not until he confronted Joe Kelly. At around 1:30 A.M., he called Alex's father and told him, "Your son raped my daughter!" Joe Kelly claims that at first he thought the call was a prank. When he realized it was *not* a prank, he woke Alex and told him what Bill Bak had said. Alex (according to Joe Kelly's court testimony) replied, "I didn't rape her, Dad; we had sex." Joe Kelly accepted that statement apparently at face value and with equanimity.

Joe Kelly and Bill Bak have different recollections of the substance of their *next* phone conversation, which Joe Kelly initiated later during those predawn hours. According to Bak, Joe Kelly called and asked him what he was going to do about the event, and Bak told Kelly he was not sure what the next step would be, because Adrienne said that Alex had threatened to again rape and then kill Adrienne if she told anyone. (Evidently Bill Bak believed Alex's death threat was hyperbolic or he would not have disclosed it to Alex's father.) According to Kelly, when he called Bak back, he told him that Alex had denied the rape; then the elder Kelly, in his own words, "went to bed and thought that was the end of it."

It is not known what, if anything, Melanie Kelly learned about Bill Bak's call to her husband.

Thus, while the entire Bak family was struggling with a

serious crisis in an intense, open, and concerned way, the Kellys were minimizing and ignoring alarming information.

The next morning, Alex walked through Tom Kelly's back door. The two were going to get high, tie three sleds to a station wagon belonging to one of Tom's friends' mother, and go joyride-sledding down the snowy banks of Christie Hill.

Tom remembered Alex giving curfew-panicked Adrienne Bak a feigned hard time about driving her home. And he sure remembered hanging around at that lame party, waiting for Alex to come back and give him, Josh, and John a ride home— and Alex *not* coming back. "So," Tom recalls, "before I'm, like, halfway through the 'Hey, what's up, Al?' I ask, 'So, d'you do her?'*

"And he just said, 'Who?'"

Tom was taken aback. "I go, 'Adrienne. Did you do her?'"

"And he goes"—Tom affects a conspicuously casual tone— "'No. I didn't even give her a ride home.'

"I said *'What?'*

"He said, 'What happened was: Some of her friends pulled up in a station wagon and they ended up giving her a ride home.'

"And I said, 'Well, why didn't you come back inside? You were our ride home.'

"And he goes, 'Aaahh, I just knew I'd party all night long.' And one of my eyebrows went up because it was, like, the lamest party I'd ever been to."

Alex's remarks were so jarringly strange, Tom Kelly just did a total erase on them and said, *"Yo*kay! Let's go sledding!"

While Alex and Tom were having a carefree time getting

---

*This is the language Tom Kelly remembers having used at the time. He recalled these exact words (expressing embarrassment and regret, eleven years later, at the word choice) in an interview with the author in March 1997. During his May 20 testimony, Tom Kelly cleaned this remark up to: "Did you fool around with her?"

stoned and sledding, Adrienne was having a different kind of day. She had awakened and come downstairs to find her mother on the kitchen phone with Jeff. They were discussing Adrienne's options: tell the police . . . or stay silent? Georgina put Adrienne on the phone with Jeff and then watched her daughter crying as she spoke to her brother, appearing "withdrawn" and not "completing her sentences." By the end of the conversation Adrienne "had slumped down and was sitting on the floor."

After hanging up the phone, Adrienne "told [my mother] I would go to the police. . . . I thought it was the right thing to do." Still, the decision seemed tentative. Adrienne remained so traumatized, she barely left her mother's side all day.

And she was still in considerable physical pain. Mrs. Bak wanted to take her to a doctor. Adrienne was reluctant. She refused to go to a hospital because "I didn't want people looking at me." She refused to go to a male doctor because "I was afraid to have a man touch me or look at me." She was even afraid to leave the house because she thought that Alex would be watching for signs that she had told someone what had happened. (Apparently Adrienne did not know that her father had revealed his knowledge of the rape to Alex's father.) So when an appointment was secured for that afternoon with Stamford gynecologist Dr. Marilyn Kessler, Georgina Bak pulled the car into the garage so Adrienne could enter from *inside* the house and thus not be seen from the street. Adrienne slumped down in the seat so that she would be invisible to passersby as her mother drove her out of the garage and down the streets of the neighborhood.

Mother and daughter sat holding hands on the other side of Dr. Kessler's desk. The doctor (as she testified on May 21) encountered "an emotionally upset young girl" during the preexamination interview.

When it came time for the physical examination, Dr. Kessler told Adrienne her mother could not come in the examining room with her. Adrienne remembers, "I was crying—I didn't want to be alone. The doctor told me she wouldn't hurt me, that she would stop if I asked her to."

Dr. Kessler had Adrienne lie down on the examining table with her feet in what Adrienne remembered as "the steel things"—the stirrups. At the outset of the internal examination, "I started hurting. I sat up and told her to stop." Although internal examinations are important to rape prosecutions, Dr. Kessler decided to forego the procedure rather than risk causing Adrienne any more "pain and humiliation." So, after observing and noting the pain and tenderness around Adrienne's neck, Dr. Kessler did only an external examination. She observed four scratchlike marks and "two ruptures of the hymen. . . . One of them was quite deep." The doctor was "reasonably certain" these were caused by "forced penetration . . . with a blunt instrument."

Dr. Kessler also noted something else—something psychological. "The patient, without being asked, kept going back to the fact that she had" willingly gone in the car. "She kept trying to give me excuses as to why she got into the car with Alex Kelly." Like many rape victims, Adrienne Bak "felt somewhat responsible for what happened."

At 6:30 that evening, Georgina Bak placed an anonymous phone call to the Darien Police Department. What if someone was sexually assaulted? What will happen if she reports the rape? What can the victim expect from the police department? These were the questions the desk officer heard from a concerned and nameless woman.

The officer explained the procedure—victim statement, medical examination, investigation—not knowing to whom he was speaking or if any assault had actually occurred. Mrs. Bak ended the conversation by saying she would have to talk to "this person" to see if she wanted to proceed.

As Adrienne recalled it during her testimony, Georgina Bak told her daughter, "You don't have to do this if you don't want to . . ." But Adrienne, who had been a mass of pain and vulnerability for the past eighteen hours, now made a calm, firm decision: "I said that I *had* to go to the police."

In 1986, when Adrienne Bak decided to report her rape to the police, police departments around the country were in the middle of a quietly significant self-education about the phenomenon of acquaintance rape, a process that picked that particular kind of violation (which *victims* had always *felt* was a crime) up off the law enforcement establishment's cutting-room floor and legitimized it as criminal behavior.

Numbers tell this story. In 1960, the Uniform Crime Statistics tabulated 9.6 forcible rapes per 100,000 people; in 1991, that number was *42.3* per 100,000. While this enormous increase may appear at first glance to be the improbable sign of a massive rape epidemic, it actually reflects something else: a shift in mainstream law-enforcement consciousness. According to rape statistics authority and Vanderbilt University sociologist MaryAltani Karpos, Ph.D., coauthor of the forthcoming academic book *The Social Construction of Rape,* it's not that there have been *more* rapes; it's just that more *kinds* of rapes are now being taken seriously by recently skeptical police forces. (It is America's local police department figures—forwarded to the FBI—that make up the Uniform Crime Statistics.) In other words, the police have become more sensitive to women's experiences and more inclusive in their definition of rape. They've gone beyond merely counting attacks by the proverbial stranger who jumps out of the dark alley (that restricted count yielded the 9.6 per 100,000 rate in 1960) to also counting assaults by acquaintances.

The official figures have, in other words, caught up with reality. For when victims rather than police departments are polled, it becomes evident that these once-"hidden" acquaintance rapes are actually the most prevalent kind of rape that women suffer. The Department of Justice's "Crime Victimization in the United States" survey for 1993 (the most recent year available) reveals that, of the 485,290 self-counted rapes, 33 percent were by a person "well known" to the victim and almost 26 percent by a "casual acquaintance"—thus, *59 percent* were acquaintance rapes. (Stranger rapes accounted for 24 percent and slightly less than 14 percent were rapes by current or former spouses or incidents of incest.)

But if Adrienne Bak had vast company in terms of the *kind* of attack she had suffered, she had extremely low odds on her side in terms of attaining justice—for the overwhelming majority of acquaintance rapes do not result in courtroom convictions. In fact, so few of them are seen through to a satisfying conclusion for the victim, and so arduous (indeed, punitive) to the acquaintance-rape victim is the legal process, that insisting on justice takes almost heroic resolve.

A look at the number of such rapes—and then at the process of elimination that slashes that figure at each step up the legal ladder—reveals the enormous anomaly of acquaintance rape conviction. Sociologist Gary LaFree, Ph.D. (author of the scholarly work *Rape and Criminal Justice,* director of the Institute for Social Research at the University of New Mexico, and Dr. Karpos' collaborator on *The Social Construction of Rape*) has found (on the basis of twenty years of National Crime Survey data) that a mere 10 to 15 percent of U.S. rapes by acquaintances *or* strangers are reported to the police by the victim. (The National Victim Center, in 1992, put that number at 16 percent.) Most of *these* are then dropped by the prosecutor or rescinded by the victim. Of the cases that are left, over half are plea-bargained.

What's left to reach the courtroom? *One to 5 percent* of all rapes. But, like upstream-swimming salmon, these resilient cases are the strong ones: Dr. LaFree's study of 900 Indianapolis cases leads him to extrapolate that about 50 to 75 percent of tried rape cases yield guilty verdicts. Good news for the victim—right?

Yes and no. For this long-range good news for the victim

actually makes for initial very tough going for her, *if* consent was the issue in her case (as it is, by definition, in almost all acquaintance rape cases) and if her perpetrator (like Adrienne's) is wealthy enough to hire a top attorney. The reason is simple: What the hovering likelihood of conviction leads a good defense lawyer to do is just about everything he or she *can* do to scare the victim and prosecutor into dropping the complaint. This often means harassment of the accuser. Of course, lawyers won't call it that. They call it investigation.

What the best lawyers will do is hire a private investigator to try to dig up dirt on the woman in a frank attempt "to derail the rape case before it gets to trial," says past-president of the National Association of Criminal Defense Attorneys Nancy Hollander, who has successfully defended men accused of rape in Illinois and New Mexico. Hollander has investigators ask her client's accuser's friends and past employers, "Does she have a reputation for lying or making things up? Does she have a history of abuse within her family that may have given her the habit of thinking she was raped when she was not?" Hollander presents whatever damaging information her investigators have dug up to the prosecutor. She's gotten rape charges against clients dropped this way three out of three recent times.

Some defense lawyers go beyond dirt-digging missions to actual spying. Attorney Marshall Stern of Bangor, Maine, for example, says, "We'll do a surveillance of a rape complainant to find out: Does she go to parties and bars? Leave with somebody? Come home drunk? You can't use these findings on the stand because it's 'behavior after the fact' and can be considered a result of the crime; but it's a bargaining tool with the prosecutor. If you say, 'See, she smoked dope here. . . .' the prosecutor may not think he has the winning case he once thought he had." Some lawyers go further yet. In New York's St. John's University case, a defense-hired investigator tried to get a date with the accuser. He failed.

If the fruits of these tactics do not have the desired effect of getting the case dropped, they can yield victim-impugning information that can be slipped into the trial.

For even though forty states, including Connecticut, have "rape shield" laws (most enacted between 1975 and 1980) that make details of the accuser's past sexual life generally inadmissible in trials, the character and credibility of the victim is of inordinate—overwhelming—importance to acquaintance-rape case jurors. In their eyes, she is as much on trial as the defendant. Gary LaFree interviewed jurors in 880 rape cases and found that acquaintance-rape case juries "find it more important that she was a drinker than that he had a gun; more important that she had sex outside of marriage than that she sustained a physical injury during the incident; more important that she was a 'partyer' than that her clothes were torn that evening. Even though ideas about women have changed in this culture—a single woman with birth-control pills in her purse will be regarded differently by a jury today than thirty years ago—still, when people don't have complete information, they fall back on stereotypes. My own students—young, enlightened kids—will say, of a rape victim, 'What was she doing hitchhiking?' Or 'How come she went to that bar?' "

Defense lawyers *know* jurors ask themselves these questions, and they are only too happy to feed into the process. Therefore, anything a defense lawyer can do to impugn the victim usually is done. As Adrienne was being driven by her mother to the police station, she could not foresee the day that Alex Kelly's lawyer would make negative references to her weight, repeatedly call her a liar, and insinuatingly tell the jury that she had been voted "Biggest Flirt" of her ninth-grade class.

And she had no idea that justice would take eleven years.

When Bureau Lieutenant (and eventually Chief of Police) Hugh McManus, Detective Ronald Bussell, and Officer Rebecca Hahn—sitting around the police station conference room's table with the frightened daughter and the concerned mother—heard the name "Alex Kelly" as the attacker, "We all looked at each other," Rebecca Hahn Nathanson recalls, "like, 'It figures. He's capable.'" Although sex offenses had never before been part of his known repertoire, the fact that all three officers had crossed paths with him was enough to make them feel frustrated and guilty. "There was a sense," Hahn continues, "that we hadn't been able to do anything to keep this from happening."

Small town that Darien is, Officer Hahn recognized Georgina Bak—as her aerobics instructor. The three officers explained to the mother and daughter that, *if* they chose to proceed, they would have few privacy protections: The Kellys would eventually get access to Adrienne's statement and medical reports; Adrienne would have to testify; there would be publicity.

The two processed the information with different effects. The mother, Rebecca Hahn Nathanson recalls, "was angry to some degree (but not banging-the-table angry; she's reserved and refined in how she talks to people), more protectively concerned about her daughter. She was as cooperative as she could be, though kind of shell-shocked. I think she felt that she wasn't able to have protected her daughter last night—now she *had* to make this part work. Mothers make things work; that's what we do.

"The daughter was scared. Very emotional. Barely able to keep from crying. She had a bruise on her back, about five inches long, that went from her lower back down to the top of her buttock. And marks around her neck—they weren't purple but you would see something had been there. She was tiny, blond, and fragile. You knew if you said the wrong thing, she'd come apart."

For this reason, Officer Hahn, when she was left alone with Adrienne to take her statement (it was rightfully felt that the victim would feel more comfortable speaking to a young woman officer), decided to just let Adrienne talk, to ask her for clarification only when she had to. She began by telling Adrienne that, however painful it was to recall all the details, it was very important that she tell everything that happened. "It was stop and start," Rebecca Hahn Nathanson recalls. "I'd get information from her and then she was struggling. So I'd slow down, back off, and reassure her. I knew if I pushed too hard she would come apart and she wasn't going to get it together to finish the statement."

Once the statement was complete, Adrienne and her mother made a decision that frustrated the police: They decided to take a day or two to think, as a family, about whether or not to press charges. They were going forward with their Vermont ski trip. The police's thinking was that the family would decide not to press charges, and though the police were not happy about the delay there was nothing they could do about it. The officers also decided to wait a day before photographing Adrienne's bruises. "Because of the state she was in," Rebecca Hahn Nathanson says, "we were afraid she was going to lose it if we did take the pictures then." At least in terms of photographs, "one more day wouldn't hurt. In fact, it might even make the bruises better" in terms of their color deepening. But the police never did take the pictures of Adrienne's bruises. Hahn Nathanson says, "It just got lost in the shuffle."

What they did do, though, was seize Adrienne's clothes. Hahn and McManus went to the Bak residence. "We got there," Hahn Nathanson recalls, "and she ran upstairs to her room, her mother behind her. And we hear this *wailing*. It's her. For a few minutes. Just *wailing*—hysterical crying, like somebody died.

"Then the mother comes back downstairs with the clothes. The mother tells us, 'She gave me all the clothes at first, except her underwear. She did not want you to see this. That's why she was crying.' Then she hands us the underwear. They are *covered* with blood."

Now it was time to draw up a search-and-seizure warrant to see if there was also blood in the vehicle.

The next afternoon—Wednesday, February 12—Bill Schwing, the young man who was house-sitting for the Molitors in the family's absence, called Tom Kelly and, according to Tom, nervously asked about Tom's doings with Alex on Monday night: "Tom, what did you guys do? Were you smoking pot in the car?" Alex may have been given permission by the Molitors to use their car, but Schwing was generally responsible for the house and the vehicles.

Tom was slightly taken aback. He replied, "No. We weren't smoking pot in the car. We were drinking beers in the car."

Schwing said, "Look, the police just came here and impounded the Wagoneer. They told me not to say anything to Alex and I don't think you should either. But . . . do I have anything to worry about?"

Tom stuttered out a no. But when he hung up the phone, he was unnerved. Alex's odd remark yesterday morning, denying he'd even taken Adrienne home. Now this. What was going on?

A neighborhood boy named Steve Devereux, who lived on 8 Wee Burn Lane, just up Hollow Tree Ridge Road and to the left of Wee Burn Country Club, was having a party the next day, Thursday, February 13. Steve attended a Stamford private school, King & Low–Heywood Thomas (its bulky name the result of the consolidation of three separate schools) and some of the partygoers went to that school. Other neighborhood kids, like Alex (who lived right around the corner) and Tom Kelly had heard about the party, which had actually started in the late afternoon. Tom got to the party after playing a Darien High hockey game with some hockey teammates. "I remember seeing Alex over at the kitchen table, sitting around playing a drinking game." But Tom felt dissociated from the party—first, because he'd just finished a game, but also for another reason: Bill Schwing's strange nervous words were

The stately Kelly house on Christie Hill (above) is just down the road from Christie Hill's intersection with Leeuwarden Road (below), where Adrienne Bak lived with her family. Right around the corner from Wee Burn Country Club (and the scene of the rape and alleged rape), this is also the place where Alex flipped Amy Molitor's parents' Nissan on September 20, 1996, and left her in the road with five broken ribs.

Darien High   Dariannus '83

Perhaps the best-looking boy and girl of Darien High's 1983 sophomore class, Alex Kelly and Mavis McGarry were, despite their wholesome looks, involved in a tempestuous relationship whose violent moments were witnessed by students and faculty alike.

When Alex reentered Darien High in the winter of 1985, after juvenile prison for his burglary arrest and drug rehabilitation, he became involved with the prettiest girl in the class behind him, Amy Molitor. To Amy, being Alex Kelly's girlfriend was something she apparently wanted so badly that not even two rape charges could pull her away from him.

Najlah Feanny/Saba Press

Darien High   Dariannus '82

Alex's older brother, Chris, was vulnerable and star-crossed—a sweet guy who adopted a proudly blue-collar persona and often fell prey to a hot temper. About a year after this picture was taken, a moped accident left him with a permanent physical disability that dogged him until his October 1991 death by synthetic-heroin overdose.

When an executive's daughter, Rebecca Hahn, became Darien's first female police officer in 1981, she was able to see firsthand how the town treated its service class and hid its problems, and how self-destructive so many of the Darien kids were. Officer Hahn arrested Chris Kelly twice, arrested Alex for the alleged rape of Valerie Barnett, and took Alex's victim Adrienne Bak's statement.

Hour Publishing Co.

Alex (right) and his buddy Tom Kelly (left), all tuxed up and ready to party at a country club event in 1985, lift glasses and flash peace signs happily. Soon, though, the good times crumbled. Tom's testimony at Alex's 1997 retrial was one of the pieces of evidence the jury found most compelling.

Alex (in shades) has a carefree smile at the Darien High graduation ceremony in June 1986, belying his efforts to stay in school through his final semester there. After being graduated early, in March, in a gesture that was called by some an eviction-by-diploma, he and his parents (with some support from the ACLU) fought hard to try to have him reinstated. They were ultimately unsuccessful.

After Alex met ski-bum-emeritus Gary Bigham while hitchhiking in France in the late 1980s, the American fugitive from justice (who passed himself off as a rich kid from Vail, Colorado) seemed a natural to star in one of Bigham's spoofy *La Dolce Vita*-on-the-ski-slopes movies.

Alex (right) lived, traveled, and shared adventurous winter sports in Sweden and France with girlfriend Elisabet Jansson (center) from 1989 until shortly before his January 1995 surrender. Alex's father, Joe Kelly (left), relaxes with the couple at an undisclosed rock-climbing locale.

Darien Police Department

AP/Wide World Photo

After three and a half months in a Zurich jail while final extradition was being negotiated, Alex returned to Darien on May 4, 1995, accompanied by police and federal marshals (left), and was promptly processed by the Darien Police Department (above).

Susan Harris/NYT Pictures

Soon after his return to Darien, Alex, free on the $1 million bond his parents put up, was joined by Elisabet, who moved in with the Kellys and accompanied Alex to his early pretrial hearings.

The defense side of *Connecticut* v. *Kelly:* Joe and Melanie Kelly stride toward the courthouse on the day Alex's October 1996 trial went to the jury (above). That trial would eventually end in mistrial. Ultimately (below), even brilliant and combative defense lawyer Thomas Puccio (who had helped win Claus von Bülow's acquittal) could not save Alex Kelly from conviction for rape. Puccio (second from left) and his cocounsel Hope Seeley (far left) walk with Amy and Alex to the court on July 24, 1997, to hear his sentence. By day's end, Alex would be sent off to serve a 16-year prison term.

The prosecution side of *Connecticut* v. *Kelly:* (Above) Prosecutor Bruce Hudock chats with a colleague in the Stamford Superior Court's parking lot the morning— June 12—of the retrial verdict. He would shortly learn whether eleven years of hard work and long, frustrating waiting had paid off. (Below) After Adrienne Bak Ortolano's emotional victim-impact statement at Alex's sentencing—which influenced Judge Kevin Tierney's sentence more than any other factor—Adrienne (center), husband, Chris (to her right), and sister Kimberly (to his right) share a moment of gratitude and closure with (from right) Adrienne's lawyer, David Golub, and Adrienne's mother, Georgina Bak.

ringing in his ears and "I was still freaked out that the car had been impounded." Tom, taking Schwing's advice from the police, wasn't going to tell Alex about the Wagoneer's impounding—but he didn't want to think he was *avoiding* telling Alex about it, either.

So he just avoided Alex.

Years later, when Tom Kelly made sense of everything, and when he was old enough to realize what had really happened, "I thought, Damn it, maybe if I *had* gone up and told Alex that the cops took the car we wouldn't have a second rape victim."

Jillian Henderson was also at Steve Devereux's party after attending the hockey game. "I had recently been in a car accident where I had a few hairline fractures in my pelvic bone," she recalls, "so I was on crutches. This was my first time out since the accident." It was less than pleasant to walk in the door and see Alex Kelly, her attacker and tormentor, "doing shots of tequila and going, 'Ooo-weee!' and being out of control . . . and Amy not there. He said out loud, in front of the whole room, 'Oh, did you break your cunt? You should put an 'Out of Commission' sign over your head.'

"And everybody laughed—like, that's really funny. Well, *I* didn't think it was funny. I left."

Before she left, however, she noticed Alex starting to pay attention to one of the girls. The girl, she would later find out, was a student at a private school nearby named Valerie Barnett. She was dressed in long johns and baggy pants and a blousy top. She had dark blond hair pulled up in a ponytail. She had a boyfriend. In fact, she had been with her boyfriend earlier that evening. According to what Jillian observed, Alex seemed interested in her. "He was making his way over to her. I think she was flattered." The two were seen talking.

The account Valerie gave to police about what happened next shows a chilling similarity between her experience and Adrienne Bak's three nights earlier. According to the police report written by Bureau Lieutenant Hugh McManus after he interviewed Valerie, Alex had introduced himself to her during the party and, in time, he overheard Valerie asking her friend, at about 12:45, for a ride home. He then offered her a ride, which she declined.

Meanwhile, according to the police report, Valerie's friend left the party and Valerie walked outside the house to have a cigarette while she waited for her friend to return. Alex came outside and sat in the car he had driven to the party—his parents' black Chevy Blazer. Because it was cold, Valerie asked Alex if she could sit in the car while she finished her cigarette. He said yes. She got in the car and, again, he offered to drive her home—again, she declined. Then Alex put foot to pedal and took off anyway, virtually kidnapping her.

According to the police report, Alex drove north on Hollow Tree Ridge Road and parked in the Wee Burn parking lot. He began kissing Valerie, and when she refused his continuing advances and told him to take her home or back to the party where she could wait for her friend, Alex grabbed her by her coat and forced her into the back of the Blazer. He followed her into the back and "forcibly kissed her while fondling her breasts." She was very scared, and attempted to get away from him by kneeing him in the groin, but to no avail. Alex ordered Valerie to get undressed, just as he had ordered Adrienne. Valerie refused and Alex pulled her clothing off. As the police report flatly declares, "Alex Kelly then pulled down his own pants after which he performed vaginal intercourse on her."

But there was another escalation in Alex's repertoire: "He then forced her to kneel and bend over while he sodomized her."

And there was a repeat of another aspect of his behavior from three nights before:

"After the assault Alex Kelly threatened to kill [Valerie Barnett] if she told anyone of the assault."

Alex drove Valerie Barnett back to Steve Devereux's house. By now, Valerie's friend had returned to the party, whereupon the friend encountered a hysterical Valerie who said, "Take me home!" The friend asked what was wrong. Valerie told her. The friend returned Valerie to her house in Stamford as quickly as possible, whereupon Valerie woke her mother and told her what had happened. The two called the Stamford police. The Stamford police instructed Valerie and her mother to go immediately to Stamford Hospital to have a rape kit administered.

While Valerie and her mother were at the hospital, the Stamford police, realizing the alleged rape had taken place not in their city but in Darien, called the Darien Police Department, who scrambled to take over. By 4:30 A.M., Hugh McManus and Ronald Bussell had arrived at the hospital as had a female officer from Stamford. Valerie told that officer that she had been, in the words of McManus's report, "raped vaginally and anally." The female officer saw fresh scrapes and cuts on Valerie's knees and back and observed that her neck was red. (In this instance, Alex had supposedly not choked her with his hand, as he had Adrienne, but had jacked his whole arm around her neck, holding her neck in the crook of his elbow to restrain her during the attack.) In addition, the Stamford Hospital doctor "observed blood on the victim's lower extremities," the police report said.

The police then drove Valerie past the Kelly house on Christie Hill, where Valerie identified the black Chevy Blazer sitting in the driveway as the car she had been raped in. She described to the officers the clothes Alex had been wearing—a disarmingly little-boy-style sweater with a motif of reindeer running across it. Back at the station, Bussell and McManus had assembled a photo array of seven white older adolescents. Valerie looked at the array and, as the police report puts it (its stilted tone serving to dramatize Valerie's certainty), "did without hesitation choose photo number 5 as being the person who raped and sodomized her in the Chevrolet Blazer on Friday, 02/14/86. Photo number 5 is that of Alex Kelly."

When Officer Rebecca Hahn arrived at the station at 7:30 that morning, Bussell and McManus and three officers were on the phone with the prosecutor's office, hurriedly working on search-and-seizure warrants and an arrest warrant. Before she could take off her coat Becky was told: "Get your stuff and get to work—they need you upstairs to take pictures. There's been a rape."

Rebecca Hahn Nathanson recalls today, "My first reaction was: 'Let me just guess who did it . . .'"

Hahn took photographs of Valerie Barnett's shoulder and knee injuries. Valerie was different than Adrienne, Hahn noted—she was strong and angry and in full control of herself, whereas Adrienne had been fragile and shaking and terrified. You could ask her questions, flat-out, without worrying about how to phrase them first so they wouldn't push her over the emotional brink.

Thus freed from the strain of having to mince her words, Hahn, while she photographed this victim, was able to let her own frustrated thoughts wander off into Monday-morning quarterbacking. "How could we have let this happen—*again?* When we just had a victim three nights ago?!" she asked herself. She did a quick mental inventory of her meeting with Adrienne and Georgina Bak: The questions answered, the statement taken, the clothes seized, the family's decision to wait a couple of days to make a decision. "Oh, man, when Adrienne hears *this* happened, she's going to feel *so* bad!" Hahn thought. Then she stopped herself: You could what-if and if-only forever, and it wouldn't get anyone anywhere. The important thing now—the *only* thing now—was to get Alex Kelly.

Detective Don Anderson was posted on Christie Hill Road, in front of the Kelly house. Alex, unaware that anything was afoot, was walking out the door wearing jeans, sweater, and Patagonia-style jacket en route to Darien High to meet Jeff

Bouvier and his wrestling teammates, there to get on the bus and go off to the FCIAC tournament in Wilton. Everyone knew he was going there to win.

Alex got into the black Chevy Blazer and gunned the ignition. It was 9:30 A.M. Don radioed in. "He's in the Blazer and he's pulling out—what do I do?"

McManus radioed back to Anderson: "Stop the Blazer!"

Hahn, by now in uniform and on patrol, was radioed to drive over to Christie Hill and back Don up. McManus and Sergeant Glenn O'Connell meanwhile got into a squad car and also left for Christie Hill, all the while radioing in for instructions from the prosecutor.

Anderson, his car light flashing, stopped the Blazer just as it reached the back side of the Wee Burn Country Club parking lot. It is at this point, Rebecca Hahn Nathanson believes, that Alex, figuring something was up, reached into the back of the car and hurriedly stuffed an article of clothing on his person.

Hahn arrived at the scene, her car light flashing. Alex was out of the car. "What did I do?" he asked, with what Hahn recalls as a "real wide-eyed expression and a very calm voice. I wanted to grab him and say: 'You know damn good and well what you did!'" Instead she simply said there was an unspecified investigation going on.

McManus and O'Connell pulled up, their car light flashing. Acting on the go-ahead from the prosecutor, Hugh McManus, whose father was Darien's first police chief, got out of the car and said, "You're under arrest for sexual assault, Alex."

Anderson turned the suspect around, planted his hands on the hood of the car, frisked him, and cuffed him.*

---

*Nine years later, Alex would give his own account of the arrest to *Turning Point:* "I was driving to school. The lights come on and the next thing I know, it's like the movies. 'Put your hands on your head' and the whole deal. I had no idea what was going on." When interviewer Forrest Sawyer asked him, "You had no suspicion that anything might be wrong?", Alex answered: "This was unbelievable. . . . It's not real. Why would I—why would I rape somebody?"

Hahn and O'Connell put Alex in the back of Hahn's car and drove him to the police station.

At the station, Alex was processed—asked to strip, his clothes seized as evidence, made to furnish blood, saliva, head hair, and pubic hair samples. He was given a green jail jumpsuit and led to a jail cell.

Armed with an additional search warrant, Hahn went back to the Kelly house and searched Alex's room. "It was a disaster area—clothes everywhere, big Grateful Dead poster. One of those your-mother-closes-the-door-every-time-she-passes-it-'cause-she-can't-stand-to-look-at-it rooms." Hahn found a small quantity of marijuana, "so we arrested him for that, too."

Later that night back at the station house, Hahn bent over a table and, tweezer in hand, picked up, piece by piece, every item of the clothes Alex had been wearing at the time of his arrest, careful not to shake anything (in a sexual assault case, evidence can be microscopic). She bagged each item and marked each bag with a number and turned the bags over to the detectives in the upstairs squad room.

Later that night when the bags were opened, it was found that inside Alex's own underwear was a pair of print bikini underwear. They had probably been left in the Blazer, and Alex, when he saw Officer Anderson in his flashing-light car, had probably quickly stuffed them onto his person so they wouldn't be found if the car was seized.

According to the police, they belonged to Valerie Barnett.

Alex was booked on two counts of first-degree sexual assault, one count of unlawful restraint, and one count of threatening. These charges related to the alleged rape of Valerie—police were still officially investigating the rape of Adrienne.

Alex sat quietly in his cell, with a blank look on his face. "If it were me—if I were an eighteen-year-old rich suburban kid charged with two serious felonies, I'd be scared, I'd be plead-

ing, 'Call my parents! Call my lawyer!'" Rebecca Hahn Nathanson says. "But Alex—it was scary—he just had *no* reaction."

Except one, that is. As if what had happened was just
another minor inconvenience that would be finessed by those
forces that kept star athletes afloat in their world of entitlement, Alex calmly asked: "Am I gonna get out in time to
wrestle tonight?"

CHAPTER  6

ALEX'S COACH, JEFF BOUVIER, WAITED AND WAITED FOR his star wrestler to show up at the bus for the Fairfield County Interscholastic Athletic Conference meet. When Alex didn't show, Bouvier got angry. He boarded the bus with the team, and they drove off to Wilton. When the team had to forfeit the match at 5:15 P.M. because of Alex's absence, Bouvier's anger turned to worry. A local newspaper reporter came to the meet and told the coach that Alex had been arrested for rape. Bouvier, whose glowing Darien *News-Review* article about Alex had just gone off the newsstand, dismissed the news as "a rumor." After the meet, Bouvier went to the Kelly home on Christie Hill and found it was no rumor.

Meanwhile, Alex was learning just how bad a Valentine's Day can be. At his arraignment at Stamford Superior Court, his bail, for the alleged rape of Valerie, was set, by State Superior Court judge James Bingham, at $500,000—an amount that the local papers would, not inaccurately, describe the next day as "unusually high." Secondly, he was remanded to none other than the infamous Bridgeport Correctional Center. Whereas

John R. Manson had been prison "lite," your typical juvy center, tucked away in the bland town of Cheshire, the BCC (known locally as North Avenue Jail) was an urban jail full of destitute and desperate adult offenders.

Situated smack in the middle of Bridgeport, on struggling-up-from-decay Madison Avenue, the BCC is barricaded by a chain-link fence and miles of razor wire, through which the expletive-rich catcalls of its clientele regularly pierce the air and land on the Portuguese- and Italian-bodega-lined sidewalks. About 1,500 prisoners are processed through a week, roughly 50 percent black and 25 percent hispanic. In the winter (as when Alex arrived) the neighborhood's homeless, anxious for warmth, commit petty misdemeanors in order to bunk down in its bars-and-tiers cellblocks, side by side with those rape and murder suspects who are too poor to rustle up bail money. Although Alex was held in the newer "37 Block" (where he got the same kind of six-by-eight foot cell he'd had at Manson), the experience clearly afforded profound culture shock for him.

And for his parents. When the Kellys came to see him, their support of him and their belief in his innocence seems to have been unconditional. The way Melanie would later describe the jailhouse reunion (on *Turning Point*), it was clear that she believed her son was the bereft one, the victim: "We went to see him in Bridgeport Correctional Facility, behind a big wall of glass. I mean, I wanted to hug him so much because he was dealing with a lot. And we were dealing with a lot, and there was no way to communicate except just look at each other. It was just awful."

Equally awful was the prospect of getting Alex out. Raising a half-million-dollar bail takes time, even for well-off people like the Kellys. Unless a party can come up with the money in cold cash (and the Kellys did not have $500,000 lying around in bank accounts), a bond is required—and, in the case of a real estate bond, this involves doing a title search, going to the town clerk and assessors for certification and records. So Alex had to cool his heels while his parents filed papers.

* * *

Arriving home from her Florida vacation to hear that her boyfriend had been arrested for rape, "Amy didn't believe it— not in the least bit," her friend says. "She said, 'Not my Alex— Alex wouldn't do that!' That was her position throughout. I remember us sitting up at night while she wrote long, long letters to him at Bridgeport."

But a male friend of Alex's says he had a very different conversation with Amy, one in which she appeared less the pious stand-by-your-man type and more the tough cynic. After Amy told this boy that Alex had pleaded with her not to go to Florida because he knew "something bad" was going to happen if she left him, the friend says he asked, "'So, Amy, what did you do?' And she said, 'I fucking went away.' And I go, 'We-ell, what do you think [about Alex's arrest for rape]?' And she goes, 'I think the kid's got a fucking split personality.'"

The Kellys, unprepared for the crisis they were now steeped in, sent their real-estate lawyer, Anthony DePanfilis, to represent Alex at his arraignment and first bail hearing, but DePanfilis was outside his area of general expertise. So Joe Kelly called Mickey Sherman, whom he had met during the burglary proceedings. Sherman—ten years in private practice after a year as a public defender and four as a prosecutor in Stamford—had made a name successfully defending a number of sexual assault defendants. Aside from getting acquittals for the recently convicted Stamford auto-mechanic rapist on two prior rape charges, he had also recently represented two defendants—a tennis instructor and a high school teacher— in their acquittals on rape and sexual assault charges. Sherman was a creative showman, and his cheeky techniques often carried the day for his clients. In the teacher's sexual assault trial, he enlisted the testimony of *all* the accuser's classmates—the trial was quite a circus; another time he had virtually no defense for a client, but upon hearing that the man's alleged victim just happened to belong to a religious group that placed great store by forgiveness, Sherman convinced the victim to beg the judge for mercy for the defendant. The tactic worked: The judge suspended Sherman's client's sentence.

Sherman's techniques could also extend to that staple of defenders of accused rapists: victim-bashing. In the rape trial of the tennis instructor, he had seized upon the alleged victim's license plate ("MMGOOD") to project to the jury her supposed licentiousness. Sherman won that trial, but was roundly criticized by victim's advocates.

In the world Joe Kelly moved in—wealthy but macho, non-white-shoe "regular" guys—Mickey Sherman was *the* man if you stumbled into criminal problems. So during Alex's first weekend in jail, Joe and Melanie met Sherman in the unprepossessing wood-frame house on Stamford's Fifth Street that houses the offices of Sherman and Richichi. The Kellys "seemed very upset and concerned; they felt Alex was being unjustly accused," Sherman recalls. He himself could not have agreed more about at least one injustice—the $500,000 bond was "obviously very, very unfair; that's *two murder* bonds!" Indeed, bails on five other recent rape cases in lower Fairfield County had ranged from between $50,000 and $100,000, meaning that Alex's bond was five to ten times higher than these others. (When asked why the bail was so high, State's Attorney Callahan had given the local press a less than satisfying answer: "We often ask for a high amount. This time we didn't cut it down. Why? I don't know."*)

---

*Today, Assistant State's Attorney Bruce Hudock, who prosecuted the case, recalls the justification this way: "You have two rapes within a three-day period of time (and although there hadn't been a second arrest, the first arrest was for the *second* rape so we knew there would be a warrant coming down for a second rape), and we also knew he was on probation for the burglaries—so that's a lot to put on a judge's plate; that's why the high bond." But someone close to the case on the other side offers this speculation: "The police department was very embarrassed that they had made a bad judgment call, when the first complaint [from Adrienne Bak] came in. They respected the wishes of the victim by not arresting Alex right then. So they made a compassionate move. *Then* they realized they had been acting too much as social workers and not as police officers. So when [the second rape report came in], they overreacted to make up for it."

Sherman and the Kellys concluded that there was a social and legal lynch-mob out to get Alex: Between the excessive bail and the front-page Darien *News-Review* and Stamford *Advocate* articles, "the attitude was, 'Somebody open the general store and fetch a rope; we gotta string him up by noon,'" says Sherman. "The police acted as if he was the Charles Manson of Darien."

News of the arrest was on all the teachers' lips when classes at Darien High resumed, after winter break, on Tuesday, February 18. The faculty (a number of whom had been called to the police station) "was buzzing about it," one social studies teacher recalls. "This was a story that's very dramatic: To have a kid who's seen the depths, risen to the heights . . . and then *this* happens! But let me just say: It did not surprise me."

As for the students themselves, they were already burdened with more than their fair share of tragedy. A month earlier, during school hours, there had been another teenage driving death: A car carrying five Darien High students had crashed into a utility pole. Fifteen-year-old Therese Evers had been killed in the fluke accident, whose lack of any attendant sybaritism (it occurred in broad daylight, after a *final exam,* of all things) was a devastating acknowledgment of life's random cruelty. While the kids were nursing their vulnerability about their safety and mortality, the midair explosion of the Challenger spacecraft two weeks later magnified their sense of bad things happening to good people.

So by the time everyone came back to school, the additional news of the star athlete's arrest and incarceration for the rape of a Stamford girl shook an already fragile student body. Remembers a young man named Mark, who was then a junior, "Girls came to class red-eyed, like they were just wiped out— like they were devastated." For those who had not heard the news, the school officially informed the students of Alex's arrest; the school policy that students not speak to any reporters who may have gotten onto campus was also firmly reiterated.

Meanwhile, Principal Velma Saire, already concerned enough about the children's delicate psyches, had been paid a visit by Chief of Police John Jordan. "He sat down in my office," Saire recalled to a journalist two years ago, "held up his thumb and forefinger about three inches apart from each other, and said, 'We came this close to two murders in town this week.'" Others in his department—chiefly Lieutenant Ronald Bussell, Officer Becky Hahn, and Bureau Lieutenant Hugh McManus took the acts just as seriously as Chief Jordan did. (All three officers would essentially be on the case until, and beyond, Alex's surrender.)

After Jordan's words to Saire, questions were raised within the school and school board about what to do if and when Alex Kelly was released from the Bridgeport Correctional Center. But before that concern could be addressed, everyone was in for another jolt, and although the police and high school faculty knew it was coming, it stunned the students: Alex Kelly was charged with a *second* rape—of the younger sister of a Darien High senior.

School was becoming a melodrama.

The day after school started again—on Wednesday, February 19—Alex was brought to Stamford Superior Court from the BCC in the jail van, to have formal charges—one count each of first-degree sexual assault, unlawful restraint, and threatening—read. Before pleading not guilty, he was, said the Stamford *Advocate*, "near tears in court as he sat handcuffed to defendants in other cases." His bail was raised by $65,000 ($50,000 for the second rape charge, $15,000 for the violation of probation stemming from his burglary charge), to $565,000, and an additional charge—possession of marijuana, for the contraband found in his room during the search on the morning of February 14—was added.

Mickey Sherman was outraged at the ridiculously high bail gone even higher. He turned his full attention to scheduling a bond-reduction hearing. ("The courts were not bending over backward to accommodate Alex Kelly," he says today.) But as he visited his young client in jail, his anger that his hometown legal system was suddenly not doing him any favors was mollified by his developing assessment of his young client. Sherman had acquired a simple motto in his years defending accused rapists: "Winning a rape case is just like winning the election for third grade class president. It's a popularity contest." Young Alex Kelly was a very attractive candidate.

Even jailed and afraid, Alex had not lost the capacity to think and speak clearly. "Sometimes you'll speak to a client who will be in an almost dissociative state—the effect of the arrest and the incarceration has put them on another planet. But Alex— Alex was consistently a very intelligent young man. His emotional state was very appropriate." If Alex performed so cool-headedly and articulately in the midst of postarrest trauma, he would only improve on the witness stand.

More important, Alex's story passed muster. "He told me the sex was consensual," Sherman recalls. "He maintained— consistently—that he was wrongly accused. I listened to his version of events and they sounded very credible to me."

(In 1991, when Alex was on the lam—and any witness-stand appearance was thus virtually foreclosed by the incriminating nature of the flight evidence—Mickey Sherman commentated on the rape trial of William Kennedy Smith for Court-TV. As he watched the telegenic if thin-lipped medical resident—and member of America's tattered first family—testify, under the gentle prodding of his attorney Roy Black, Sherman was as frustrated as a revved-up coach abruptly benched by his star athlete's Olympics-eve injury. Alex "had a magnetic personality, a real presence, an aura, *charisma!*" Sherman would fruitlessly rhapsodize. Compared to how Alex could have come off looking, Willie Smith "looked like a wimp on the stand—like a *shnook!*")

If Alex Kelly was in jail on a huge bail, on unproved charges of *two* rapes, who *else* at Darien High could be vulnerable? Some of the kids got worried. All of this was so *new*. To help address the questions hanging in the air, the faculty augmented the normal curriculum with informal talks, in law and government and history classes, about the legal process and constitutional rights. When these impromptu sessions did not allay the students' worries, the school scheduled seminars with lawyers and social workers on the workings of the criminal justice system and the problems and myths surrounding rape. "It was discussion as might occur between members of an extended family," assistant school superintendent Robert Laber told the Stamford *Advocate*.

Through all this information-sharing, "the parents were about evenly divided," says a woman who was then the head of a major town-school organization, "between those who knew the Kellys and were strongly supportive and those who knew them and assumed the worst. But I think the town reacted pretty well. There was not a huge outcry of 'He's innocent!' *or* 'He's guilty!' People were willing to wait and see what the facts revealed, to not prejudge. Mostly, there was a sense of sadness among the parents, sadness that the rapes might have happened and sadness that someone may have made up an accusation."

A less decorous version of the town's divided opinion is given by Rebecca Hahn Nathanson, who bluntly recalls: "Darien was literally split in half. There was a lot of nastiness—people just jumping down each others' throats. In the stores, in the bars, at the golf clubs—you name it: Alex's arrest could not come up as a topic of conversation and not get ugly. Did he do it? Did he not do it?: The 'fors' and the 'againsts' were just very passionate."

Did the rape accusations and the arrest prompt high-schoolers' parents to talk with one another about improving communication with their kids about intimacy, respect, sex, drinking, and values? "No," says a board of education member, although the incident "caused people to be introspective about something they were not used to [being introspective about]. To the majority of people, it was: 'Oh, my gosh . . .'" The most concerned people, she recalls, "were the kids. They were worried that Darien—that their life-style—was going on trial. They were worried that people were going to ask questions about what they did at their parties." *Were* such questions asked by parents? "No. Not that I know of." The woman pauses to think about it, then says, "You know, I don't think the parents ever *did* know much about the kids' parties."

But if the parents attempted a wait-for-the-facts attitude and continued their almost willful know-nothing approach to their children's social mores, Alex's friends were opinionated (though, truth be told, they didn't seem to be taking the charges too seriously). "A lot of the boys were laughing at it: 'Why would Alex have to do something like that?'" recalls one of his friends' sister. "Alex had so many guys in his corner who couldn't fathom him having to go to this kind of length to have sex with a girl, and those guys sticking by him were the hotshots. To them, the only thing he was guilty of was cheating on Amy."

Almost as if to bolster this chorus of supporters, the Darien *News-Review* published an article which struck a similar cheerleaderly note. The paper quoted Alex's sports teammates (and only his teammates) in various states of shock and support. "Gary Kirsch, [a wrestling] team cocaptain said he thought the arrests were a mistake. Dan Byrnes, also a cocaptain, and John Paterniti, a fellow football player, also expressed their concern and disbelief." The boys raved about his physical skill, and Jeff Bouvier remarked that Alex "has been a coach and a leader by example." Bouvier allowed: "We knew of his past, but he gave us no indication he was capable of these crimes."

With no sense of inappropriateness or even irony apparent on the part of the speaker, reporter, or paper, Bouvier also noted that "It was a joy to watch [Alex] wrestle" because those he wrestled "were afraid of him."

To girls who knew better, that stubbornly blind jock loyalty to Alex—and the extolling of his ability to frighten people—

was simply unbelievable. Margaret was afraid. Jillian was furious. Julia West found it "so frustrating! I was dating this guy and he said, 'No way could Alex have raped a girl! Alex is the mellowest guy!' I said: 'Are you *kid*ding?! He is *not* mellow! He has a dark side!' But I couldn't tell him *how* I knew that." As angry as she was, the outpouring of support for Alex only hardened Julia's fear at being found out as a victim. "I was horrified that people would know my story. My mom said, 'You've got to go to the police with your story!' but I was petrified that if I did, first of all, all of Darien would know, and secondly, they'd make me go up on the witness stand and I'd be torn to shreds."

(Julia kept her silence all the way through the arrest, Alex's flight, and the two trials, although the attack continued to affect her. "Much later, I was kiddingly wrestling with this guy, and he pinned me down, playfully, and I totally freaked out and started crying. And he had *no* idea why. But it was so scary to be with someone who's that much stronger than you who's exerting that power—and you have no power at all.")

Meanwhile, the news of the arrests sent tongues gleefully wagging in the city in which Alex was charged, and would be tried: Stamford. Though Stamford shares with Darien the fact that many of its residents are corporate employees (Clairol, GTE, Nine West Shoes, and GE Capitol all have headquarters in Stamford), that's about the extent of their resemblance. Unlike Darien, eight-times-more-populous Stamford is ethnically diverse (70 percent white; 30 percent black, hispanic, Asian, with almost a quarter of its residents' primary language being something other than English) and *not* dominated by wealthy father–led traditional families. Fully half of Stamford's 110,000 residents are single, divorced, or separated, and its $28,000 average per-capita income is almost half that of Darien's.

Though downright lovely by most urban standards—its traffic-friendly one-way streets course down sloping hillsides into a Seward Johnson statue-studded town center—Stamford ("The City That Works") also accommodates gritty-kitschy stuff: strip malls, convenience stores, a few downright ugly buildings, even urban blight. It is the real world next to Darien's dollhouse—and, among Stamford residents, there is plenty of quiet resentment of Darien's pristine image. "People in Stamford are *thrilled* that [the Alex Kelly rape case] happened *over there,*" says someone in a high-level position for the city, "and they have felt that way since the beginning."

But Stamford's barely disguised glee at its next-door neighbor's bad fortune was not the opprobrium that the country club executives were worried about. *Their* antennae were trained on the site of their board meetings: Manhattan. So when the Kelly rape arrests made *The New York Times,* those executives old enough to have squinted through the media glare at Judge Eielson's 1964 roundup of liquor-serving corporate-VP dads girded for a reprise. Though the accused rapist's father was (thankfully) just a local plumber, some of the teenagers attached to his wild-partying crowd had more embarrassable families: One father directed advertising for the world's most advertised product; another family included the founding namesake of a major publishing company; a third father had been telephoned in his overseas hotel by an official informing him and his wife that the girl who'd had sex with more than one boy in their home in their absence was, lucky for them, *not* under sixteen.

So there was perturbed stoicism among the briefcase-clasping Metro North elite, who knew that the liberal press in the city in which their companies were headquartered never quite minded catching Republican Connecticut corporate towns with (in this case, literally) their pants down. If Alex Kelly had lived in Larchmont or Nyack, New York, or in Montclair, New Jersey—in a suburb where urban newspaper writers and editors slept, raised their own teenagers, and occasionally harbored untidy secrets, or if Alex went to any elite private school in New York City—might not the *Times,* some of these Darien executives' wives wondered, have acquired *slightly* colder feet about the story?

To the younger townsfolk, it wasn't so much that Alex was from Darien specifically as that he was rich and white. The police and prosecutors were bending over backward these days to prove they weren't racist—that was the opinion of the young, male drinkers at The Post and at Lock, Stock and Barrel. With neither girl seriously injured, they complained, Alex would *never* have gotten that half-million-plus bail (or his picture in the papers) if he'd been a poor black kid.*

On Monday, March 3, seventeen days after he was jailed, Mickey Sherman went to Superior Court to arrange a reduction of Alex's bond to $200,000. It had taken Sherman longer than expected to secure a court date (he does not think this was simply a problem of an overcrowded calendar but, rather, that animus against his client had something to do with the delay) and the process of documenting the ownership and worth of the Christie Hill house (it was appraised at $450,000) had been drawn out by technicalities.

Once all the papers were in order, Joe and Melanie drove to Stamford Superior Court, hoping to finally take Alex home.

---

*This sentiment was the flip side of the one held by some members of the black community, as the 1980s progressed and questions about the role of race (and class) in the perception of sex crimes intensified through a series of high-profile New York area cases: the 1986 purportedly "rough-sex"-motivated killing of teenager Jennifer Levin by white preppy Robert Chambers; the 1988 assertion (largely thought to be a hoax) by black upstate teenager Tawana Brawley (and a coterie of advisors including Reverend Al Sharpton) that she had been raped by a white police officer or assistant district attorney; and the 1989 gang-rape and near-killing of a white Wall Street professional ("The Central Park Jogger") by black youth. In the attention surrounding each case, it was argued by some that when affluent whites are the victims or perpetrators of sex-related crimes, they are viewed by the white press and public differently (the perpetrators, like Chambers, with much more shock and puzzlement; the white victims of black rape defendants, like the Central Park Jogger, with much more sympathy and protectiveness) than when the alleged victim (for example, Brawley) or perpetrators (the Jogger case defendants) of an alleged interracial sex crime are poor and black.

But Assistant State's Attorney Bruce Hudock was not going to let Alex Kelly out of jail easily. A large, looming man of Czech-Irish background, and a lifelong resident of the area, Hudock (then 34) is given to theatrical sarcasm and somewhat broad humor—his answering machine features a goofily stentorian Walter Cronkite imitation. But such marks of the man are deceiving. Hudock carries himself in the courtroom with the touching self-consciousness of one who has spent much of his life trying to let others know that his daunting physique does *not* represent his sensibility—he calls to mind those huge, tender bears in contemporary children's books. The image of sensitivity is apt: By the time he got the Kelly case, Bruce Hudock had established as his trademark a compassion for rape victims. Rare for a male prosecutor, he seemed to understand their anger, humiliation, long-lingering terror, and their sense of having been made "damaged goods." And if he didn't know all this before he prosecuted State v. *Amarillo* in 1982, he certainly learned it afterward.

In the winter of 1982, a young female college student was sitting in her car parked on a Port Chester, New York, street, eating an ice cream cone, when a stranger—one Jairo Amarillo—brandished a knife, forced his way into the car, pushed her over to the passenger seat and took the wheel, and, after robbing her, drove her to a Greenwich, Connecticut, parking lot, where he made her perform fellatio upon him.

In meeting after meeting with Hudock, the traumatized victim could not describe what had happened to her. But the prosecutor's sensitivity and patience eventually enabled her to trust him. She agreed to testify. The testimony proved difficult and during the grueling cross-examination (by Amarillo's defense attorney Kevin Tierney, who would eleven years later face Bruce Hudock from the bench, as the judge in the retrial of State v. *Alex Kelly*), she broke down sobbing. Hudock won a conviction for Jairo Amarillo on first-degree sexual assault, kidnapping, and robbery charges, but the ordeal weighed heavily on the victim. She was never quite the same. One day, not long after the trial, Hudock learned that while driving her car, she—accidentally?—crashed into a tree. She died in that accident.

The death drove home to Bruce Hudock just how lasting the scars from sexual assault can be, even after justice has supposedly triumphed—and he is said to have had Jairo Amarillo's rape victim in his mind every time he walked into a rape prosecution.

So Hudock's first move in arguing, on Monday, March 3, against Mickey Sherman's requested bail reduction for Alex Kelly was to upgrade the two counts of unlawful restraint, (one for Adrienne's, and one for Valerie's, incident) to counts of first-degree kidnapping. (Once charged with these upgraded crimes, Alex pleaded not guilty.) Hudock also informed Judge Bingham that Alex had choked the two victims and had "subject[ed] them, in my opinion, to brutal assaults." Further, he made the point that, in committing the second attack, Alex had defied a clear warning. "The [father of the] victim from the first incident did notify the defendant's father that [Alex] would be charged with rape, and yet the defendant four days later at another party gets involved with another victim." Hudock declared: "I see a trend, if the allegations are true, of an increasingly violent nature."

Sherman and Hudock—the bronzed, skilled, media-minded defendant's advocate and the passionate, gentle-giant prosecutor—were used to sparring in this courtroom on an almost daily basis: amiably but fiercely. Sherman took swift issue with Hudock's "increasingly violent" characterization. "There were no gross beatings," he protested, in his low, soft, seductive baritone. "There were some marks on someone's arm, but this is not a 'brutal' situation."

Judge Bingham agreed enough to reduce the bond to $200,000. He set these conditions for Alex's release: Alex was to abide by a five P.M. daily curfew, was ordered to attempt no contact with the victims, and he was mandated to submit to a psychiatric examination to determine whether he was a danger to the community.

The evaluating psychiatrist was allowed to be chosen by Alex's own parents (pending approval by Hudock), a privilege to the defendant that, experts in such cases estimate, occurs in about 20 to 50 percent of criminal rape cases.

"If a psychiatrist feels he should go back [to jail], he'll go back in," Mickey Sherman cavalierly offered. (This, of course, did not happen in Alex's case. Neither did voluntary counseling. When asked if Joe and Melanie Kelly ever expressed to Sherman the sense that their son might have a sexual aggressiveness problem, Sherman says, without any hesitation, "No. They did not think Alex had a problem that required treatment.")

By hearing's end, prosecution and defense each came away with something: Hudock now had a raft of charges against Alex Kelly—for the attack against Adrienne Bak, first-degree sexual assault, first-degree kidnapping, and threatening; for the attack against Valerie Barnett, two counts of first-degree sexual assault (the second count reflecting the alleged anal rape), one count of first-degree kidnapping, threatening, and possession of marijuana. And Sherman won his client's release, on $200,000 bond, from the Bridgeport Correctional Center.

As huge a relief as it was for Alex to be out of jail, the news he faced was chilling: If convicted of everything, with maximum penalties, he could face a *lifetime* in prison.

Since the Kellys seemed adamantly to believe their son had done nothing wrong, renormalization of his life was a key order of business. Even before bail was made, they had started preparing for this. The Friday (February 28) before Alex was let out of BCC, Melanie Kelly had met with Darien High administrators. They told her that they thought it best if Alex did not return to school, and they offered him, essentially, home tutoring.

Melanie took issue. She wanted her son to have the advantages of classroom learning. As she expressed it to the local press a few days later, "I'd like him to be able to go back to school. I wouldn't expect it to be a perfect situation. We're dealing with a very volatile issue."

Alex took matters into his own hands. Despite the school's request, he showed up at Darien High for classes the day after he was freed, Tuesday, March 4. Kristen Bak—Adrienne's older sister and the first person Adrienne had run to right after the rape—was in the cafeteria in the morning, and, as she recalls (in a letter she wrote to the judge for Alex's July 24 sentencing), "I was stopped dead in my tracks when I saw him [there]. I dropped my books." She ran, screaming, and spent the rest of the day in Principal Velma Saire's office, "too afraid to go to classes."

Largely because of Kristen Bak's reaction, Alex was told he *could not* attend classes; he was placed on a ten-day suspension, the never-quite-stated reasoning for which would land the school in escalating controversy. The terms were quickly—and nervously—improvised: Teachers would come to his home to tutor him. And, if the school administration did not let him back in after his suspension was up, he was entitled to a hearing.

Mickey Sherman went on the media warpath, vowing to exhaust all means—taking the high school to court, if need be—to get Alex back in school. "He has no reason to be home," Sherman said. "Obviously, they believe he's some kind of danger to the school, which is ridiculous. The Darien Board of Education apparently doesn't recognize the presumption of innocence."

Those words, of course, sent fur flying. "We are being careful in observing Alex's due-process rights," assistant superintendent of schools Robert Laber asserted. But the Fairfield County ACLU warned that, although the school appeared to be within its rights in suspending Alex,* they had better

---

*Connecticut law allowed administrators to suspend students if their "conduct endangers persons or property, or is seriously disruptive of the educational process, or . . . is violative of a publicized policy" of the board of education (which meant anything from swearing to bringing weapons to school).

quickly set up that promised hearing to determine readmission.

Loyalists rallied: Amy welcomed Alex back into her life. No matter what she may have quipped to his friend about him having a "split personality" after hearing about the attacks, "she believed him," her friend maintains. "They went back to the same relationship as they had before—having sex in the same room in her house, like they had before—with the Molitors seemingly accepting him back in their home." The Kellys' parish priest telephoned the president of the Darien Board of Education, offering to write a letter supporting Alex's readmission.

Made confident, perhaps, by the support of his parents, the easy forgiveness of his girlfriend, the support of his wrestling and football teammates and his wrestling coach (as published in the local paper), and by the votes of confidence from his friends and his clergyman, Alex sought to do something ambitious: to get himself an alibi. And for this he turned to the boy who had been with him the night of Dan Anderson's party, the boy who used to look up to him as the Christie Hill wild man.

So after he had been home from BCC for about a week, he called Tom Kelly.

When Tom heard the voice he'd been hoping he'd never hear again, he felt "really uncomfortable. Alex says, 'T.K., what's goin' on?' I didn't want to get *near* this guy."

But Alex disregarded any discomfort he may have sensed in his neighbor's voice and said, "There's something I have to ask you."

Tom said, "Go ahead."

Alex said, "Nah. I'd rather come down and talk to you."

Ten minutes later, Alex arrived at Tom's back door. The two teenagers sat at Tom's kitchen table—"the long way": Tom at one end, Alex at the other, as if they were embarking upon a war summit. "And Alex took a deep breath and asked, 'Is there any way'"—Tom bites off each word slowly, to re-create Alex's deliberateness—"you can say you saw me come back to the party?'"

Tom was stunned. He says today: "I thought about it, and I said, 'How can *I* say I saw you come back to the party when I was with other people the whole time, and you didn't come back—and they didn't see you come back.' I said, 'There is nothing more I would like to say than I saw you come back to the party. But my circumstances prevent me from being able to lie for you.'" ("I wouldn't have lied for Alex, anyway," Tom says today. "But I made a real logical case for why I wouldn't.")

After Alex left, Tom Kelly felt shaken. He told his brother about what Alex had asked him to do (he *had* to tell *someone*) and then he made his brother promise to never tell anyone about it.

But Alex's request preyed on Tom.

Out of sheer awkwardness, kids started shying away from Alex's older brother. "People were afraid to ask Chris about Alex," a female friend of Chris's says. "People were afraid to call Chris. It was so uncomfortable, such a weird subject— people just . . . well, backed away from him." Already isolated and self-conscious because of the limp and physical limitations he was left with after his moped accident, Chris was now further marginalized by his friends' embarrassed diffidence.

Graduated from Darien High and working for his father now, Chris Kelly was already used to criticism and humiliation. "Because of the accident, when Chris had to go to the bathroom, he had to go right away," sometimes necessitating abrupt stops at the shop between jobs, Chris's friend Jay Bush says. If these pit stops got in the way of the work flow, his father upbraided him. "Joe used to make him cry in front of guys all the time," Jay recalls. "Nothing Chris did was enough" for Joe. "If he did ten service calls a day, it should have been twelve. And with his [accident-weakened] back, Chris shouldn't have even been working. Joe should have given him administrative jobs." (Eventually, at one point, Chris would go to work for Joe Kelly's rival.)

The isolation and stress on Chris Kelly would worsen as the months passed. "About a year later," the female friend says, "I ran into Chris at a party and he started to cry. He said, 'Why do people feel so awkward talking to me? *I'm not* Alex! I am *so* lonely.'"

But by the second week of March 1986, it was Alex who was lonely. He wanted to go back to school! He was tired of the dauphin/leper treatment, the teachers trooping to his house; he longed to be back on campus, hanging out as usual, basking in his charisma. "Alex still had a lot of support among his friends and peers at school—kids who believed him," Mickey Sherman says. "He thought he was being treated like a convict, shunned and banned. He thought [the school was] punishing him before he'd ever been convicted of anything. And I agreed with him." Good news came in the form of the psychiatric evaluation: The doctor the Kellys had selected came up with what Sherman termed a "very favorable" evaluation. He was "not a danger to students, the community, or anyone," Mickey Sherman declared on March 12; therefore, Alex should be readmitted to Darien High several days *before* his ten-day suspension was officially over.

Hudock, who knew that the entire Bak family was feeling the effects of Adrienne's rape and Alex's threat to her, reiterated that Alex *was* a threat.

Sherman countered that he was "more interested in mending fences right now" than taking Darien High to court; still, *if* he had to take the school to court, he would.

Facing either a high-profile court suit by the Kellys or great distress for the Baks, the administration of Darien High scrambled with their rock-and-a-hard-place options.

They came up with an inspired solution: They would give Alex his diploma early! He had enough credits, what with having repeated much of his senior year after his two months in juvenile prison in 1984 and his four subsequent months in rehab. So, on Thursday, March 17, the school announced "Alex Kelly was graduated from Darien High. . . . He has successfully completed all graduation requirements." This was done, assistant superintendent Laber said, in the "best interests of [Kelly] and the students."

If the already ducking and cringing Darien school system *had* wished to call attention to itself, it could not have found a better way to do so. To the school's and town leaders' dismay, the instant graduation made local headlines, and got big play in the dreaded *New York Times*, as a far less benign gesture than intended. The Stamford *Advocate* was the bluntest: "School uses diploma to evict rape suspect."

Alex, Sherman said, was angry and frustrated. And, although the last quarter senior year education in *any* high school is largely gratuitous, Melanie Kelly complained that Alex would suffer academically if he did not complete his high school courses, and (in a query whose indignance might not sit well with anguished parents of high-school dropouts) she intoned, "Does the school have the right to *foist* a diploma on you?" Revealing the strength of her conviction that her son was the real victim in the events of the last month, Melanie said, "He's got a big enough black cloud hanging over his head. To further stigmatize him would be overwhelming."

Mickey Sherman assailed the school's tactic as "morally, a cheap shot" born of Darien's "mass hysteria." Even the Connecticut Department of Education's own attorney waxed "very suspicious about the [Darien school] board's authority" to force early graduation, and opined: "The reason behind this is discipline." The local *and* state ACLUs also jumped in. "An absolute denial of education on the basis of speculative fears of harm," said the chairman of the Fairfield County chapter; the Connecticut chapter's executive director said the school was wrong to "punish" a student "for things . . . allegedly [done] outside school property."

There seemed to be no end to supporters of Alex Kelly's education rights. Meanwhile, Adrienne Bak was having regular nightmares. As Georgina Bak put it in a statement read by Adrienne at Alex's sentencing, on July 24, 1997, her parents watched their "vivacious" girl become "withdrawn" and "scared": afraid to open the front door.

"The Kellys and I always shared the determination to win," Mickey Sherman recalled, in an interview with this author before the hung-jury trial and the retrial. "They were always adamant that they wanted to prevail in this case, and I agreed with them. There was never any defeatist tone in anyone's mindset here."

So when, in mid-April, State's Attorney Eugene Callahan presented Alex with a plea offer of a twenty-year sentence, Alex and his family flatly turned it down. Bruce Hudock told a reporter that the state makes a plea offer when it feels it has a strong case. Still, the answer from the Kellys was no.

Standing before Judge Bingham with his head bowed and his hands folded behind his back, Alex, for all his touted surety on the plea issue, must have appeared vulnerable. Did he know how momentous this decision was?

"You realize the choice is yours, Alex," Judge Bingham gently but firmly said. "You understand what you're doing?"

Alex indicated that he did. (Years later, he would tell *Turning Point* of the offered plea deal: "What kind of life would I have had for something I did not do?" Did he ever consider taking the plea? Forrest Sawyer asked. "No," Alex answered, adamantly. "Because I knew I didn't do this, so why should I go to jail for that?")

Then Sherman spoke up for him. "He's electing a jury. He realizes he may face a sentence longer than the twenty years offered by the state." Sherman was understating. Each of the three counts of sexual assault carried a twenty-year penalty, and the kidnapping carried twenty-*five* years. Including the marijuana-possession charge, Alex was facing a maximum (though extremely unlikely) *ninety*-year prison term, if convicted on all charges for both alleged rapes.

It was quite a risk. But the Kellys were unmovable: Alex *was not* guilty. There would be *no* plea. (Melanie Kelly was also still fighting for Alex's school reinstatement, an issue Sherman had dropped. She told reporters that she and Joe had consulted "an expert in education law" to continue the battle.)

But if the family was employing denial in their decision to nix the plea deal, Mickey Sherman was employing something else: his confidence in the witness-stand power of his attractive client. His plan? "All I have to do," he shrugs, reliving the moment, eleven years later, "is show the jury that the defendant may not have committed this offense." Sherman's strategy was "to basically try to pick apart everything the victim says that might be inconsistent with common sense. To bring in forensics experts. The strategy is simple: 'Alex, what happened? Let's try and show that the state can't prove its case and we'll put *our* side out."

Indeed, in acquaintance rape cases* (where the fact that there *was* sex is conceded to by the defendant and the only issue is the victim's claimed lack of consent), the defense almost always has the advantage. Lack of consent is very hard to prove. It's always hard to prove a negative—that you *didn't* do or feel something—and when only two people know the

---

*Although the style of both alleged sexual assaults was as sudden and violent as any classic "stranger rape," the fact that Alex and both girls voluntarily socialized together, at least slightly, before the incident makes the context one of "acquaintance rape." ("Date rape" is sexual assault committed in the context of an actual mutually agreed-upon social, one-on-one encounter.)

truth about it, and only one of *them* (the accuser) bears the burden of proof, then the difficulty multiplies severalfold. In both rapes that Alex was charged with, the girls had willingly gotten into his car and there had been alcohol at both parties. And they were all *teenagers*—teenagers at *night*: Hormones, mixed signals, impulsivity and flirtation rule. An encounter that one person might call rape, a jury might view as merely a muddled, later-regretted surrender of judgment.

Although Bruce Hudock and the Darien police did not acknowledge such and do not to this day, Adrienne's case was, from a jury-presentation standpoint, thought to be the far stronger of the two cases. (Sherman thought it undeniably was, and that the prosecutors' choosing to present it first proved that they thought so, too.) Even though Valerie had been raped anally and Adrienne had not, and even though Valerie had had a rape kit done at a hospital and Adrienne had had no internal examination, Adrienne was a virgin when she was raped. Also, a number of witnesses saw Valerie and Alex talking amiably at Steve Devereux's party.

Though prosecutors and victim's and women's advocates vehemently believe that such factors as a woman's possible flirting with an alleged rapist (or even consensual foreplay) are irrelevant in determining the accused rapist's guilt, jurors can be swayed by these factors. In addition, in cases in which the accuser is a virgin, a prosecutor is going to want to tender that information to the jury. In a crunch, an accuser's virginity often carries the day—it's the hook on which jurors can hang the whole thorny consent question: If she had *never* consented before, in her *whole* life, then it is believable that she also did not consent on that one specific occasion.*

---

*The importance of an accuser's virginity might be said to be illustrated by comparing two of the best-known recent acquaintance rape cases: that of William Kennedy Smith, in 1991, and that of Mike Tyson, in 1992. Though both men's accusers had willingly gone home with them, Patricia Bowman was given a ride home to the multiroomed family estate where she knew other family members of his were staying. Washington, on the other hand, went to Tyson's *hotel room* with him, and no one else was expected to be in

So it made sense that Adrienne, the virgin, would have her day in court first.

If Alex could win *that* case, then the other might be dropped. And if it were dropped, then Alex was home free.

Of course, this entire hopeful scenario, for Sherman, rested on one supposition: That the judge would rule that the two cases would be tried separately.

Alex was allowed to participate, capped and gowned, in the Darien High Class of '86 commencement ceremony. ("I have one memory of my high school graduation," Kristen Bak wrote in her sentencing-day statement. "Alex Kelly right behind me in line.")

Although Mickey Sherman would soon complain that Alex was relentlessly followed by the police and kept from having a "normal day-to-day life-style," by many of his peers' accounts Alex was essentially unconcerned that summer, bopping around to parties and events as if nothing had happened— even when he ran into people he had recently hurt.

He and Amy went to a party given by a close friend of Julia West's (the friend was one of the girls who had referred to him as "Alex Kelly, M.R." *before* the arrests) and his nerve in doing so astonished and appalled both girls. Julia says, "I was, 'Ohmigod!, I can't believe he's here! He was so scary to me, but to everyone else he was so . . . *not* scary! My friend said, 'Alex, I hope you get exactly what you deserve!' And he was dumbfounded. He just scowled at her."

This was the period when, partying at a Dead show, Alex ran

---

that room. By these facts, it could be argued (in the course of determining consent) that Desiree Washington must have known that sex was on the agenda, while Patricia Bowman might have thought she was just signing on for a social evening. Yet there were differences between the two accusers: Patricia Bowman was a 29-year-old mother of a little girl while Desiree Washington was a teenager who had never before had sex.

Washington's assailant, Mike Tyson, was convicted.

Bowman's alleged assailant, William Kennedy Smith, was acquitted.

into Jim Hunter and acted as if there had been no bad blood
between them. (Jim turned and walked away in the middle of
Alex's jovial greeting. "If I hadn't," Jim says, "I would have
decked him.") Yet fear lay beneath the veneer of bravado: On
another occasion that summer, Alex walked into a friend's rec
room where that friend and an older fellow Alex did not know
were playing Ping-Pong. "Hey, anyone got a bong?" Alex
asked. When Alex's friend said the older fellow was a Connecticut State Trooper (it turned out that Alex's friend was just
joking), "Alex," an eyewitness recalls, "just about jumped out
of his skin. He was in a panic. He almost kissed the guy's feet.
He said, 'I didn't mean that! I didn't mean that! I was just
kidding!' He thought he was going to be taken away right then
and there."

Yet, it was almost as if he *wanted* to get taken away. He
seemed to relish playing chicken with the authorities. "We
were responding to calls all summer," Rebecca Hahn Nathanson remembers, "about him being out after curfew, Alex
violating his restrictions by drinking at parties. Someone
would call and say, 'Alex Kelly's at a party at such-and-such'
and we'd get in the car, and when we got there he would
immediately run out of the house, and the kids would walk
around"—affecting a mock-clueless whine—"'What happened to Alex?'"

On the Fourth of July, when the police raided a party at a
house whose yard was on a cliff overlooking the Sound, "the
minute the police came," a guest says, "Alex sprinted to the
edge of the cliff, took a dive into the water, and swam across
the water to Rowayton."

Alex felt dogged. Looking for a place where the Darien cops
wouldn't follow him, he sought permission, through Mickey
Sherman, to move to Colorado. Bruce Hudock—so victim-
focused that his concern about the Baks' distress apparently
blinded him to other dangers—actually thought it would be
better for Alex to be far away, so, in an extremely naive move,

he granted permission for Alex to relocate far from the Darien police's watchful eyes, and he did not seize Alex's passport. Alex rented an apartment in the town of Leadville, close to Aspen, and got a job at an A&W. But before he took that job, he exercised his prosecution-granted freedom, and took advantage of his lawyer's very loose rein on him: In violation of his bail, he took a several-weeks-long secret vacation to a Club Med in the Bahamas.

What was Alex feeling when Bahamian authorities stamped his passport on August 2 without any suspicious looks or troublesome questions? Did he get a rush? Or was it more quietly eye-opening, the realization of how easy it was to slip out of the country?

A Darien police investigator gives this account of what happened once Alex got to the resort island:

After vacationing at Club Med, Alex ended up working there as a windsurfing instructor. There, he met two sisters from California; the younger was thirteen. At one point, a photograph was taken of her, her sister, and Alex Kelly. Everyone was smiling, their arms around each other.

On her family's last night at Club Med, the girl attended one of the Club's evening functions. Alex "sidled up" (the police investigator's word) to the girl "and convinced her to go for a walk on a darkened part of the beach." There, on a chaise longue, "He commits a sexual assault on her that is very, very similar to the other ones that we now know about," says the police investigator.

Does "very, very similar" mean: A hand around the neck and a threat?

The police source answers: "Yes."

Two people who saw the investigative file on Kelly recall the file mentioning that, after the forced sex, which the girl objected to, Alex just walked away and left her there.

The police source: "So she goes back to her room, distraught, upset. Her sister says, *'What happened?!'*" just as Margaret's sister had done when Margaret came in from the woods; and as Adrienne Bak's sister Kristen had done, after Adrienne banged on the front door; and as Julia West's two friends had done, after Julia walked back to the party; and like Jillian Henderson's friend Kimberly Marengo and like the boys who saw Darcy alarmed and then crying after she jumped off the bed and ran out of the room. As with so many of these other girls, the girl told her sister only after making her sister promise never to tell anyone.*

Mickey Sherman says he never knew, back in 1986, about the trip to the Bahamas.

Shortly after Alex's return, they began working on their defense. "Alex consistently, adamantly denied *ever* having forced *anyone* to have sex with him," Sherman says.

Two weeks before Alex had winged off to glamorous Club Med, Bruce Hudock had scored an unglamorous but meaningful (and, as it would turn out, highly consequential) victory in the state appellate court system. A few years earlier, Hudock had won a conviction against a Stamford podiatrist named Lawrence Morowitz, who sedated a female patient who came to him for foot surgery and, once she was anesthetized, he sexually assaulted her. During that trial, Hudock had brought in (over defense objections) testimony about another female foot patient's similar attack three years earlier by the good doctor.

---

*Her sister kept her promised silence. Then, nine years later, when Alex was brought back to Connecticut in handcuffs and his photograph and story appeared in *People* magazine, the girl and her sister saw the article and recognized Alex as the boy who, she would later tell police, raped her on the beach in the Bahamas. Her sister called the Darien Police Department, saying that although she was still very reluctant to talk about the incident, it *was* Alex Kelly. When asked if she had proof, the sister told the police about the picture. The FBI in California picked up the photograph from the girl's sister and Fed-Exed it to the Darien Police Department. The young woman gave a statement, and offered to testify at Alex's trial, as did Diane Sales. The testimony of both young women was disallowed by Judges Nigro and Tierney.

After his conviction, Morowitz appealed. The trial court had erred, his lawyer claimed, in part because, one, prior testimony's "prejudicial impact outweighed its probative value, the two assaults being neither sufficiently similar nor proximate in time"; and two, the charges resulting from the earlier assault had been dismissed and the records erased following the defendant's successful completion "of accelerated rehabilitation."

On July 15, 1986, the higher court denied Morowitz's appeal. Hudock had not erred in introducing the testimony because the testimony revealed "striking similarities between the incidents . . . relevant to establish a common scheme or plan" and therefore the "probative value of that testimony outweighed its prejudicial impact." (The records' erasure did not matter because "the challenged testimony was based on personal knowledge independent of police, court, and prosecution records.")

This fresh affirmation of the right of a Connecticut prosecutor to bring in collateral testimony, from a second victim, in a sexual assault case meant that Bruce Hudock now had a good chance of having both Adrienne's and Valerie's complaints brought into one trial, before one jury, whether a joined trial (two separate cases with two separate outcomes—the jury can convict on one and acquit on the other) or with one victim's testimony bolstering the other's in the first victim's trial.

The higher court had said something very important: Additional-victim testimony, when *"strikingly similar,"* is *not* too prejudicial to the defense to be included in a sex-assault case.*

---

*It is up to the trial court judge to decide if "rape signature" testimony *is* strikingly similar enough to be included. In William Kennedy Smith's trial, Palm Beach Judge Mary Lupo disallowed the prosecution-proffered testimony of three women who gave statements about alleged attacks by Smith. Judge Lupo ruled that they were not similar enough to outweigh their prejudicial impact.

In early September, on the strength of *Morowitz* and other precedent, Bruce Hudock filed a motion requesting that both rape charges be combined in one trial. Mickey Sherman was ready for him. Employing a creative strategy, as he often did, Sherman had hired a Stamford market research firm, Leterman Associates, to survey residents to prove that jurors could be prejudiced or confused if both cases were joined. Indeed, Leterman Associates found that 60 percent of those polled would have trouble separating the cases.

The two litigators argued in front of Judge Bingham at Norwalk State Superior Court.

Hudock said that Sherman's telephone survey was "unscientific" and that the judge would instruct jurors to hear each case separately; therefore, they could not be confused. Yet Hudock knew he would have a tremendous advantage if one jury heard both cases: Intent, a major issue, could be proved—with two women describing such similar attacks, there was almost no way a panel of jurors could come away thinking that Alex Kelly's aggressive advances were the result of a mere misunderstanding.

"The major issue" in joining the cases, Hudock conceded, is that the defendant must testify in both or in neither.

Sherman did not use that point to try to get out of the joinder. "It's our intention to have him testify in both situations," he said forthrightly. His client *was* the defense, and he seemed not to care who knew it. Still, he wanted the freedom to change tactics. Joinder would be "unfair," Sherman said.

Joinder was "the rule," Hudock rebutted. Sherman hadn't shown the "extreme exceptions" that justified separate trials.

His client would "not get a fair trial" if the cases were joined, Sherman insisted.

A week later, Bingham ruled for the prosecution: There would be one trial. Relying on *Morowitz* and other decisions, Bingham determined that Connecticut case law promoted joinder when similar crimes were allegedly committed by one person within a short period of time. The judge said there was no showing of "substantial prejudice" when rape cases were joined. He also said that "the [state] supreme court says the economy and expedition of the judicial administration is of paramount importance."

Alex Kelly would have been severely disadvantaged if the cases were joined—and for a judge to join cases for the cavalier reason that doing so would save time and taxpayer money is almost shocking—an abridgment of defendants' rights.*

Mickey Sherman was furious. "To say that economy and expedition of the judicial administration is paramount over someone's opportunity for a fair trial is . . . very wrong," he responded at the time. Even today, the usually genial Sherman gets angry just thinking about the joinder. "I was extremely pissed off," Sherman remembers now. "To join the trials for the most stupid reason imaginable—to expedite matters and save money! But I knew it wouldn't hold. I felt that as we picked a jury, we would voir dire them on the same questions the market research people asked, and the answers would come out substantially the same and the trial judge would be convinced that this was not going to work—that the trial would not be fair.

"And he would separate the trial."

After being delayed several times for procedural reasons, Alex's trial was scheduled to begin on Monday, February 16, 1987, almost exactly a year after his arrest.

About ten days before his trial, Alex came back to Darien for a short trip. It *may* have been at this time that he got together with his old girlfriend, Mavis McGarry. Nine years later, Mavis

---

*Bruce Hudock had argued for joinder on the basis of judiciary expediency, but says he would not make that argument today. And, further, that if the cases had been joined and Alex had been convicted, the conviction would probably have been overturned on appeal.

would tell Darien teenager-turned-writer Mike Paterniti (whose younger brother, John, had been one of the football team members who had been quoted in the Darien *News-Review* as supportive of Alex right after the rape arrest) for his article in *Details* magazine: "I came to visit him in Darien. We were driving back from the airport, and he told me"—referring to the rape charges—"he was set up, that he never instigated anything. He started crying. He told me he was going to bolt."

It is also more than likely that Alex saw Amy at this time.

On this trip home, Alex got together with some friends, including Tom Kelly and a boy named Bill Keating. (Although T.K. had felt distinctly uncomfortable about Alex since the day after Dan Anderson's party—and especially since Alex had asked Tom to lie for him—his own neighborhood loyalty still held sway, to some extent.) During a game of quarters, Alex astonished the group by taking out twenty-four nitrous oxide "whippets" and doing them three at a time. While the others were amazed at his ability to withstand something that would cause them to turn blue and black out, Alex was saying, "What a great buzz!" and extolling their virtues as an aid on the ski slopes.

That Alex could indulge so heedlessly in thrill-seeking just a week before his double-rape trial amazed Tom.

"Are you worried?" Tom Kelly asked him.

"Not at all," Alex answered. "Everything's gonna be fine."

Which was surprising, Tom thought—damn surprising—given the ninety-year sentence he was facing.

Alex went back to Colorado. He had quit his A&W job (actually, according to a coworker who was interviewed after he fled, he "just didn't show up one day") and had gotten a job at the B-List Clubhouse at the Copper Mountain Ski Resort. He had moved to a condominium in the town of Frisco, sharing it with other young men.

On February 12, Mickey Sherman—slipping in a last-minute Vail ski vacation before opening arguments—drove over to the Copper Mountain Resort. Melanie, Joe, and Russell Kelly were there as well, visiting their son. Sherman met with them and Alex in the Kellys' suite to discuss trial strategy.

In both Alex's October 1996 trial and his May 1997 retrial, Mickey Sherman would be called to the stand by Alex's subsequent lawyer Thomas Puccio to testify to a remark he had made to Alex during that Copper Mountain suite conference: Sherman had told his young client that he was not getting a "fair shake" by having the two cases joined.

In looking back on the Kelly family's mood and demeanor during the conversation, Sherman said (in a conversation with this author before the retrial), "Were they angry? Yes, of course. Were they upset? Yes. Were they panicking? No. This was a family that handled matters very rationally, very intelligently."

With the trial set to start the week of Monday, February 16, 1987, the Kellys left Colorado that weekend to go back to Darien.

Here is the way the departures went:

Joe Kelly, asserting a knee injury that needed medical attention, definitely left on Saturday, February 14. Melanie and Russell were to leave on a 10:45 A.M. Continental Denver–Newark flight from Stapleton Airport on Sunday, February 15. Alex was to have taken a flight later that evening—also a Continental Airlines flight from Denver to Newark. (He was originally booked on People Express, Mickey Sherman would soon volunteer, but that airline's buyout had forced him to change his flight.)

Melanie did, indeed, drive herself, Russell, and Alex to the airport in a rented car, which she returned to the car rental before they checked in.

Just before Melanie's 10:45 A.M. flight was to depart, she and Alex hugged and bid a very emotional farewell in full view of other departing travelers. In fact, the reason the authorities know this is that a bystander witnessed the dramatic farewell and later reported it to the police.

That farewell was the last known sighting of Alex Kelly before he fled, authorities say. Thus, the authorities have always believed, and have repeatedly said that Alex dropped out of sight via a flight that originated from the Denver airport on Sunday night, February 15. That is the official story.

On Sunday afternoon—while Melanie and Russell were in flight from Denver—the Darien police got a frightened phone call from the girl—a tall, thin blond named Laura—who was living with Chris Kelly in one of Joe Kelly's two-family houses, this one on Old King's Highway. "She's hysterical, crying and carrying on," Rebecca Hahn Nathanson recalls. "She claims he hit her. We go over there—the house is trashed, somebody tore it apart. And Chris is agitated and she's agitated."

Two friends of Chris, a husband and wife, recall that, at this time Chris had also, as the wife says, "vandalized Laura's car so she couldn't drive it, couldn't leave him."

When Officer Hahn got to Chris's apartment, Joe Kelly was there. Based on information she had ascertained at the time, the officer believed that Laura had "reached out to Joe first, to get him to try to calm Chris down, and that Joe was already on his way over when Laura decided that she couldn't wait for him to get there and called the police."

Joe's presence did not thrill Officer Hahn. This was a man who had given her a tongue-lashing the *last* time she arrested Chris. *Then* she had arrested Alex, on the rapes, for which he was going on trial, *tomorrow*. Now here she was again—trusty scapegoat girl-cop: redheaded, freckle-faced Rebecca of Sunnybrook Darien—to arrest his other son for assault.

Yet, astonishingly, Joe Kelly's not pugnacious but conciliatory manner was different.

"He walks up to me and says, 'You know I really owe you an apology for that night you came to arrest Chris. I shouldn't have yelled at you.'"

His contrition shocked Officer Hahn. She laughed a startled but grateful laugh, said, "O-kay . . ." and accepted the apology. "Joe was as mild and meek as a lamb" as Hahn and her partner took Chris Kelly down to the station and arrested him on assault charges. "At one point he even said, 'You shouldn't have to be doing this.'"

The apology that Officer Hahn unexpectedly received from Joe Kelly may well have been the first and last apology anyone in Darien law enforcement would ever get from him. And it may have contained the regretful understanding, at last, that something malignant had taken root in his sons, and had flourished in this town—this town he himself had grown up aspiring to—in a more troublesome way than Joe Kelly could have ever imagined.

Thinking about it after the fact, Rebecca Hahn Nathanson believes that Joe Kelly's contrition may have been a form of guilt. "Here, one of his sons was about to run and the other was going to be arrested any minute. As a parent, that's got to be a tumultuous place to be in, emotionally. And maybe he just needed to gesture regret and apology to those of us who were dealing with his sons."

Alex's trial was now scheduled to commence on Wednesday, February 18.

On Tuesday, February 17, in the middle of a job, Jay Bush had to unexpectedly return to a site where Joe happened to be, to pick up materials. Driving back to the site, Jay drove past what he observed to be the Kellys' other car. Jay Bush says today that he is *certain* that he saw Alex driving that car and Melanie sitting next to him. When Melanie saw Jay, she had a look on her face, he recalls, "like she or Alex wasn't supposed to be seen." The look struck Jay as odd because there was no reason for him to imagine that Alex *wouldn't* be in town: His trial was to start the next day.

Not thinking anything of it, Jay, upon arriving at the site, said to Joe, "Hey, I just saw Alex." Joe surprised Bush by quickly insisting, "No, you didn't." Jay said, "Yeah, I did." Joe—oddly, Jay thought—said, *"No,* you didn't." Jay Bush says today: "Joe made a point of saying to me, *five* times: 'No, you *didn't* see Alex. That was *not* Alex.'"

Jay is positive that he saw Alex, with Melanie, the day before his rape trial started.*

The FBI, police, and prosecutors always assumed that Alex had fled from Colorado—a supposition supported by (indeed, generated from) the sighting of Alex bidding his mother that emotional good-bye at Stapleton Airport, and a position that the Kellys themselves advanced from the beginning. But Jay Bush's account indicates that Alex *did* return to Darien. Was that very public, emotional Denver airport farewell two days earlier a ruse designed to keep authorities from checking any New York–to–Europe airline passenger flight logs past Sunday? And in this way to enable Alex to get a big head start on anyone looking for him? Or was it a genuine farewell, emotional because Alex had yet to make up his mind about whether he was coming home to stand trial or was fleeing? And because his mother genuinely did not know if she would or would not see him again? And, if that is the case, did Alex's coming back to Darien signal that he was still planning (until, at least, the very last moment) to go through with attending his trial? One can only speculate.

In any event, the Darien police, having put credence in the theory that Alex disappeared from Denver on Sunday, February 15, never checked to see if his name was on any *New York* area outbound flights (or California airport outbound flights,

---

*Jay Bush was interviewed by the Darien Police as part of their general information-gathering after Alex fled. He wasn't asked, at the time, any questions that would require him to mention his sighting of Alex, and because he was employed by Joe and Joe had made it clear to Jay that he wasn't supposed to have seen Alex, he did not volunteer that he had seen him.

for that matter) in the two days after that.*

On Wednesday, February 18, Judge Martin Nigro (who had presided over Alex's burglary proceeding) struck his gavel and called court to order in *State* v. *Kelly*.

The defendant was not present.

"I would like to tell the court my client is on his way here," Mickey Sherman said, an hour after proceedings were to begin. But he had no idea of the defendant's whereabouts. Alex Kelly, he guessed, was either "unavoidably detained . . . or he is not coming, or not coming now because he is scared."**

Judge Nigro revoked the Kellys' $200,000 bail, termed Alex's absence "willful and intentional," and ordered a first-degree failure-to-appear warrant for his arrest, along with a $400,000 bond.

Alex was now a fugitive.

Alex left behind a farewell letter to his father. On Copper Mountain Resort stationery in Alex's neat if hurried printing, it reveals Alex as a young man able to express love, respect, and appreciation. In short, it reveals his emotional potential—and it reveals an idealized relationship which, had it been real, might have enabled him to realize that potential.

Alex starts the letter by telling his father there is so much

---

*They did check Denver outbound flights subsequent to Melanie's 10:45 A.M. flight and found none booked under Alex Kelly's name. However, in 1986, a passenger did not need a photo I.D. matching a ticket to travel within the United States. Any flight Alex may have taken to the New York area may well have been booked under another name, as might any New York–California flight he may have taken on Tuesday night, February 17. However, if he flew out of the country from New York, California, or anywhere else in the U. S., the flight would have to have been booked under his real, passport-matching name. There is no indication that the Darien police or FBI ever found, or looked for, such a U. S.–Europe ticket from anywhere but Denver.

**Five years later, Mickey Sherman would say he had spoken to Alex the day after his disappearance. During that postflight conversation, as Sherman would later tell the FBI, "I did everything I could to try to persuade him to come back, but it didn't do any good."

he has never told him and how Joe Kelly has been the "best" father possible. "I just hope someday I can be half the man you are. I really did try to make you proud of me."

He expresses regret that life has taken this course and entreats his father to focus, with pride, on the positive things that he, Alex, has accomplished. He himself feels positive, certain that he'd be successful in his own way. "Thank you for everything you have done for me throughout my whole life. Someday I will return everything. Love, Alex."

ALEX KELLY WAS GONE—JUST *GONE*—AND THE DARIEN police were virtually helpless to find him.

Not only did the police force lack experience with, and resources for, an international fugitive flight, but minor bad luck dogged them. First of all, Continental Airlines, because of an internal record-keeping glitch, was not able to retrieve its records from microfiche to ascertain if Alex had turned in his (alleged) Denver–Newark ticket for a ticket from Denver to another destination. On top of this, the Rocky Mountain trail had gone instantly cold. Alex (the Darien police found out from their Colorado counterparts) had picked up his last Copper Mountain Resort paycheck on February 14, and said good-bye to his condominium roommates the next day, and taken all his belongings with him, including his skis. None of the fellows he'd roomed with knew where he was headed.

Thirdly, Alex may have benefited from the fact that Melanie now worked at a local travel agency. A year or two earlier, she had taken a job there, and *if* calls to him in Europe were made from the agency's phones, there would be no way of knowing, since travel agencies routinely place dozens of calls in any given week to European cities.

Then there was Alex's lawyer's attitude—appropriate for a defense attorney but conspicuously unhelpful, nonetheless. When asked by the Darien *News-Review* if Alex had contacted him, Mickey Sherman bluntly said, "If he did, I probably wouldn't tell you, and I doubt I would tell the authorities."

The Darien Police Department did enlist the aid of the National Crime Information Center, a computer linkup of nationwide police departments, but this service is useful only if a fugitive gets arrested in another U.S. jurisdiction, something Alex Kelly would certainly be careful to avoid.

On March 1, Bruce Hudock filed a motion to have Alex tried in absentia—it would have been the first time the state of Connecticut had conducted such a trial—but he thought better of the gambit almost immediately, withdrawing his request a day later, noting that any verdict that resulted from such a trial would almost surely be overturned on appeal. He also drafted a letter to the U.S. Attorney in Bridgeport as a first step in requesting the assistance of the FBI. If it sounded as if Darien authorities were stumped, well, they were. Lieutenant Hugh McManus conceded, "There is not a lot we're going to be doing actively."

While the authorities were rustling around in this desultory manner, the young man they were searching for was safely overseas. Alex had left the Netherlands (when he arrived there, or where he arrived from, remains unknown) the day— March 1—that Hudock had filed the motion to try him in absentia. He entered Italy that same day.* Thus began a period of wanderlust: On March 12, he entered Greece. (One day later, and unbeknownst to Alex, the U.S. Attorney's office

---

*This itinerary comes from the stamps on Alex's passport, which were enumerated by FBI agent James Larner at Kelly's trial.

officially charged him with unlawful flight to avoid prosecution and authorized worldwide extradition.) A little over a week later, Alex journeyed to Egypt. Between March 21 and July 13, he crisscrossed Egypt, Turkey, then went back to Italy and back to Greece.

Egypt, Turkey, Greece, and, later, Morocco, Tunisia, Hungary: Amazingly, Alex was choosing the most dangerous borders for a fugitive to navigate. All of these countries were entry and exit paths for terrorists, revolutionaries, and drug-traffickers. They were next door to police states. They were countries where border and airport checks could be expected to be stringent, random, and unforgiving. Yet he was traversing them as freely as if he were driving between Stamford and Darien.

"I couldn't stay in one place," is how Alex explained it on *Turning Point.* "Too many questions came up, so I would move. Every time I walked by a policeman, it was the most amazing thing. It was a fear so strong, it's a physical thing. And I'd feel it in my fingers and my toes. Every minute, every single thing I did was affected by my situation."

Half a world away from Alex's bazaars and cafes, in his drab, low-ceilinged, pine-paneled Stamford office, Bruce Hudock was telling the press, in a roundabout way, that he was coming up with goose eggs. "The rumors" of Alex's whereabouts "encompass the globe," he said. "He has been mentioned to be living in several foreign countries, although none of the rumors have been confirmed." The Darien police's first assumption was that Alex had not fled the country, so the Leadville, Colorado, police and Summit County sheriff's department (where Frisco, the Colorado town Alex had last lived in, is located) had also been looking. But no longer. "We've exhausted pretty much every lead we've had here," a sheriff's detective there said. "I doubt he'll show up back here. There's nothing to keep him here or bring him back."

But if the local prosecution and law enforcement were frankly empty-handed, the FBI, which had been on the case for about five weeks, had acquired some leads while combing Colorado for friends Alex may have made there. On April 12, someone reported to Special Agent Milo Downing the claim that Alex's parents gave him $10,000 in cash before he left the state. Another source said that Alex had spoken of having a $600,000 trust fund which he could not have access to until he was twenty-one but which had been modified to enable him to attend school in Europe until (as Alex is said to have said, with naive wishful thinking) "this whole thing blows over." (The FBI would eventually stand by both of these early tips as probably true. When both cash figures were posited to Melanie Kelly on *Turning Point,* however, she said: "Lie. Absolute lie. No way.")

With the forfeiture of Alex's $200,000 bond, it was still an open question whether his parents would lose their house (which they put up as bond collateral), or whether the prosecution would release them from the full obligation and settle for a cash payment of $140,000. (Bail forefeitures are typically "compromised" to lower amounts.) Even if Joe and Melanie *did* lose their house, Mickey Sherman assured the press, they wouldn't hold it against their son. "They do not feel as though Alex burned them," Sherman said of the couple who, three years earlier, had had to pay a $100,000 restitution for Alex's burglary thefts. "They are really concerned about his welfare. They are not angry with him, that I can tell you."

To some Darien High teachers, Sherman's report of the Kellys' sentiment answered a long-asked rhetorical question. As one of the then-teachers puts it, "There were times in the past when we'd all sit around and ask: 'To what extent will a parent go? They'll write the kid's paper; they'll argue, to us, that they *didn't* write the kid's paper; they'll argue for a better grade on the paper. . . .'" But when Alex jumped bail and the Kellys took the possible loss of their house in stride, "we finally had our answer. *That's* how far parents will go!'"

* * *

Alex apparently sent Amy a letter. "It was sent," her friend remembers, "from somewhere between Colorado and his next destination." The letter, the friend says, contained "a full description of his fear, and that he didn't think he was getting a fair trial. He said he loved her and didn't know when he'd talk to her again." The letter, the friend says, "absolutely tore her apart."

On May 4, after a one-day jaunt to Egypt, Alex reentered Turkey. Although he would later assert, on *Turning Point,* that he worked in many of the places he visited—"picking grapes and working on farms . . . working in restaurants; I washed so many dishes, people used to joke that I was the 'dish technician'"—he seems to have opted for outdoor sporting activity at every opportunity. He spent some time mountain climbing with two Canadian girls in Cappadocia. While there, he met a young man named Terence Dunne, from Charlottesville, Virginia. (Ten months later, Dunne spoke to the FBI.) Alex obviously felt relaxed and confident enough not only to use his real name with Terrence Dunne but also to tell Dunne that he was from Darien—"and Vail" (Alex had started adding the Colorado resort town to his biography). Most stunningly, Alex told Terrence Dunne that he was wanted for two rapes in Connecticut. He also told Dunne that he wasn't working—that his parents were sending him money.

As soon as Amy graduated, the Molitors moved from Darien to Florida, where they owned property. "They just picked Amy up and left," is how Amy's friend puts it. Amy was too worked up over Alex—his flight had made things not better but worse. Her parents hoped that removing her from the site of their relationship might enable her to cut her ties with the past and move on with her life. She enrolled at the University of Tampa.

* * *

In August—while Alex was in Italy—Connecticut Governor William O'Neill authorized a $20,000 reward for information leading to Alex's capture. At the same time, Mickey Sherman pleaded with Judge Nigro to let the Kellys keep their home, which was just about to go into bank foreclosure to satisfy the rearrest bond. "We're saying it is still very likely he might come back," Sherman said. "All his family ties are here and all his friends are here. It's quite possible he might return."

The fight for the Kellys' house would turn into a major battle. Early in September, Judge Nigro ruled that the Kellys, indeed, had to pay the full $200,000 and that the state could force foreclosure. Tenacious Sherman continued to fight that decision and six months later won a reversal.

How did Sherman effect this victory? "I whined and groveled," he says today. His emotional argument started with the premise that it is normally a bail bondsman, not a family, who forfeits the bond when a defendant flees. If the Kellys did lose their home, they would be losing much more than a standard bail bondsman would lose on the flight of, say, a Colombian drug dealer—and that bail bondsman had no personal connection to that defendant. And since, if and when Alex returned home, the Kellys would lose *him* as well (to imprisonment on flight charges, at the very least), why punish them doubly? Sherman also had something else to hold over the state's head: When the sheriff had come to serve Joe Kelly with the foreclosure notice, he had accidentally run over and killed the Kellys' dog. And now the state was trying to take their *house?*

In March 1988, the state gave in and accepted the compromised figure of $140,000, rather than, as State's Attorney Eugene Callahan said, "face the prospect of extended litigation." (It is frankly doubtful that the Kellys would have really lost the house if they'd paid the $200,000, since they could have liquidated other assets to satisfy the bond.) Bruce Hudock today says the "compromise" bail settlement was still one of the highest cash bonds ever settled in the jurisdiction.

* * *

At about this same time, Sherman dangled in front of the press's nose the tidbit that Joe and Melanie Kelly had recently traveled to Ireland and that "everyone thought that meant they went to visit [Alex], but I don't believe that." (A large hole in Alex's itinerary does appear during this period of time—between Alex's arrival in Italy, on July 13, 1987, and his probable arrival in the Soviet Union on February 16, 1988.)

Whether or not the Ireland trip was made by one or both of them, and despite the united-couple front that the Kellys were presenting to the media, sources say that Joe and Melanie Kelly had separated briefly during the period right after Alex's flight. Melanie rented a house in Tokeneke, telling the realtor (according to someone to whom that realtor spoke) that she could no longer take Joe's "mental and physical abuse" of her.

But the separation was short-lived. Some believe that when Joe found out that, if they divorced, Melanie would get half of everything they owned together, and that there was no way to effectively fight such a fifty-fifty money settlement, Joe made up with her.

In early 1988, the brand-new Fox television show *America's Most Wanted* approached the Darien Police Department. They wanted to feature a segment on Alex Kelly's alleged crimes and his disappearance. Hosted and coproduced by John Walsh—the former businessman who had been turned, by his young son Adam Walsh's 1981 murder, into a full-time reformer of the criminal justice system—the show was a novel combination of true-crime reenactments and a televised version of a WANTED! poster or a police radio.

The bargain *AMW* implicitly presented to local police departments was straightforward: You help boost our ratings, and we'll help catch your fugitive. In other words, in exchange for the right to be able to treat the show's viewers to a somewhat sensational dramatization of a recent crime whose perpetrator was still at large, Walsh and his producers would train massive national public attention on that fugitive—plastering his picture, vital statistics, identifying characteristics, and habits on the screen, and providing a toll-free number for viewers to call if they spotted him. With *AMW*, everybody got to be an armchair bounty hunter. Of course, a police department and town government had to withstand the tabloid presentation of events that some would much prefer remain private. And the town had to be willing to watch itself identified with a sensational crime—in this case, a sensational *sex* crime.

Darien's response to *AMW*'s offer was predictable. "The police department didn't want it, and the town didn't want it," Rebecca Hahn Nathanson recalls. She herself saw value in the town cooperating with the production—"I thought: 'Alex did this and we *know* he did this—we *arrested* him on evidence. This show can help. Why aren't we cooperating?'" Others in the police department's rank and file agreed with her.

Still, the town power structure disapproved of the enterprise, and, after the producers had begun work on the segment, key access was shut down. But *AMW* very much wanted to do the story, so its researchers, writers, and producers forged ahead.

America's Most Wanted aired its Alex Kelly segment on Sunday night, April 17, 1988. It immediately spurred controversy. In the view of many in town, the segment sensationalized and misrepresented the case. But a viewing of the segment shows it to be largely realistic—the actor who played Alex was well cast and the depictions of upper-middle-class high-school life were authentic. However, the scene of Adrienne leaving the party with Alex showed her bouncy and laughing, not hesitant; and a subsequent scene showed Alex and Valerie kissing before her alleged rape occurred. Still, without the cooperation of the police for the details of the case, the producers had been forced to rely on guesswork.

After watching the show, Bruce Hudock (who had reluctantly agreed to be interviewed on the show only because Mickey Sherman had said yes, and Hudock did not want the defense view to be the only view presented) angrily told the Darien *News-Review*, "They took every opportunity to make the program into as much of a peep show as they could." He pronounced the depiction "an injustice to the victims." But it is Hudock himself who appears in the broadcast saying, "Rape is rape, whether it's a date rape or not. I don't see a difference in my mind," unwittingly helping to lend the impression that the rapes were of a somewhat lesser magnitude.

At the end of the segment, John Walsh scolded the town. *"America's Most Wanted* was promised full cooperation," he told the viewers. "Then something happened. A wall of silence was put up. The Darien Police Department refused to cooperate. People were pressured not to speak. But some in town refused to be intimidated." After reeling off a short, perfunctory list of Alex's identifying characteristics (including a "distinct, howling laugh"), Walsh said, "It's not much to go on."

Lieutenant Hugh McManus denied pressuring people not to speak. He claimed that the department had declined to cooperate because, since they believed Alex was out of the country, Alex was outside of the show's viewing area. Yet in the broadcast, both Hudock and Sherman had said that one of the places Alex might well be was Malibu. And after the broadcast, many of the calls that came through the *AMW* switchboard (the call sheets for which were given to the Darien police) had placed Alex at outdoor sports havens, resorts, and Grateful Dead concerts (John Walsh had told viewers Alex was a Deadhead) in California, which he might have attended in mid to late February.*

---

*Alex would eventually be featured (without the Darien Police Department's cooperation) on *America's Most Wanted* four separate times, as a result of which he was "positive[ly]" (according to the FBI) identified by viewers in Greece, India, Turkey, Dutch St. Maarten, West Germany, and Ireland. (All but India, Ireland, and Dutch St. Maarten are places he is known to have spent time in.) In addition, three anonymous calls were made to the show about Alex: On June 6, 1989, a woman claiming to be a friend of Melanie's

A month after the controversial *AMW* broadcast—in mid-May 1988—Julia West was finishing her sophomore college year abroad. She found herself in Greece. "It was my last day, and I had time to kill before the airport, and I was sitting at this little cafe, down the hill from the Acropolis. And I notice this guy a few tables away and he was kind of cute. He had long hair in a ponytail. And I was looking at him some more and I realized: Oh my God, it's Alex Kelly!" (Alex's passport does show time spent in Greece during May 1988.)

Julia steadied herself. "I was just about to say, 'Alex . . .?' Then I sucked in my words. It was: Oh my God, I don't want him to know I'm here!

"He turned, and he was looking at the Acropolis behind my head, so I was looking directly at him. He saw me—I *know* he did. And then he vanished into thin air. He was *gone.*"

Actually, Alex had run into people he knew in other places. Darienites would come home and speak of Alex sightings; later, Alex confirmed them. He told *Turning Point:* "I bumped into people and they'd say, 'You're Alex Kelly!' And I'd—I would speak another language. I would try my best to get out of there or else I'd say, 'No, I don't understand,' and walk away."

After Greece, Alex entered Tunisia via Turkey on May 29; then, on June 4, he arrived in Morocco.

Although the police attached number-tracer registries to both the Kellys' home phone and Joe Kelly's business line (these are legal for police departments to employ, since a conversation is not being overheard; a number is simply being

---

said Melanie had opened a bank account in one of the Carolinas to send Alex money (Melanie's father was, at the time, living in Hilton Head, South Carolina); on June 28, 1989, a woman said Alex was living in Ireland with relatives; and on June 1, 1990, a man who claimed to be a friend of one of Joe Kelly's employees said Alex was living in Ireland. None of the information in these phone calls, however, was ever confirmed as accurate.

logged into a computer), they did not do the same trace on the travel agency. Perhaps it's because there were too many lines to tap, and since any travel agency has legitimate business calling Europe, separating real from false leads would be almost impossible. Melanie would later say that she made her calls from pay phones. "We assumed that every [phone in the house] was bugged; we lived like that for years," she told Forrest Sawyer. Then, by way of illustrating her hardship, she rhetorically asked, "You know what it's like to put eighteen dollars' worth of quarters in a telephone? It's crazy . . . [I was] shaking."

As if he were abroad on, say, a class trip or a student exchange program, Alex asked his parents to send money, and, according to friends in Chamonix, he received it. Alex wrote long letters to his parents, likely using a relative living in another Connecticut town to facilitate the correspondence. In Alex's letters, he signed off with the self-consciously cryptic signature "Your Friend," yet the bodies of the letters did not attempt to disguise the fact that he was a son writing to his parents.

Alex entered Portugal on August 2. He spent most of August and September journeying back and forth between Morocco and Egypt. On September 14, his passport bears an indeterminate stamp. He spent most of the fall of 1988 in Hungary.

But where did he go after Hungary?

Just as Julia was certain she saw Alex in May 1988, Amy Molitor was, according to some of her friends, shaken by an Alex sighting in early 1989. Amy had started her sophomore year at the University of Tampa and was dating a fellow student named Scott, a good-looking boy, talented swimmer, and, according to a dormmate of his, "a real nice guy." "She was just getting over the hump of Alex," says her friend from Darien. "She was moving on with her life.

"Then, one night, at this same time, she supposedly got a knock on her dorm door. She opened it and . . . she believed that she saw him. At the end of the hallway. She ran out. But he was gone.

"She sincerely believed that she saw him. (When she told me, *I* believed it. I thought: That's Alex—he loved the game of risk.) And that sighting of him ate her up."

Could Alex have slipped back into the country in early 1989? Though unlikely, it is possible; Interpol did not post him on their wanted lists (in 176 countries) until later that year. Alex's passport does not show a 1989 U.S. entry (or a U.S. entry for any year before his January 1995 surrender), but this is not a definitive indication of lack of entry. After all, although Alex's only 1989 passport stamp was Denmark, it is known that he also spent time that year in France, Sweden, and Germany.

In fact, it was in West Germany, during the fall of the Berlin Wall—on September 18, 1989—after at least thirty-nine previous border crossings, that Alex had his only real brush with the law. He was stopped at the Badishe Personbahnhoe railway station, while on a train crossing from Switzerland into West Germany.

The German border guard checked Alex's passport number on a handheld computer. "He looked at it and said, 'You're wanted in America," Alex would later tell *Turning Point.* "And I said, 'It's a mistake. What do you mean?' And they said, 'All right, we'll have to check this out.'"

Interpol was called. The version that made its way around the police community is that the Interpol computer just happened to be down at that particular moment, and in the ensuing lack of communication, Alex was declared free to go. An hour later, the guards found out they had just released a fugitive.

But Alex's own version, given to Forrest Sawyer, is much more dramatic. Essentially, Alex fled. "I was going through cars and cars, and the train is moving and I was trying to open the doors to jump off the train, but the train doors all locked. The train finally stopped to let another train go by on the track, so I opened up the door and I jumped down an embankment and I rolled down into this farmer's field. I couldn't believe it!"

It was right after this near-capture that Alex, now twenty-two, decided he needed a place or two to roost in, in a more or less permanent fashion.

But this did not mean he would stop taking risks. On the contrary, the place where he chose to spend his next few years was one of northern Europe's capitals of daredevil skiing.

You come to the Chamonix valley if you are prepared to die on the slopes, and you come if a life devoid of skiing would *seem* like death to you. You come to butt heads with the mountain.

From the 15,800-foot high point of Mont Blanc, Aiguille du Midi and the encircling sprawl of lower peaks look like the knuckled claws of a giant, many-fanged sphinx: Grand Canyon–like, veined by ridges, brown on the bottom and capped by swaths of celestial white that bleed into the clouds that streak the light blue sky. So high, so far from cities, so unpolluted, the diorama's colors are as sharply exaggerated as the hues of colorized movies.

Mont Blanc is laced with crevasses, hundred-foot-deep sinkhole-type fissures that result from slowly shifting glaciers. Under the film of deceptively placid ice, the crown of the mountain is as skeletal as a skyscraper under construction. The "extreme" ski movement was started on these peaks by legendary skiers Sylvan Sudan, Patrick Valinsant—and by Jean Marc Bouvan, who died in a cliff jump. Bouvan is not Chamonix's only martyr. About ten to twenty skiers die in these French Alps each year. (Fifty more skiers, ice climbers, and paraponters—hang gliders—are hurt each year in accidents.) Most succumb in avalanches, but some, like Bouvan, tempt fate with their wild-man antics: climber Patrick Donaldson lost his life through an unlucky thrust of his ice pick; snowboarder Bruno Villy plunged to his doom when his board hit a snow hole.

The names of these legendary skiers are the subject of casual awe among the ruddy-faced young ski bums—largely Scandinavian, with a sprinkling of Americans, Canadians, and Australians—who, wrapped in down-filled neon nylon, clomp down the cobbled streets in insulated boots, hoisting their skis across their shoulders. They live in small hotels and apartments in this town of three- to five-story, balconied, wood-shuttered Alpine buildings whose ground floors house cafés and bread, cheese, tobacco, ski, and souvenir shops. The *étrangères*, as the foreign young set—who coexist with Chamonix-Mont-Blanc's 9,700 permanent residents and its seasonal influx of "Gumbies" (clumsy American tourists)—are called, hang out at night at the bars here and in next-door Argentière. Back in 1989, the hot spots were Mill Street and Revant, a Swedish-owned bar with an English chef and a Polish manager; today Marseilles is the place, along with Le Samoyede, where an American husband and French wife serve Tex-Mex cuisine to flaxen-haired kids who grew up on sardines and spaetzle.

To the American male étrangères plunged into Chamonix's mating game, the Swedish girls are tens: calm, beautiful, and *born* cool. They never fumbled in backseats of cars or relied on the tacky facilitation of keg parties; many have been sleeping with their boyfriends one bedroom over from mom and dad since they were fifteen. The American ski-bum girls, on the other hand, are—once the guys get over here—suddenly so *American*. "After five years in Jackson Hole," says Argentière fixture Gary Bigham (originally from Michigan), "they've lost all their femininity: They chew tobacco, wear baggy clothes, and dress like their last boyfriend."

Filmmaker, photographer, musician, and ski fanatic Bigham has a house that doubles as a bed-and-breakfast called Vitamin Ski (where young photographers and writer-skiers—who could have grown up in Darien—bunk out when they're on assignment for *Outside* and *Men's Journal* magazines) and his band, The Crevasse-Holes, does Kinks, Doors, and Animals covers at all the local venues. Every hip expatriate outpost has someone like Gary Bigham—an older brother figure, a one-man welcome wagon.

One day in 1989 Gary picked up a hitchhiker—a good-looking, outgoing American guy with a long ponytail. His name, the guy said, was Alex—and he was, he said, from Vail, Colorado. Gary bought him a drink and "thought he was one of the nicest guys I ever met here. To me, he was never just another kid. We hit it off right away. I'd say something cocky and he'd say something funny, in a goofy voice. He was just a *great* guy. And he was a real mountaineer. He was absolutely like everybody else: a ski bum."

Gary Bigham always made his Chamonix–Argentière ski buddies perform in his films, and he roped in Alex Kelly, just like everyone else. For a spoofy film titled *I'd Rather Be Skiing Than Happy With You,* he had Alex cavort, in ski wear, in a sauna with girls hoisting champagne glasses. When stills from the film (as well as photographs Bigham shot of Alex for a Patagonia catalog) appeared in *Details* magazine in 1996, accompanying a story about fugitive Alex's surrender, Bigham was upset that the photos' intentionally over-the-top sybaritism misrepresented Alex's life in Chamonix.

Chamonix and Argentière are not jet-set playgrounds. Not like Vevey, where Diana Ross and her Norwegian industrialist husband Arne Naess have a grand log cabin, and where David Bowie and his wife Iman winter. Not like Courmayeur, the Fellini-worthy, boutique-filled resort on the Italian side of Mont Blanc, where people drive Ferraris and put fur coats on their poodles. (Not that Alex and his friends wouldn't, once in a while, drop down into Courmayeur, just for the kick of it.) No. Chamonix and Argentière are for people who are there for the slopes, not the scene. Chamonix is about as chic as Minnesota.

In conversations with Bigham in Chamonix, in the winter of 1997, he manifested a decidedly protective attitude toward Alex. But then, so did most of the valley's étrangères that this author met. They couldn't believe the great guy and ace skier and ice climber they'd hung out with for several winters had committed any rapes. American Alex? Alex Kelly? A rapist? It wasn't possible! At a time when almost all of Alex's old Darien crowd thought him guilty, most of his Chamonix friends from six and eight years back were wholly convinced of his innocence.

It is possible that this place served to bring out the best in Alex. He was inhibited by his fugitive status from risk-taking behavior that was criminal rather than athletic; and the atmosphere of cheery equanimity that pervaded the place may well have been a good influence.

Another Chamonix étrangère who met Alex that first season was Alex Frandel, a young skier and parapont instructor from Carlisle, Massachusetts. "For Alex and me, it was just a ski-bum relationship. What did you ski today? Where's the party tonight? I never saw any side of him but a mellow one. But, hey, wait, in retrospect maybe he *was* a little nervous. Like the night after a party, he'd be embarrassed. (But then, *I*'d be a little embarrassed.) Gee, I don't know, come to think of it, maybe he *was* hiding something. . . ."

"A lot of people come to Chamonix to hide out," Gary Bigham affirms. "It's so easy! Man, they'll never find ya here! Everybody just walks around with a big smile on their face after being in the sun too long. Nobody thinks about last names. All anyone talks about is skiing. Actually, when I first got here, years ago, there *was* this guy here, a drug dealer, he got lost in an avalanche. They never found him. The FBI came. Interpol came. They didn't want to believe the guy vanished in the snow, but he *did!*" No such FBI or Interpol agents, though, ever came to Chamonix to look for Alex.

Alex was alone his first season in Chamonix. But when he came back in the late winter of 1989 he came with a Swedish girlfriend—a ten—Elisabet Jansson: blond, pretty in the very natural, slightly bovine young Liv Ullmann mold. "They were a couple who were always together," Gary says. "After a few years with Alex, she took on his mannerisms. She'd laugh like he did. She'd say things the same way."

Elisabet was a student in nearby Annecy, France, near Grenoble. Her parents, Mats and Mona, were franchised owners of one of a chain of upscale supermarkets on the Swedish island of Klädesholmen. Between ski seasons, Alex moved in with the family and worked at the store, picking up Swedish (so much that, by the time he surrendered and came back to Darien in 1995, he spoke with a slight Swedish accent) and adjusting to the stern, sensible, work-ethic values— though not without grumbles.

In letters he wrote to his parents (found when the FBI raided their home in 1994), Alex, playing the loyal boyfriend (and, perhaps, comparing the Janssons to his own indulgent parents), complains extensively that Elisabet's parents "say how easy [Elisabet] has it but she doesn't get a penny from them. She pays her own way. She is paying for school with her own savings." But Alex noted that his girlfriend's laudable industriousness was not appreciated by a mother with a martyr complex. "She thinks she is the hardest-worked and everyone else is lazy."

Alex seemed proud of his own industriousness and defensive about Elisabet's mother's lack of tolerance of his outdoor pleasures. "I work for them for about five dollars an hour and a lot of responsibility and am always willing to work on projects for nothing, painting their houses [the Janssons owned two houses, on different islands], cutting their grass . . . anything they ask but I am still lazy in her eyes because I might take a day climbing every other week. They are great people (at least Mats is great) and we all get along (I totally kiss ass) but it is nice getting out of her grip."

To flee his nagging quasi-mother-in-law (and his fears of being found), Alex joined his peers at Chamonix–Argentière during the winters of 1989, 1990, and 1991. He and Elisabet took long overnights on Mont Blanc. Despite the fact that one of Alex's letters to his parents raved about the Christmas present he sent them ("You can have a nice French picnic . . . the paté is special"), Gary Bigham says that Alex did not act like a rich kid. "He and Elisabet lived in dumpy little apartments—just the cheapest things. About ten by twenty feet. I remember this one cell-like studio they had (if you could even call it a studio)—almost just a closet with a foldout bed.

"They lived for the outdoors—people here do. They would go on eight-hour hikes up Mont Blanc: Carry their food, make a 'bivvy' [hollowing out a snow cave to sleep in], or crash at one of the *refuges*"—the dorm-style ski huts that are free preseason and go for twenty to thirty dollars a night peak season, during which they're crowded with randy-smelling climbers. Then they'd ski down the ungroomed, "unruffled" slopes.

Alex liked telemark skiing—the lighter equipment enabled longer, back-country climbs, and the greater risk that came from its unstable mooring (the skis tend to swirl under you) was exciting. "He did some radical telemarking," Bigham says. And he and Elisabet went paraponting, which he taught her, and ice climbing.

At night Alex was in a group of noisy English-speaking étrangères who hung out at the ground-floor bar in one of Chamonix's hotels. "I would cringe a bit when this loud group of guys—Kiwis and Canadians, and Alex—came in at night," says the bartender there, a young Canadian named Mark Hanson. "They arrived very drunk and they would drink until we closed down, but they were generally harmless. Alex had an amazing capacity for drinking tequila, and they would play a little game called liar's dice—you pass the dice around and take shots of tequila if you're caught bluffing." Sort of like a Chamonix version of quarters.

Mark bartended at night to support himself in Chamonix. His main reason for being there—his main reason for being, period—was skiing. He was a highly accomplished telemarker, and he and the exuberant American drinker soon progressed from a mere bartender-customer relationship to ski partners. Mark was struck by Alex's "resilient energy—he'd go home after drinking all night and then bounce up to ski as if he had ten hours' sleep." Soon they were regularly going on all-day treks up and down the north face of Mont Blanc, sometimes with their Swedish friend Ville Wimell.

There were strict rules for these jaunts: You had to start at dawn because you didn't want to miss the first lift—with everyone racing for the powder, by noon all the skiable slopes were tracked out. Once at the top, you carefully avoided the infamous crevasse-pocked death chutes, especially the particularly treacherous *poubelle.* Instead, Mark and Alex and Ville picked their way to the safe *mer du glace* chute and headed down.

Not that it wasn't risky. Once Ville, skiing ahead, crashed down a chute and found himself on a thin ledge of glacier, staring down at a crevasse that might have been two thousand feet deep. He yelled back to the others not to venture there and raised himself up as softly and deliberately as he could manage. He did not fall and die. Afterward, Alex said, 'Boy, we almost lost you.'" They all skied down together.

Alex Kelly described, to *Turning Point,* the reason he skied and ice-climbed when he was on the run in terms similar to those used by O. J. Simpson to describe why he had become a compulsive golfer: The need for intense concentration on a physical task erased everything else in the world but that one physical moment.

Ville Wimell liked Alex—and was struck by his casual generosity. After a ski, "he would buy five guys hot dogs. He'd buy them drinks. He didn't show off, but it was clear he had enough money to be able to do what he wanted. He'd kid that his parents were rich, like: no big deal."

But it was Mark who got closest to Alex. The young Canadian man's gentle thoughtfulness may have enabled Alex to open up. "When you got beyond the barrier of the gregarious facade and the obnoxious act (which I see now was maybe his way of diverting people away from asking too many questions about him), he was a sensitive, emotional person." Alex shared with Mark information that seemed innocent then, but has attained some significance in hindsight: "That he had somehow found a way to use invisible ink on the entries on his Eurail pass, so he could go longer without having to get a new one. (You can only get them outside of Europe, in the States or Canada.) He could just keep going and going. I tried to get him to show me how to do it. He always promised he would, but he never did." His parents always seemed to be sending him things—"He would say, of some piece of equipment, 'My mom sent me this for my birthday.'" But the word "Darien" was never mentioned. Nor was there any mention of rape charges.

Alex's concern for his brother, Chris, was something that particularly struck Mark Hanson during their skis in the 1989 and 1990 seasons. "He talked about that there were a lot of family problems and that he really missed his brother. He talked about his brother's drug abuse and that his father had a very hard time dealing with him. I got the sense that Alex and his brother had a pretty traumatic childhood. I think his father was very strict. It seemed that something was happening in that family, that it was almost a little dysfunctional."

Alex's parents visited him in Chamonix at least once. Mark Hanson didn't meet them but Gary Bigham did. "I remember running into Alex and his folks at the post office. He said, 'Gary, these are my parents.'"

But if he was offhand with Gary—acting like a regular American ski bum entertaining his folks for a few days—with Mark, he was a little more willing to hint at the real reason he'd become an expatriate. Mark recalls a remark Alex made that Mark thought, at the time, was just figurative. Of the mountain huts he and Elisabet stayed in, "I remember him saying—and, at the time, I thought he was just kidding or exaggerating—that if the police ever came for him, he was ready to go."

Mark Hanson also remembers something else: Being "surprised that Alex became so taken with Elisabet. It was odd for an off-the-wall, high-energy person like that to be happy with a soft-spoken, slightly withdrawn girl like Elisabet." (Ville Wimell describes their relationship similarly. "He was the dominating one between them, no question about it. Usually that's how a relationship works—one's outgoing and one's shy.") Mark Hanson says he saw a great closeness develop. "I think he was truly faithful to her and committed to her while he was with her." Echoing the phrase a friend of Amy Molitor's said she had spoken after the rapes—that Alex had a "split personality"—Mark Hanson says: "That's what I mean when I say that Alex was really *two* people."

After two or three seasons in Chamonix, Alex and Elisabet moved on to the much more remote and exotic town of La Grave. For all its extreme-skiing drama, Chamonix is a blandly wholesome ski town filled with tourists, a straight two-hour drive by superhighway from Geneva. La Grave is something else entirely: A fortresslike medieval outpost of only 455 permanent residents, three hours from Grenoble, reachable only by navigating thin, rickety bridges bearing DANGEREUX! signs over several-thousand-foot drops and driving around spiraling roads up mountains so desultory, even the Nazis forgot there were towns in them. La Grave's natives harbor a pugnacious insularity befitting their environs: When the large corporation that was building its 7,000-vertical-foot ski lift put up its pylons and cables, the townsfolk dynamited the construction sight—not once, but twice—until they forced concessions. The company could build its ski resort but was banned from constructing restaurants, grooming facilities, or establishing a ski patrol or security in La Grave, making it a definite *non*resort for dedicated skiers.

If the FBI was seriously looking for you, La Grave would be a great place to thwart them.

From 1991 on, Alex and Elisabet wintered here: drinking at the mountain-peak-hugging chalet La Chaumine (if you sneeze as you make the last hairpin turn, your car just might plunge off the unrailed one-lane-wide dirt road into the valley below) and holding an *après* ski table at Café Les Glaciers, across from the Alp'Ser'Vit mini-grocery, on the town's small main street, behind which fifteenth-century stone buildings give off on winding, cobbled, sharply inclined alleys.

Whereas the Chamonix-Argentière crowd had found Alex amiable, "a lot of people here in La Grave did not like him," says Swedish ski guide and La Chaumine regular Paul Fobe. "He was really loud. He had this 'Here I am, I'm the biggest, best skier in the valley; I'm the coolest guy here' attitude. He was always bragging about everything he was doing." Contradicting Ville Wimell's opinion, Fobe says: "And she was just the same. Loud. They didn't like her, either." (Interviewed in the winter of 1997 in La Grave, Fobe goes on to volunteer: "But his younger brother Russell, who is here in town now: *he* is just the opposite.")

Both fellow students at Darien High and courtroom observers during Alex's trial had noticed how deeply enmeshed he seemed to become with his girlfriends. Alex affirms this in a letter he wrote to his parents from La Grave. "We are used to having 24 hours together." He goes on in the letter to say that Elisabet's time at school, which gives them "a couple of days a week apart" is something of a healthy break from the closeness because "we both meet a lot more people and get to know the people the other person met also. We also have a lot more to talk about when we are together." What is striking—even poignant—here is Alex's potential to be a loving partner. Maintaining a healthy relationship is important enough for him to write about such matters to his parents.

However, it appears that there was another side to Alex's

and Elisabet's relationship, and that turbulence erupted between them in La Grave during at least one of these winters.

An investigator who worked in concert with the FBI on the Kelly case gives this account: When Alex surrendered in 1995 and returned to Darien with Elisabet, a young man with a German name who had known them there and who was now living near Darien called the prosecution and told of having partially witnessed a violent fight between Alex and Elisabet that started at night and continued into the morning. Someone who perused the investigative file on Kelly says that Elisabet may have received a black eye the night of the fight and that the next morning, the altercation involved both Alex and Elisabet taking hammers to each others' mountain bikes.*

In early summer 1990, Elisabet and Alex traveled to Stockholm to take in a Grateful Dead concert and spend time with Ville and his wife. The foursome went biking and swimming. Afterward, Ville directed them to what he described as the coolest hotel in town—it was a beautiful place that looked like a castle and, at the time, Ville did not understand why Alex was so resistant to staying there. "It was Langholm Hostel, a reconditioned prison. Alex said, 'I'm gonna *pay* to be in a prison?!' It was funny!"

Before the Stockholm trip, Alex had celebrated his twenty-third birthday, May 8, in Dublin. He was joined there by his parents, who flew over on May 2 and back on May 12— information that was later ascertained by the FBI.

While Alex was celebrating his birthday with his parents and partying at Dead concerts with his new Swedish girlfriend and friends, he was blissfully unaware that, across the ocean,

---

*The author attempted to call the young man who made the report to the prosecution, but his two most recent listed phone numbers were out of service. In January 1997, Elisabet Jansson was interviewed, in Swedish, by an assistant to this author but she politely refused to answer questions about Alex Kelly, saying, "That's in the past." The author traveled to La Grave in March 1997 to find Ms. Jansson and saw her briefly at Café Les Glaciers, but Ms. Jansson left before any questions could be put to her.

the activity that he was criminally charged with had just become a mobilizing issue on American college campuses. The year 1990 was the year that alleged student-on-student sexual intimidation and abuse—its existence, and colleges' unpreparedness for preventing it, investigating it, and effecting policy against it—leaped to the forefront of concerns that students were rallying, leafletting, and talking to the media about.

For Alex's female peers, the brand-new concepts "acquaintance rape" and "date rape" were giving voice and shape and boldness to years of choicelessness, and were recasting humiliating indignities as sanctionable wrongs and coercions. All around the country, college girls sat up at night, looking back on their high school and college nights—and interpreting a lot of unpleasant treatment in a newly politicized light. Had they been pressured? Violated? Or merely demeaned? (And was being merely demeaned a violation in itself?)

Acquaintance rape occupied many deans of students' agendas as the 1990–1991 school year continued. Guidebooks were published, orientations and discussion groups scheduled, speak-outs and "Take Back The Night" candlelight marches held. And in the grand, recent American tradition of major campus issues, reformist overkill descended: After protests arose when two female Antioch students who claimed they'd been raped by male students found that the college had no rape crisis services, Antioch responded, in February 1991, by instituting a much-publicized Sexual Offense Policy, which required that male students obtain verbal permission for every stage of foreplay and sex entered into with a female student.

That policy (known in the media as "the kissing contract") was widely ridiculed—it was, indeed, a sitting duck for ridicule. "Date rape" is a dangerously amorphous concept to begin with, and the act of penalizing sexual behavior that begins as consensual is pocked with civil-liberties land mines and invites absurdist dogma. But the policy, clumsy though it was, was at least an administrative attempt to brake on a slippery slope of sexual misunderstanding and to shift the burden of responsibility for reading signals from the female to the male. And beneath the zealous overcorrection lay a real complaint that needed redress. While college deans grappled with how to make that redress, female students were sharing their personal stories in their dorm rooms, in class discussion, and in term papers.

Adrienne Bak was one of these students.

Of course, the term "acquaintance rape" minimizes what happened to Adrienne, and although it defines the context of her attack (she and Alex were peers and in the same social milieu; she accepted a ride in his car after both were at the same party), it does not adequately describe the rape itself. (It was a violent rape, with no consensual foreplay, and it included a death threat.) Adrienne's trauma from that evening had never healed. As a student at Northeastern University in 1990 and 1991, she was still having nightmares. ("In my dream, he never got to the killing part; I would always wake up as soon as he had me down with him on top of me," she said, in a postverdict interview she gave to *The New York Times* and the Stamford *Advocate.*) She was still so instinctively wary with men, she could barely have normal dates.

Adrienne Bak married her pain to this new campus climate. She turned her obsession with her rape into a personal crusade. Almost every term paper and research paper she wrote was either directly about or "dedicated" to the subject of rape. She "wanted to do something about it"—her rape and others'. "I 'preached.' I went around writing down and telling people what happened to me. I always wanted to tell everybody what had happened because many people think it couldn't happen to them." (Not dissimilarly, Jillian Henderson had also by now started working as a domestic violence hotline worker in Maryland.)

In the process, Adrienne says, she discovered how widespread sexual abuse really was among girls just like herself. "Usually one out of five women that I'd tell had a very similar story." All over campus, Adrienne ended up talking to "a lot of women who were abused and a lot of women who were molested."

But a question remained. As empowering and healing as it was to talk to—and get angry among—other women, how would a young man react? Was that same sensitivity available? Could a man ever take it as seriously? Even if you and your girlfriends had stopped thinking that being a rape victim made you damaged goods, had young men stopped thinking it, too?

In 1990, Adrienne had begun dating Christopher Ortolano, a tall, handsome, solid-looking fellow Northeastern University student two years older than she. Still, she "didn't know what his reaction would be" to the part of her history that she had not yet revealed.

One night, as she and Chris were taking a walk after a restaurant dinner, "I told him I really loved him and wanted to make sure that he was the right person for me." The disclosure she was about to make was thus fashioned as a kind of test. Since Adrienne already knew she loved Chris Ortolano, she was every bit as vulnerable to his failure of that test as he.

"I told him that I was raped," she told the *Advocate* and *Times,* while he sat next to her during the interview.* "He got upset, and he asked me what happened, and I told him everything.

"When I told him, I cried. We cried together."

In September 1991, Alex went back to Chamonix. He skied with his friend Mark Hanson, and he seemed, once again, worried about his brother Chris. "Alex was very concerned because Chris had a *big* problem with drugs but he was doing

---

*Chris Ortolano attended every day of both trials, and immediately leaped up to accompany his wife to the court hallway every time a recess was called during her testimony and cross-examination.

them again. He certainly had a fear that Chris was headed down a certain path and I think he was troubled by that."

In fact, the year before, Chris Kelly had entered a drug rehabilitation program, and his good friends were happy for him. They thought he had learned to live with the lingering pain from his injury; they thought he was on his way to achieving a certain peace with himself. Still, to some, there was a loneliness that seemed to come from a baffling irony: He was the son who was there, yet his father seemed to prefer Alex. And as Alex's brother, still living and working in the town that his brother had fled, he was increasingly avoided, by neighbors and former friends. Even if the avoidance sprang from awkwardness, it was still isolating. He didn't deserve to be punished for acts that were not his doing—and he didn't have the resources to rise above his own discomfort and resentment.

For a while, in early 1991, Chris seemed to be getting his life together. Then, somehow, he lost his footing and—ironically, while in a drug-rehabilitative program—he started using heroin.

Jay Bush learned of Chris's last day of life—October 2, 1991—from someone who had seen Chris with Joe—and from Chris himself.

Apparently, as Jay learned from someone who witnessed this scene, Joe had gotten angry when Chris, on his way to a job he was doing with Jay, had stopped at the shop to use the bathroom, making Chris late for the job. Joe's anger had made Chris cry. When he arrived at the job site, "I said, 'What's wrong?'" Jay Bush says. "He says, 'Ahh! I've had it with my dad! He's such an asshole! I can't take any more.'

"So we did the job. I knew it had been a bad few days for Chris," Jay says. Chris had been keeping Jay abreast of his life. "He had just blown the motor in his car, so he had no car. He went to a real narrow cove with his boat—a real expensive boat—and rips the out-drive right out of the boat, which costs $3,000. So now he gets hit with *that* expense. He's got no car, he's depressed as it was. And his dad had just ripped into him."

That evening, Chris dropped by Jay's house and told Jay about the fight he had had with his father in the interim. "So he goes back to the shop," is how Jay recalls the story. "He says, 'Listen, Dad, I've got a date tonight. Think I can take the van home?' And Joe starts yelling at him about how he didn't give Joe a ticket on some job he just did. Joe said he couldn't take the van, but he could take the spare truck, which was a piece of crap. So Chris says. 'How the hell am I gonna take a date out in the spare truck?' And Joe says, 'Well, it's either that or nothing.' So Chris storms out of the shop and says, 'Man, I've had it!'"

When Chris left Jay's house, after telling him this story, Jay and his wife thought that Chris was going on his aforementioned date. Instead, he apparently scored—and used—synthetic heroin. "If we had knowledge of his drug use," Jay's wife says, "we would have gotten him help."

The next morning, Joe Kelly was telephoned by the two young women who lived in the unit below Chris. Chris's Doberman was running around as if he needed to get out and the women didn't have a key. So they called Joe, asking him to come over.

When Joe opened the door, he saw his son sprawled on the kitchen floor, surrounded by synthetic heroin and needles. Chris was dead.

Officer Rebecca Hahn was called to the scene. When she saw Joe Kelly on the sidewalk with the dog, she immediately guessed what had happened. "He looked heartbroken," Rebecca says. "He was just so sad. This was a different Joe Kelly that I saw, this time. The look on his face said: 'How could it come to this?' There was just . . . so much sadness."

* * *

Jay Bush and other close friends believe that Chris's death was a suicide, not a drug overdose, although it was never officially declared as such. The death of someone so young—in this case twenty-six—especially by his own hand, always prompts a particularly raw and alarmed kind of grief, undiminishable by the usual comforts, such as the sense of a life well lived or a long period of physical suffering mercifully ended. It is simply a time of terrible sadness.

Old family friends—those who had shared young parenthood with Joe and Melanie—felt injustice at the grim upending of life's first rule: that a child should never predecease his parents. To these middle-age people, Chris's funeral held a there-but-for-fortune pathos. "I think I will never forget that funeral as long as I live," Joe's old friend Frank Heral says. "It was packed from pew to pew. Before Pastor [Edward] Danks spoke, they put on a tape of the song 'I Just Called To Say I Love You' and there wasn't a dry eye in the house."

Many of Chris's fellow twelve-step members attended. His mentor in the program, whom he was supposed to call the minute he found himself with the urge to reabuse, "felt terrible," a friend of the man says. Why hadn't Chris reached out to him that night, instead of driving into the city? How had he failed Chris?

Great sympathy flowed toward Melanie. Her middle boy had been charged with a terrible crime and was gone—and now her older son was dead. She had always been a loving mother, those who had car-pooled and volunteered with her knew. What had she done to earn *this*?

"I remember watching Melanie—she was just trembling," says one of the young women who, as a girl, used to visit her. "The minister was saying how sad it was—that Chris had had a sort of tortured life, but here we had all thought he was on an upswing. And now, this happens." At the burial, "Joe was stone-faced and Melanie looked sedated," the young woman continues. "It was so sad watching her go up and kiss the casket as it sank into the ground. There was a huge wreath on it with a note: 'Love from Alex.' We just assumed Joe and Melanie put it there." At that moment, most guests didn't let themselves focus on whether or not the Kellys were in contact with their fugitive son. It seemed unseemly—or at least uncharitable—to even think about the subject.

But, back at the Kelly house after the burial, this young woman—who had always perceived that Melanie was unhappy and who had never harbored good thoughts about Joe because she thought that he had caused her unhappiness—found herself uncomfortable. "I didn't know what to say. I really didn't like Joe, but on the other hand, I pitied him. So I just said, 'Chris was a good boy, Mr. Kelly. Chris was a good boy.' He had a bit of a tear in his eye. He looked as if he was trying to keep pleasant thoughts. Melanie was walking around being greeted. She was trying to hold it together. I'm sure she was on the brink."

A simple image caused this woman to pull back her sympathy. "I saw Joe's relatives, taking pictures. Just walking around, snapping snapshots. At first, it seemed such an inappropriate thing to do. And then I thought: Oh God, they're taking pictures to send to Alex! They must be in contact with him.

"I just stood back and separated myself from the death of Chris and began to think, Maybe the Kellys *aren't* so innocent. Maybe they're hiding Alex. Maybe they're financing him."

Thinking that Alex might show up, the Darien Police Department had posted surveillance at Chris's funeral. Some officers sat in an unmarked car, watching the funeral home. Others milled around outside the Noroton Presbyterian Church, where the service was held. And a few kept an eye on Spring Grove Cemetery from the police station, right across the street.

"Melanie was very vocal afterward, to anyone who would listen, about what awful people we police were and what we were doing to the family and how we didn't have any respect for them," says Rebecca Hahn Nathanson. "But we found out, afterward—through the grapevine—that Alex was *this* close to coming in."

Still, whether or not their surveillance was justified, the criticism stuck. The department was taken to task for having violated a grieving family's privacy by callowly viewing the funeral as an arrest opportunity. "After that, they didn't want to put too much pressure on Joe and Melanie," Nathanson remembers.

Jay Bush was at the Kellys' one day shortly after Chris's death. "Melanie was crying. She had set up a shrine to Chris in the apartment over the garage. She was hanging on to anything he had—his bed set, his dresser, his brand-new Harley, all his clothes." She had already made part of the basement into a shrine to Alex. She'd assembled all his sports trophies and favorite T-shirts in one special area. "She would go to each room," Jay says, on the basis of what Joe told him, "to feel close to her sons."

It is not known how Alex reacted to the death of his older brother, or how much the death affected him. But accounts of other young people who have fled questioning or charges, gone into hiding for years, and eventually turned themselves in (those of political radicals Jane Alpert, Stephen Bingham, and Katherine Powers) abound with tales of how the inability to give and receive comfort when a loved one died helped them conclude that prosecution was preferable to such dire emotional isolation.

It seems that, by late 1993, Alex was beginning to sense what a desolate trap a young fugitive's life can become, despite all the earmarks of sybaritism.

On January 3, 1994, he wrote a letter that may have been his last attempt to convince himself, and his parents, that he loved his exile life and wanted to make it permanent.*

---

*In quoting from Alex's letters, the author has left Alex's misspellings and uses of upper and lower case intact. Punctuation errors have also been left as is, except when ellipses make it possible to make sense of the sentences.

After having had "a great winter," he reported that he just returned from three weeks in Corsica. He rhapsodized about its natural beauty in travel-brochure terms, and spoke of cracking open a sea urchin ". . . and hundreds of fish . . . come and eat out of your hand." Of course, his recent time had also been filled with rock climbing, scuba diving, skiing, and ice climbing.

Referring to a previous trip he and his parents had apparently taken to Norway, he thought it would be "fun if you guys came back this year." They could go rafting, biking, climbing, or sailing, he proposed. Alex's list of inducements had either the insouciant—or the slightly desperate—sound of someone whose paradisical life is starting to feel hollow. Alex declared that he loved this life—"I would love to live like this forever"—but he was beginning to feel something was missing: a young adult identity and the work that would feed it. He'd mapped out in his head some kind of business he could develop in the mountains. But the lack of identity papers was stopping him from proceeding with his plans. Once he got those all-important papers, he'd "get my shit together and go for it."

What was helping to bankroll this half year of idyllic outdoor life was his work, during the other half of the year, for Elisabet's parents. It was just about the only work he could do without documentation. His unique predicament as a fugitive—and his time-warped development as a stuck-in-limbo ex-high-schooler—dovetailed with the labor needs of this no-nonsense couple on this insular patch of land.

The result was a quaintly old-fashioned arrangement, almost a folkloric paradigm: Alex as the poor-but-decent young stranger from a faraway town, receiving sustenance from the mother, indenturing himself to the father, and earning the hand of their comely daughter through the conflation of his simple self with their bustling family enterprise. He—and Elisabet—received free room and board (the better to save for the skiing and scuba-diving vacations) and he got paid for his work at the Janssons' store, and he was expected to shoulder extra—future-son-in-law—labor. "Mats and Mona are very happy to have their slaves back," he wisecracked, of his and Elisabet's return to the island.

At some point during their travels together, Elisabet learned that he had been accused of rape in America. She believed in his innocence. ("That's not him. That could never be him. That's not the person he is," she told *Turning Point.*)

Alex had helped move Elisabet's parents into their new house. Then he had painted the house, an arduous task in the wind and rain. He knew he lent exoticism to the traditional life on Klädesholmen. Who is this good-looking ponytailed American boyfriend that Mats's and Mona's daughter has acquired? the neighbors benignly whispered. The gossip he incited left him amused. Still, some things in his beatific tableau of a life were distinctly unlyrical. "I hate doing that trip [back to Sweden]," he declared. "It scares the shit out of me."

Two weeks later (judging from another letter), having survived another frightening border crossing, Alex was back with the more pedestrian problem of yet again playing the merry sportsman, while his mate was pursuing a future. Elisabet was immersed in her school exams while Alex was skiing—alone. He was doing a lot of reading—the *International Herald Tribune* and General Norman Schwarzkopf's memoir (which had made him dream of joining the military), and learning French (he had already mastered Swedish). Still, he seemed to be living the prematurely vestigial life of a forced retiree, or a too-young house-husband.

All the skiing and ice climbing in the world could not make up for the fact that, without identification papers, life could not go forward. So while his in-laws toiled at the store and while his girlfriend put herself through college, he turned his attention to a new task, not explicitly mentioned in his letters. He had written to a group of companies in Moscow, Switzerland,

and England and had gotten back what he cryptically referred to as "some very interesting answers." The price for whatever these companies were selling was $5,000 to $15,000. Whatever their product was, he promised his parents, "I won't jump into anything stupid."

He closed the letter by imploring his parents for money. "I am broke at the moment." he said. (With boyish earnestness, he assured them: "I have substantial savings but it's just not in my pocket." Just what savings he was referring to is not clear.) He indicated to his parents that the money situation was urgent.

But it is another letter—written slightly earlier than these other two, over a period of weeks in the pre-Christmas 1993 months—that showed the true desperation that had apparently started to eat away at him. He was a full-time vacationer in a world where others had jobs and careers, straining for meaningful things to do with the surfeit of hours. To his credit he had read seven books in two months and was looking for people to trade books with. But this self-administered education did not make up for the real college education everyone else was receiving.* "I wish I could study here like Elisabet," he pined. But to be a college student in Europe, you needed identification papers, so that was out. Life was on hold.

If being a student was out of the question for a person of Alex's circumstances, employment prospects were even grimmer. The declining economy—even in Sweden—had heightened authorities' vigilance about undocumented workers. Revealing that the Janssons were uneasy about his not having work papers (though it is unlikely that they knew anything about the rape charges), he wrote that there was concern at the store that an official would inquire about Alex's papers. He

---

*In the spring and summer of 1987, Mickey Sherman had frequently mentioned that Alex had applied to three Colorado colleges. Asked in 1997 which they were, Sherman said he did not remember, but he thought that there had been one admission.

was the most worried of all because "I don't have squat to show them."

He then referred cryptically to a scheme that "Russ" was going to put in motion, with Joe and Melanie's help. It is not clear exactly what the plan consisted of. It may have been an attempt to be granted Irish citizenship (Americans with Irish-born parents and grandparents are entitled to dual Irish-American citizenship* and thus can get an Irish passport.) Or it may have been an attempt to take on his deceased older brother's identity and apply for a passport as Christopher Kelly.**

Whatever the plan, Alex clearly sounded desperate. "Please get Russ going on this thing," he wrote. "Get him going." (Apparently, the Kellys were complicit in this plan, because he said that they had told him the plan would take several months.): "Every day is borrowed time for me now," he wrote. And without the papers "I am a sitting duck."

Alex seemed to understand that, by running, he had only locked himself inside a different kind of prison—a prison of constant leisure and constant movement. "It seems like I have such a great life and I do I guess but believe it or not I would love to get something started." He had finally realized, "You may think things get better as the years go by but it is the same and worse than day one."

After telling his parents how much he missed them and would love them always, he signed the letter, as usual, "Your Friend."

Time had finally stopped standing still for Amy Molitor. Her friend says that she'd convinced herself she'd never see Alex again. "Alex's name never came up when we wrote each other. She had moved on with her life." She had done well in

---

*Alex did eventually apply for Irish citizenship; it was granted to him in January 1997.
**Shortly after Chris's death, Joe Kelly sent away for a copy of Chris's birth certificate.

college, although her course of study was not academic. As a physical education major, "She was a pretty good student, a B student, . . . did her projects and did a good job with them," the chairman of the department, Dr. Eric Vlahov, told *New York* magazine. "She was a real spunky person, real sweet, energetic, somebody I thought could really go places if the right things happened." After graduation, she lived in Vero Beach and then in Miami, and worked as an athletic trainer. She was still involved with Scott, whom her friends liked a lot.

In May 1994, Joe and Melanie visited Alex—it is not known whether in Sweden or France, but the family, together with Elisabet, apparently spent some time in the mountains.

By this time, a tough agent with the FBI's Connecticut Fugitive Task Force named Ralph DiFonzo had taken over the Kelly case. Special Investigator DiFonzo (who is invariably described as being, physically, a cross between "The Commish" and Billy Joel) *liked* being a headbutter. He enjoyed making people uncomfortable. His predecessor, in the words of a case insider, "did what he could do with it but got frustrated." But getting frustrated was not Ralph's style. "He's in-your-face. His attitude was, 'Who do these people [the Kellys] think they are?!' He went *right after* the Kellys."

DiFonzo approached the Kellys repeatedly, asking them (as he paraphrased one of his conversations to *Turning Point*), "You sure you don't want to tell us what's going on? We understand. It's time. It's going on too long. He can't stay out there forever." The result? "They didn't talk. They didn't give us clues. There was no dialog. There was nothing."

DiFonzo posted WANTED posters, with Alex's photograph, all over Darien, including right outside the Four Seasons Travel Agency, where Melanie Kelly worked. Melanie, claiming the posters were harassment of her, had them removed.

DiFonzo called the Kellys "scum" and "losers," to their faces, for hiding their son—hoping that in their ensuing anger, they would yield one piece of information that would reveal where Alex was.

"He was obnoxious with them," Mickey Sherman says. "He was a button pusher."

"Melanie *hates* DiFonzo," the investigative insider says, with some glee. "He saw right through her little 'proper Darien mother' act. He saw just who she was. The mention of his name makes her *crazy.*"

DiFonzo* told *Turning Point,* "The arrogance of the family, the arrogance of Alex, their total disrespect for law enforcement in general. . . . Eventually, we had to force somebody's hand."

And so, on July 14, 1994—in what some people believe was a long-overdue act—DiFonzo marched into Superior Court and filed an affidavit and application for a search and seizure warrant.

DiFonzo planned a surprise attack on the Christie Hill house. He was seeking everything: "photographs, slides, photographic negatives, videotapes, home movies of Alex Kelly, D.O.B. 05-08-67, address books, personal telephone books, lists of telephone numbers, documents indicating the whereabouts of Alex Kelly, records of residence, telephone statements, telephone bills, telephone toll records, United States passports belonging to Joseph Kelly, Melanie Kelly, Russell Kelly, financial records, credit card statements, bank statements, records of safe deposit box rentals, personal correspondence from the subject, Alex Kelly, personal diaries and personal writings containing information about Alex Kelly, travel records, receipts of airline tickets, records from wire transfers," the warrant enumerates.

DiFonzo's search warrant was granted.

At five A.M. on July 18, DiFonzo and his agents, and members

---

*The author had several conversations with Special Agent DiFonzo in the winter and spring of 1997, during which he repeatedly said that the FBI had given him orders not to talk about the Kelly case to anyone.

of the Darien Police Department, rang the doorbell at 105
Christie Hill Road, waking up the Kellys. The warrant was
handed to Joe, who then had to let the agents in.

Apparently, when the police walked in the house, they saw
that Melanie had photographs of Alex in Europe right out on
display, in her office, for anybody to see. Then they caught her
standing in the second bedroom, in her bathrobe, trying to
shove something onto the shelves of a closet: presumably
hiding material that would have given them information about
where Alex was. (Melanie admitted as much to *Turning Point:*
"I ran and grabbed some photos . . . and foolishly tried to stuff
them into something that I figured they probably wouldn't
find, but what could I do?")

The investigative source goes on: "They made her sit
down—once they serve you, they're not gonna let you roam
around; you have to sit down until they're done. Ralph interviewed them while he was there, and one of the things he
asked them about was traveling in Europe. One of them
admitted that they had been to Europe—gave the date—and
whoever it was (I don't remember if I was told it was Joe or
Melanie) got a kick from the other, under the table, and the
conversation ceased.

"Melanie was still sitting at the breakfast table, in that
bathrobe, at nine in the morning." At some point Melanie was
allowed to get dressed. The entire search took seven hours.

DiFonzo searched Melanie's purse. In it was a letter she had
written to Alex two days earlier and had not yet mailed. The
envelope was addressed:

> Elisabet Jansson
> Granitv. 2 44074
> Hjalteby
> Sweden

Of the FBI's finding this envelope (and in a statement that
reveals a somewhat chilling morality), Melanie bitterly told

Forrest Sawyer, "I could just sit there and think how incredibly lucky they were. Nothing else, just luck."

As soon as DiFonzo found that letter, he left the house and went to the Darien Police Department, where he initiated a chain of calls. He called the FBI in Washington. The FBI in Washington called the Legal Attaché of the American Embassy in London, and officers there faxed Interpol in Stockholm, who then contacted the public prosecutor in Kungälv, Sweden.

In the meantime, DiFonzo's men seized twenty-eight items including an "Ireland passport in the name of Joseph Thomas," a copy of a document called *Treaties and International Agreements* (which details different countries' extradition terms), many pictures, postcards, bank statements, Alex's birth certificate, a Eurail pass booklet, letters from Alex (including those quoted in this chapter), two Union Trust safe deposit box keys (DiFonzo then requested, and received, a search warrant for these), and documents from numerous accounts at Union Trust, Gateway, and Chase banks. (The accounts, a source says, yielded little useful information. Like many people with substantial assets, the Kellys opened, closed, moved, and rolled-over certificates of deposit too frequently for the flow of their money to be easily traced.)

What happened after the FBI and police cleared out of the Kelly house? According to the Swedish police report of its interview with Mona Jansson (conducted on August 5, 1994):

At 2:30 in the morning, Swedish time (8:30 P.M. Eastern Daylight Time), the Janssons' phone rang. Elisabet's parents were staying in the main house; they had not seen Alex and Elisabet (who were staying at the "summer house") in a few days. Mats picked up the phone—they thought an alarm had gone off at the store—and when the speaker proved to be English-speaking, Mats passed the phone to Mona, who spoke and understood English better than he did. It was Alex's mother Melanie on the line. She asked if Elisabet was home and where Alex was. Mona told the Swedish police that Melanie sounded very excited.

Since Alex and Elisabet were at the Janssons' other house, Mona gave Melanie that phone number. Mona went back to sleep, believing that something bad had happened to the Kelly family. Perhaps Alex's father was sick?

The next morning, July 19, Mona told Elisabet that Melanie had called. Elisabet told her mother that Alex had left on July 16. In her own interview conducted by the Swedish police on August 3, Elisabet said that she had last seen Alex on July 16 (two days before the FBI raid on the Christie Hill house) when the two had decided to put their relationship on hold—and that he was wearing a backpack and about to hit the road. Since Elisabet, in due time, would follow Alex to America (both of them wearing matching friendship rings), it is possible that this July 16 breakup story was a fiction, meant to keep the FBI away and protect Elisabet. More likely, Alex had received a call from Melanie and taken off.

But whether Alex really left on the sixteenth or after a call from Melanie, by the time the Swedish police "converged on the town where Kelly had been living" (as a Connecticut Fugitive Task Force press release put it) on July 19 (the day after the raid on the Kellys' house), Alex was gone.

Although the raid yielded proof that the Kellys knew where Alex was, the idea of charging them with harboring a fugitive was out of the question. Eventually Bruce Hudock would tell *Vanity Fair* magazine that he declined to prosecute Joe and Melanie because it would be difficult to try "a blood relative for something each and every juror would look into their hearts and think about what they might do under similar circumstances." In truth, the sentiment in Darien after Chris Kelly's death would have made the bringing of such charges a very unpopular thing to do.

But Joe and Melanie could no longer plead ignorance about where Alex was. The raid had proved they had been in touch with him, had even visited him. Before July 18, 1994, their stance was that they would never have told their son to turn himself in. (In the *Turning Point* interview, Joe Kelly said that had Alex wanted to come home he'd have had a ticket waiting for him. But telling Alex to turn himself in "would be making a decision for his life. . . . I could not take that responsibility." And Melanie Kelly said, "I don't imagine that any mother would expect her child to sit in a cell for fifteen years for something that is untrue.") But after July 18, the Kellys no longer had the luxury of such feelings and principles. The whole equation had changed. The authorities now held the power. And the task of any lawyer representing Alex Kelly now was to advise the family on how to best manage Alex's fugitive status. That, frankly, meant coming up with the best terms for surrender.

Alex did have one positive incentive for returning, however. Connecticut case law had changed in the seven years he had been away. If Alex came back to face trial, he would almost certainly face separate trials, not the joined trial he would have faced at the time that he fled—the joined trial which had contributed to his fleeing in the first place.

There was also another development.

When the search of the Kellys' home was reported, and it was finally clear that the Kellys had been in contact with their son, Adrienne's and her family's determination for justice was fired by furious revulsion. (Reflecting her feelings at the time, Adrienne told the Stamford *Advocate,* after the verdict, "I think it's unbelievable that they . . . prevented me from going to trial, prevented me justice. And financed Alex Kelly for eight years.")

The Bak family hired attorney David Golub, a prominent civil litigator (recently chosen by the state of Connecticut to represent the state in its suit against the U.S. tobacco industry) to become Adrienne's advocate and personal attorney.

Eight-and-a-half years after she was attacked in the Jeep Wagoneer, Adrienne's life was still defined by the rape. The trusting love relationship that she had with Chris Ortolano (they would marry the next year) had only underscored the salience of her trauma. She was still having nightmares. She was still afraid that Alex would come back and make good on his threat to her.

Golub hired a private detective to try to determine where Alex Kelly was hiding. "We believed we knew where he was," Adrienne would tell the *Advocate* later. "They [Golub and his investigator] were getting faxes of pictures" from Europe. "He knew that he was going to be caught."

As the Kellys may have already known (from looking through their copy of *Treaties and International Agreements*), Switzerland had an extradition agreement with the United States that contained a very attractive loophole: A person charged with a crime in America who surrendered in Switzerland could not be extradited for the crime of failure to appear in court (a charge which adds five years to a sentence) or for violation of probation (a still-pending charge for Alex, which would have added to any rape-conviction sentence the balance of his unserved time from the burglaries). Alex's flight would be exempt from prosecution until thirty days after he was released from prison on the charge for which he was tried and convicted, if he was convicted.

Someone close to the case concludes that Mickey Sherman was unwilling to become involved in the process by which Alex was moved safely to Switzerland. But Sherman's reluctance was moot. Alex's flight had made his attractiveness to a jury very problematic. The Kellys needed much more than a good local attorney. They needed one of the smartest, most aggressive, and most intimidating criminal defense lawyers money could buy. Through their personal lawyer and friend, Fred Tobin, the Kellys made contact with attorney Thomas Puccio.

Tom Puccio was the kind of man Joe Kelly could be expected to like. Puccio, like Kelly, was a tough, ambitious self-made man who had made it in the white-shoe world. Just as Joe

Kelly had moved from the projects of Stamford to prosperity in adjacent Darien, Puccio had crossed the bridge from Brooklyn (where he'd grown up the son of a purchasing agent father and secretary mother, and had been educated at nonelite Fordham University and its Law School) to Manhattan, where, as an assistant U.S. attorney prosecuting corrupt politicians in the Abscam hearings, he locked horns with Harvard and Yale Law alumni. As Joe Kelly harbored a chip on his shoulder about his executive neighbors, so, too, Puccio was said to have been "intensely conscious" (as *The New York Times* put it) of the social and reputational disparity between his adversaries' alma maters and his own.

After thirteen years as an assistant U.S. attorney (winning convictions for, among others, New York City policemen accused of stealing heroin in the notorious French Connection case), Puccio struck out on his own as a defense attorney, working for various law firms, including the prestigious Millbank, Tweed, Hadley and McCloy. His intensity ("Tom only has one gear—overdrive," Washington lawyer Irving Nathan told the Washington *Post*), and killer instinct made him professionally admired but personally unpopular. When he sustained one atypical, high-profile loss (against then U.S. Attorney for Manhattan Rudolph Giuliani, in the case involving Bronx Democratic leader Stanley Friedman and the city's Parking Violations Bureau), fellow lawyers bought each other drinks in celebration. "I think that happened because they were jealous of Puccio," says defense attorney Paul Rooney, who, as a onetime U.S. attorney, successfully prosecuted mobster Carmine DeSapio for extortion. "Tom's won cases that are damn hard to win."

Puccio's tour de force moment was his defense of Claus von Bülow during von Bülow's second trial in 1985. The Danish husband of American socialite Martha (Sunny) von Bülow had had his earlier conviction for her attempted murder (she languished in a coma after having sustained insulin poisoning) overturned on appeal, and the lawyer who had crafted that appellate victory, Alan Dershowitz, had recommended Puccio to von Bülow.

It had not been easy evoking juror sympathy for the unctuously arrogant defendant (whose previous defense lawyer had almost as much hauteur as he did), nor had it been easy to win an acquittal when the state had as insulin experts two of the world's most authoritative blood-sugar specialists, both of whom testified that the only way the victim could have fallen into her coma was through exogenous insulin (i.e., insulin injected from the outside)—and the only person in the room who could have done the injecting and then disposed of the needle was Claus von Bülow.

"Tom did an excellent job," says attorney Michael Armstrong, who watched the trial (and who represented Sunny von Bülow's children in a subsequent suit). "The first and most important thing he did was bully the trial judge (in a perfectly legitimate way) to make rulings which I think were wrong but were to the advantage of his client. Then he cross-examined the medical experts and took their certainty about the exogenous insulin—the strongest evidence the government had—and effectively turned it against them, making them seem, to the jury, too sure for their own good." He won von Bülow's acquittal against what seemed to be considerable odds.*

If Puccio had made a supercilious European bon vivant palatable to an American jury and had forced favorable rulings to chip away at a very strong prosecution case, could he also make a spoiled American bail-jumper similarly sympathetic—

---

*To some in the legal community, the best move Puccio made was *after* the trial when, angered by Alan Dershowitz having written a credit-usurping book on the von Bülow legal triumph, *Reversal of Fortune,* (which was later adapted into a movie in which Ron Silver portrayed Dershowitz and Jeremy Irons won the Best Actor Academy Award as von Bülow), Puccio told the New York *Daily News* that a book about the von Bülow acquittal written by Dershowitz was equivalent to a book about the World Series written by the bat boy.

and tease out sufficient reasonable doubt in two rape cases the state had had eight years to refine?

The Kellys were betting he could.

Freshly hired, Puccio flew to Europe to meet with Alex. European legal negotiations on behalf of jet-set clients were something he did well: He had represented tennis player (and international partyer) Vitas Gerulitis on a business matter, had consulted for the Louis Vuitton Company, and had met—in Switzerland—with lawyers for extremely wealthy American oil trader Marc Rich.

Puccio began his long dance of negotiation with the FBI on behalf of Alex Kelly. The talks took months.

Nobody knew where Alex was during this time.

On January 19, 1995, a phone rang in a Zurich police station. As spokesman Eric Landis of the Zurich police later announced to massed cameras and microphones, "Mr. Kelly phoned from an office of a lawyer in Zurich to the police here in Zurich and he asked if he could turn himself in. And we said of course, and he arrived here in this building along with his lawyer, and we put him in custody."

CHAPTER 8

IT TOOK THOMAS PUCCIO THREE AND A HALF MONTHS to negotiate what he thought were suitable enough terms for Alex to finally waive extradition and agree to return. (Getting rid of the narcotics charge that Hudock had added onto the rape and kidnapping charges was one matter that took some time.) So Alex sat in a Swiss jail until May 4, when Lieutenant Commander Ronald Bussell, who had made it his personal mission to see Alex brought to trial, flew to Switzerland to bring his prisoner home with him.

When Alex deplaned in New York, Bussell and an FBI man were at his side. His hair was shorn, and he was wearing a red plaid shirt with a white T-shirt underneath, brown work pants, and work shoes. When he arrived at the Darien police station—his ankles and wrists shackled—reporters and on-lookers shot him questions—"Why'd you do it, Alex?" He smiled, as if he did not quite understand that it was a hostile crowd he faced.

The Kellys put up their Christie Hill home and other proper-ties to secure the $1 million bond the court now demanded. On

Turning Point Joe Kelly would later declare that he "didn't hesitate for a minute," because "he's my son."

My son: poignant words, those. In a tragic stroke of irony, Alex's newly hired attorney, Thomas Puccio, had just gone through the most horrible thing that can befall a parent. On a Sunday in late February, while he was giving his sixteen-year-old son, Matthew, a driving lesson near a boat basin in Westport, the boy lost control of the car, and the car rolled down a steep embankment, into the water. Matthew could not be rescued. After an interval of time when (as William Glaberson reported in a December 29 *New York Times* profile of Puccio), "some of [Puccio's] closest friends said . . . they were not sure if he would regain his equilibrium," Puccio seems to have understood that the only alternative to unbearable and debilitating grief was intense work. And since the work he had already committed to consisted of helping a couple save a son from prison when they had already lost another son to death, that intense work now acquired a personal resonance. Puccio could, as he put it to the *Times,* "relate to [the Kellys] trying to save their son."

One of Tom Puccio's fortes is spin control. As he put it in his book, in an uncharacteristically hackneyed way, a good defense lawyer should "[a]lways tell reporters things are going great, even if 14 nuns have just taken the stand to identify your client as the man who pulled the trigger." Appropriately, then, on the day that Alex was returned to Darien, Puccio—a lean man with clumps of wispy hair encircling a bald pate—stood on the Stamford Courthouse steps in front of Joe and Melanie. His famed combativeness deftly sheathed in a blasé veneer, he almost shrugged as he told the crowd of reporters, "I'm not going to try the case right here, but I think you'll see that when these allegations are scrutinized under cross-examination, they'll fly away." In tone and substance, his message was: Much ado about nothing.

David Golub, Adrienne's lawyer, took the opposite approach. Golub is a short, slight, cerebral-looking man, but his aggressive swath of broom-bristle mustache suggests passion. Standing on the same courthouse steps, he shot back, angrily and adamantly: "It is *outrageous* and *irresponsible* for Puccio to call anyone in this case who has complained a liar! The evidence in this case is *overwhelming.* There are two brutal rapes, committed within a matter of days with the *exact* same methods."

As Mickey Sherman had done, Thomas Puccio hired a pollster to determine whether or not Alex could receive a fair trial in Darien. But whereas Sherman had hired a Stamford market-research company, the worldlier and more connected Puccio hired a major national opinion-shaper, Dick Morris, who had had fourteen years of on-and-off association with President Clinton. Puccio did not foresee that such a grand gesture at the service of a very simple task (determining whether or not pretrial publicity had poisoned the local jury pool against Alex Kelly) might entail liabilities greater than its benefits.

Since Alex's return home was four days before his twenty-eighth birthday, Melanie threw a small birthday party for him. She served birthday cake and champagne to Russ Pinto and Russ's girlfriend Camden, Cy and Junie Clark, and a number of other friends. If the notion of a champagne fete for a fugitive son's homecoming sounds odd—well, it was perceived as such, even to some of this group of loyalists. "I thought it was the most bizarre occasion," says one guest. "Alex walked around, being witty with his new Swedish accent, but he was wearing an accessory you don't usually wear at your birthday party—an electronic ankle bracelet.* We all tried not to look at

---

*A condition of his bail, the ankle bracelet enforced Alex's nine P.M.-to-six A.M. curfew thusly: During the curfew hours, the bracelet sent a pulse signal to a modem attached to the Kellys' house telephone. If Alex was ever beyond a certain distance from that modem (and that distance included his mailbox), an alarm would go off in the bracelet security company's main office in Minnesota. A security agent in the Minnesota office would then immediately call Darien police Lieutenant Commander Ronald Bussell. The whole notification process took ten to fifteen minutes.

it. It was awkward." The countries Alex had visited during his eight-year idyll, were also, for legal reasons, "the taboo topic of the evening." Given so few outlets for conversation, "Everyone was sitting there, just staring at each other."

Yet, for all the strangled words, the women present were not exactly immune to Alex's charm. Says one, "He was so cute and charming. There was a sense that there was no way those charges could be true."

For the most part, that's how it went: Those friends of Alex's who had always been loyal apparently remained so, yet even the most loyal friends had questions, one remarking to another that it was wrong for Alex to have fled; another saying, "He's my friend, even if he is a rapist." But for most of Alex's peers, whether they still lived in the area or just came back to visit, he was living in a time—and a perception— warp. "It was like O. J. Simpson coming home to Rockingham after the not-guilty verdict," one young man says. "He thought all his friends would be just as he'd left them, in terms of their thinking he was such a great guy and believing in his innocence. But they had changed"—in terms of how they viewed him and how they viewed the events he was part of—"and he hadn't."

Alex's bail terms promoted a kind of enforced extended childhood. He had to be home with his parents between nine P.M. and six A.M. He was not allowed to drink alcohol. He had to wear the electronic ankle bracelet. And, fully ten years behind his peers, he had just now enrolled in college: Norwalk Community-Technical.

Shortly after Alex's return home, Elisabet flew over from Sweden to join him. She moved in with the Kellys, and the couple, now engaged, went about making their Darien life into as close a version of their European one as possible. They rock-climbed at an indoor climbing wall in Stamford. They went skiing. (Alex could partake of outdoor activities as long as he stayed in Connecticut. He was allowed out of the state only to visit his lawyer.) And one day in August he went skydiving.

A young woman named Briana joined Alex, Elisabet, Russ Pinto, and a few others for that expedition. Everybody got up in the dark and left at 6:00 A.M. Actually, the outing was supposed to start before dawn but, Briana says, "we had to wait for Alex because he had his curfew. Alex and Elisabet came over to Russ's house." It was Briana's first introduction to them. "He seemed like a nice, normal guy, and Elisabet was a sweet-heart."

The group drove, in two cars (Alex driving his parents' car, Russ driving his own car) two hours away to Connecticut Parachutists' Incorporated, in Ellington, Connecticut. Then they all sat in a classroom for two hours of instruction. They were all taking tandem jumps (each new diver hooked up to an experienced "jumpmaster"), as novices must. And they were doing static line jumping—where the parachute opens automatically—rather than actual skydiving, where the jumper pulls his or her own cord.

In two separate groups (one after the other), they boarded the plane, all suited up (jumpsuit, leather beanie) and fully harnessed, from crotch to shoulder, each person hooked up to his or her jumpmaster by four clips. When the small plane reached half the altitude of 14,000 feet, two by two, "we stood on the edge of the open plane door—it was so cold up there, even though it was summer—and put one foot out and held on and the jumpmaster got behind us and said, 'One, two, three, jump!' And we jumped!

"It's terrifying for the first three seconds of free-fall and then it's . . . the most heavenly, unbelievable feeling." The new diver communicates with his or her jumpmaster (who is virtually on top of the new diver) through hand taps and hand signals. The jumpmaster maneuvers them both onto dips and turns (directed by the new diver) as both drift slowly, slowly back and forth and downward through weightless air.

When Alex hit the ground, his opened chute flapping in billows all around him, "He was yelling, 'Yahoo! Yahoo! That was awesome!' He basically said that was better than anything he'd done so far."

On the car ride back, Alex spoke of other thrill-seeking activities on his agenda. "He said the next thing he wanted to do was cliff-jump, which is, like, *lethal.* That's when you literally have a parachute in your hand and you jump off a three-thousand foot cliff and if it doesn't open in time, you're dead. He said he wanted to go to one of those waterfalls in Venezuela. He said, 'Yeah, it's crazy. It's one of the scariest things you can do. But I'd love to try it.'"

Alex's parents were essentially charged with supervising him. What did they think when he told them of his plans to rise before dawn and spend the day skydiving? Had they ever questioned his obsession with thrill-seeking sports or considered that there might be a link, in some people, between those activities and other risk-taking behavior? And did they suggest, perhaps, that he tone down his activities? One can only wonder.

The next day, the skydiving group continued its camaraderie. Briana and other friends joined Alex and Elisabet at the Pintos' house for a barbecue. Everyone was having a fine old time, says Briana—"eating steaks, hamburgers, corn on the cob, drinking Buds. I don't remember how it was brought up, but we were talking about the fact that Alex had to be home by nine and couldn't leave the house until six. And I asked him if he was under house arrest."

Briana had meant it as an innocent question. But "Alex got angry. He said, 'No. I am *not* under house arrest! I haven't been tried yet!'" Alex's anger intimidated Briana and made her feel as if *she* had done something wrong. "I felt bad. I guess I stepped on his toes a little bit."

What did she do?

"I apologized to him."

* * *

The same unembarrassed entitlement, defensiveness, and strange optimism that Alex had exhibited during the skydiving expedition and the next-day barbecue seemed to remain with him in November, when he attended the Darien High Class of 1985's tenth reunion. The night before the actual party (which was held at Giovanni's restaurant, on the border of Stamford and Darien), a smaller dinner was held at the Black Goose Grille. Jamie, the girl who had once shared a kiss with Alex in the Christie Hill woods, was the first member of the class to arrive. "And Alex," she remembers being surprised to recall (figuring that this most notorious alumnus might have skipped the reunion) "was the *second!*" But, on the contrary, "Alex told me that his lawyer had suggested he go, to make himself as publicly seen as possible." Jamie asked him about his upcoming trial. "And he just said, 'I'm not too worried about it. My lawyer and I are pretty confident that I'm going to get off.'"*

Indeed, some things were going well for Alex—and by his own making. He was studying hard and getting good grades at his junior college. By the end of the semester, he would make the dean's list.

At the same time that Alex was waxing confident about his future, Amy Molitor was pondering her own. She was in New York City, trying to decide whether or not she should let herself be lured back into a relationship with her old boy-friend.

Amy had moved back from Florida shortly before Alex came home. She was living with her brother, Tyler, on the Upper East Side and bartending at a bar called Iggy's. Her relation-ship with Scott was in one of its down cycles. A friend from the old Weed Beach–Keg Club crowd saw Amy a lot during this period. As of November 1995, this woman says, "Amy had yet

---

*According to Professor Elizabeth Schneider of Brooklyn Law School, a specialist on crimes against women, male defendants in rape cases are generally more optimistic about their chances of acquittal than defendants charged with any other crimes are.

to see Alex, but he'd been trying to get in touch with her. He'd been calling her, calling her, calling her.

"She was afraid to see him. First of all, she hadn't seen him in ten years or something. And secondly—I remember this vividly; we were sitting in the kitchen of her apartment, and I had been dying to ask her about [the charges against Alex] but I wasn't going to pry." By the end of the conversation, however, the friend was convinced that Amy wondered about Alex's innocence.

"She was afraid to see him because she thought he might manipulate her and try to, like, sucker her back in. She was afraid she would weaken—that's the sense I got. I figured she was also afraid he wanted her to speak at his trial. I was afraid for her because I knew he had been tracking her down."

What Amy seemed most afraid of, in terms of getting back with Alex, was her parents. "She said: 'And my family would *kill* me.' And then we just kind of laughed, because it got kind of heavy."

In time, Amy began seeing Alex again. Elisabet was still living with the Kellys, but Alex was, increasingly, leaving Elisabet alone all day. According to one friend of Russ Pinto's, "Russ told me that every single day Alex would leave Elisabet and go out and hang out with Amy. So Russ would go hang out with Elisabet because he felt bad for her." According to the friend, "Russ says he said, 'Elisabet, this is not fair to you.' And Elisabet said, 'Alex has to do what he has to do right now.'"

At some point in early 1996, Elisabet Jansson went home to Sweden.* Alex and Amy resumed their relationship, and Amy

---

*Telephoned at her mother's house in Stockholm, where she was visiting (she now has her own apartment in Gothenburg, when she isn't in La Grave) in January 1997, Elisabet told a Swedish assistant to this author: "I don't want to talk about Alex. That is in the past now."

divided her time between her best friend Whitney Roberts's house in Rowayton and the Kellys' house on Christie Hill. (Living with girlfriend *and* parents—either his or the young woman's—was now standard practice for Alex. Perhaps it provided a kind of enforcement of good behavior.) Amy had taken a job as a bartender in two of the hip new bars in the downtown area of South Norwalk: first the Paris, then the Savoy Supper Club. Then she went to work tending bar at the new, eponymous bar-restaurant that Back Street owner (and Wee Burn member) Doug Moody opened in Darien.

In March, Puccio's pollster Dick Morris's poll results were in: The Stamford jury pool had, not surprisingly, been saturated, over the course of ten years, with publicity that had biased many potential jurors against Alex Kelly. Puccio drafted a motion for a change of venue. But some knowledgeable trial watchers wondered: If his motion were to be granted, would it not be a case of "Be careful what you wish for"? For although Kelly's notoriety in Fairfield County was a distinct defense liability, the members of that singularly wealthy jury pool might perhaps be less inclined to harbor lethal class resentment toward a young criminal defendant who'd spent the better part of eight years skiing in Europe.

There was another kind of be-careful-what-you-wish-for attached—not just to the poll but the pollster: If Puccio had thought big-league player Dick Morris would intimidate the opposition or earn him points in the spin-control department, he might have been pleased with Morris's new stature. Morris had just been hired by President Clinton to craft him a strategy for the 1996 election that would appeal to those conservative Democrats who had rebelled and had voted in a Republican Congress. But Morris's new stature would prove to be a double-edged sword for Alex Kelly.

In early May, Judge Nigro denied Puccio's notion for a change of venue, and a week later, on May 16, the assembled female Republican members of the U.S. Congress sent an angry letter to President Clinton, asking him to fire Dick Morris. Although they made sure to assert their belief that Alex Kelly, like any defendant, deserved legal counsel and that Dick Morris had a right to help him, it was an "outrage," the Republican women wrote, that the President should rely for counsel on social issues on a man who had demonstrated an "insensitivity to women's concerns" and "lack of ethical judgment" by going to work for the cause of a double-rape suspect. Representative Jennifer Dunn of Washington said Morris had done "the worst thing an advisor to the president could be doing at a time when crime and crimes against women are such a deep concern to the American people." Nevada Representative Barbara Vucanovich seconded, "The President says he's against violence against women, but with a nudge and a wink he takes his advice from Dick Morris."

White House spokesman Mike McCurry responded by admitting that President Clinton had known about Morris's work on behalf of Alex Kelly when he'd hired him, and the Clinton-Gore campaign dismissed Morris's work for Kelly as irrelevant, with campaign spokesperson Ann Lewis (an otherwise vocal feminist) saying, "This is an effort by partisan opponents to try to stir up a nonissue." Indeed, as the Cleveland *Plain Dealer* reported, "Democratic women in Congress have been mostly silent" about the Dick Morris–Alex Kelly connection. "One noted anonymously that 'if this were a Republican president and Dick Morris was helping an accused rapist, you know we would be screaming. But it's not worth picking a fight. We just want to win in '96.'"*

The public outrage of the Congresswomen of their dominant political party just added to the headache the Kelly case was

---

*Three months later, when Morris's gossip about President Clinton to a Washington call girl was revealed in a supermarket tabloid, Morris resigned as the President's election strategist.

giving to Darien. In February, *Vanity Fair* had come out with an article on Alex's return to Darien, and *Turning Point* had aired its segment in April. For a town shrouded in privacy and rectitude, this kind of attention was excruciating. People impatiently whispered, "Why aren't they *moving?*" But no For Sale sign appeared at 105 Christie Hill Road. In fact, when a prominent Wee Burn family called a plumbing hot line with an emergency, who appeared at their door to do the job? Joe Kelly.

In that sense you had to admire the man. He did not run from his class roots or from the town that wished him and his son gone. To hell with them. He was not going to be moved from his house, from his work. Or from what (it must be assumed) he thought were his principles: taking his son at his word against all evidence to the contrary, and condoning his son's fugitive status rather than having him submit to an unfair legal system. The only trouble is, what Joe Kelly deemed courage (Joe had told Forrest Sawyer that Alex was "brave" to have fled), others called cowardice.

And none more so than young women. They in particular did not like Alex Kelly, and—things had changed a lot since the eighties, when so many girls had been peer-pressured into intimidated silence—some did not mind going out of their way to tell him so.

Early in the evening of July 19, three such young women sighted Alex at Jimmy's Seaside, where he was hanging out with good friend Junie Clark, who tends bar there. The events that ensued show what could happen when young women acted less deferentially toward Alex than, for example, had Briana (who had apologized to Alex after mistakenly mentioning "house arrest" at Russ Pinto's barbecue).

Jimmy's Seaside has both a front bar and a back poolroom. The young women were in the poolroom, and when Alex walked back there, one of the girls, upon recognizing him, "started provoking him, calling him a rapist—they were literally trying to start something with him," says a young woman who received an eyewitness account from one of the bar's customers. A man who received an eyewitness account from the bar manager also heard that the young woman had called Alex a rapist and had asked him, challengingly, what he was doing out in public.

"And Alex came back at her with a verbal obscenity," the young man continues. "He said—these were his exact words: 'Fuck you, you stupid cunt.'" (In *New York* magazine, the remark was quoted differently—as "You better take that fuckin' [pool] stick and use it, because it's the only stick you'll ever get.") "So the other girl came into the front bar and told the manager, 'Alex Kelly's back there; he's causing trouble.' She's getting riled up, saying, 'Maybe you should do something about it.'

"The manager then proceeded to go to the back bar. He grabbed Alex and said, 'Hey, Alex, maybe you should come up to the front of the bar and stay away from these girls. I'm not gonna kick you out, 'cause that would be ridiculous, but maybe you just better stay away from them.' Alex said okay. He came to the front bar." Meanwhile, the girl who did not go to the front bar had gone to the bar's pay phone and had called 911, claiming "something like, 'Alex Kelly is down at Jimmy's Seaside right now. He's drunk and harassing us.'"

By now the manager had convinced Alex that it might be best for him to leave voluntarily. Just as Alex walked out the front door, the police arrived. Alex was later charged with breach of peace and interfering with a police officer. (Since it was an on-site, not a warrant, arrest, the details of Alex's interference with the officer are not recorded.) He was released on a $2,000 bond. He eventually pleaded not guilty.

By now, even Alex's close friends had begun to disapprove of his behavior. Russ Pinto told another friend (according to that friend) that "Alex was going out and partying [presumably before his curfew]" instead of staying in every night, reading books, and waiting for his trial.

* * *

On the evening of Friday, September 20, Alex and Amy were leaving a dinner party that Amy's best friend Whitney Roberts and her boyfriend had hosted. Alex was driving Amy's car—not a Jeep Wagoneer this time, but a white Nissan. He was driving fast along Hollow Tree Ridge Road at 8:55 P.M., presumably trying to get home before his curfew.

Alex zoomed past a radar post, and when an officer clocked him doing fifty-five miles per hour in the thirty-mile-per-hour zone, the officer pursued Alex. Alex then sped ahead of the pursuing officer, ignoring the police siren and flashing lights. Rounding a sharp curve on Leeuwarden Road, Alex lost control of the car. It flipped onto its hood. Amy was hurled onto the pavement. When the officer approached, Alex took off into the woods.

Having seen Alex flee, the officer first started to give chase, then went to the Nissan to see if there was an injured passenger. There he found Amy, called for an ambulance (a similar call was not placed by Alex), administered first aid, and called Lieutenant Commander Ronald Bussell. When Bussell arrived on the scene, he found Amy "badly injured" and called for a state trooper with a police dog. No admission was made by Amy, who was in too much pain to talk or breathe easily, about who had been in the car with her. The police dog followed the trail left by the human scent through the woods to the Kellys' front door. An officer accompanied the dog. Summoned to the door, Alex told the officers that he did not know about any accident.

When the ambulance arrived, emergency medical workers lifted Amy onto a stretcher and took her to Stamford Hospital, where she was treated for five broken ribs and scalp lacerations. As reported in *The New York Times*, Amy was (according to an affidavit filed with arrest papers) "reluctant to talk to the police at first but [she] later said Mr. Kelly drove her car." And Alex, having already lied to the police, did not turn himself in until three days later: Monday, September 23.

When Alex finally turned himself in to police on Monday

afternoon, he was charged with a felony and two misdemeanors: evading responsibility after a serious accident and engaging the police in pursuit and interfering with police officers— as well as speeding. He was released on $5,000 bail, which was supplied by Joe.* His curfew was tightened to six P.M. to six A.M. and he was now not allowed to leave the house unless accompanied by a parent. The arrest headed the local news. At his arraignment with Puccio at his side, Alex pleaded not guilty. It was less than a week before jury selection began for Alex's rape trial. Puccio requested, and did not get, a change of venue. As Puccio's own nemesis, Alan Dershowitz, (who, as appellate lawyer and media hound, seemed never to meet a colleague's misfortune he and his publicist didn't like) told *The New York Times,* "The best-laid plans of lawyers are often ruined by clients."

The types of women's issues Connecticut is best known for may be those of style rather than substance, but appearances can be deceiving: The state that gave us headbands over blond pageboys and *Martha Stewart Living* is also the state that produced two of the most singularly important and influential judicial victories for women in the last two generations. The fight to make a woman's private decision to use contraception a Constitutional right and the fight to require police officers to protect women who are being beaten by their husbands were both launched—and won—by tenacious Connecticut women: Estelle Griswold, the executive director of Connecticut Planned Parenthood, who battled the Catholic Church all the way up to the Supreme Court to triumph in 1965's *Griswold* v. *Connecticut* (which kicked off the entire prochoice movement), and severely battered wife and mother Tracey Thurman, who took on America's entire law-enforcement

---

*By now, the Kellys had paid $100,000 restitution to the victims of Alex's house burglaries, $140,000 in bail forfeiture when Alex fled, $1 million to keep him out on bail after he surrendered, $2,000 for the Jimmy's Seaside incident bond—and now $5,000. $1,247,000 in all.

establishment to win the 1984 U.S. District Court decision *Thurman* v. *Torrington Police Department* (which initiated the country's movement against domestic violence).

So it should not have been a surprise that a mass of victims' and women's advocates crowded Judge Nigro's small courtroom on October 15, 1996, or that a young woman like Adrienne Bak Ortolano—who had pursued her case against her rapist for almost ten years—would have come from Connecticut.

Jury selection began on Tuesday, October 1. Six jurors were to be seated. (Connecticut, for purposes of judicial expediency, seats juries of six—not twelve—except in cases where death or life in prison are possible sentences.*) Connecticut is also one of the only states in which jurors are voir dired one-on-one and privately: When each prospective juror is interviewed by prosecutor and defense, he or she is the only juror in the witness box. During the voir dire sessions for this case, some of the questions the prospective jurors were asked were: "What is the reputation of Darien?" "Are you familiar with a drinking game called quarters?" and "Do you believe a person is capable of making a false allegation of rape?"

The process lasted two weeks. The defense had access to noted jury consultant Paul Tiger (though he was not present in the courtroom); the prosecution did not use a jury consultant. (Many prosecutors are bothered by bringing experts in to handicap and select jurors; it strikes them as a cynical tactic that reduces individuals to group stereotype.) Though Hudock did not know it at the time, his eschewal of this tactic may have hurt his case as much as Marcia Clark's rejection of a jury consultant had helped doom hers.

In truth, Hudock did not pay much attention to jury selec-

---

*Another unique feature of Connecticut trial is its dispensing with opening arguments.

tion. He told courtroom reporters he was looking for the same kind of law-and-order jurors as he would choose for any other criminal case. He was also looking for parents of daughters. (Puccio—who referred to Adrienne, during jury selection, as the "so-called victim"—was looking for parents of sons.) Hudock had been pleased with his selection of two solidly married women in their forties, so when he came upon a third woman in this general category—a mother of two daughters, no less—he may have dispensed with some elements of critical scrutiny. First of all, this heavy-set woman with dark curly hair was divorced—and in the crude game of handicapping jurors, a divorced person means someone who might develop a crush on an attractive defendant. Secondly, she was of European background and had attended school in South America, yielding a wild-card factor in terms of her cultural fix on acquaintance rape. The sexual mores she best understood *might* be stricter (predisposing her, say, to disapprove of girls who drink at parties and then get into cars with boys) *or* they might be more permissive. (She might view American suburbs as puritanical places where girls who'd had impulsive first-time sex would ricochet into paroxyms of guilt right afterward.) In short, she was unknowable. And although she had spoken, during voir dire, of her belief that all criminal defendants deserve a fair trial, Hudock had apparently taken her recitation of what was after all an American justice-system truism as the enthusiasm of a recently naturalized new citizen. Others thought it might be a red flag for prodefense tendencies.

The press would eventually nickname this juror "Mrs. Doubtfire."

Like any good defense lawyer, Puccio let few things pass unnoticed. He was creating a record for appeal: He complained about how late he had been served with the state's witness list, asserting that "Hudock flagrantly violated the rules. . . . This is trial by ambush." He objected strenuously to Hudock's speaking at a function for the Stamford Rape and Sexual Abuse Crisis Center, calling it inappropriate (Hudock refused to cancel), and he complained that Hudock had refused to seat any jurors who did *not* have prior media knowledge of the case. He tried—and failed—to subpoena Adrienne's psychotherapy records. He renewed his motion for change of venue and he requested sequestration. (Both of these motions were denied by Judge Nigro.)

By Friday, October 11, a jury of three women in their forties and fifties and three men (one in his twenties, one in his thirties, one in his forties) was impaneled.

And then, like a thunderclap undoing all the work of the last two weeks came the news of the zero-hour plea bargain negotiations.

On her evening broadcast, News-12 Connecticut's Audrey Honig (whose excellent coverage of the case—along with that of the premiere Kelly scribe, the Stamford *Advocate*'s Dan Mangan—was the most authoritative) reported that plea-bargain talks had started. These negotiations eventually collapsed, but the fact that Alex had even considered pleading guilty was tantalizing information.

Puccio swiftly and categorically denied Honig's report that there had been plea talks, saying that there was "no possible resolution of this case short of trial. There never was and there never will be, with a plea of guilty or anything approaching that."*

On the trial's opening day—Tuesday, October 15, 1996— press and spectators lined up in front of the courthouse for hours before the doors opened. Alex and Amy strode through a phalanx of photographers and TV cameramen, in a manner that would become their trademark: hand in hand; he, in blue blazer, khakis, shirt, and tie (he wore this precise costume so

---

*On February 14, 1997, the fact that there had been plea talks was confirmed by Judge William Hickey, Jr., who asserted that he had overseen these talks. Puccio responded by calling these talks standard "pretrial discussions."

unwaveringly over the course of both trials that he inadvertently became, to some viewers, an object of ridicule); she, her shiny, blond, blunt-cut hair against her overtanned, careworn face. She appeared to have aged more than he. With her briefcase and dark suit, she looked more like his slightly older, Manhattan-based fashion-editor sister than his bartender girlfriend.

Inside the boxy, low-ceilinged second-floor courtroom, Alex sat at the defense table with Puccio and Puccio's Connecticut cocounsel, attorney Hope Seeley, whose knowledge of the state's law made her just as important to the defense as her far-more-visible colleague. Hudock's cocounsel, Maureen Vallerie Ornousky (the daughter of John Vallerie, who had been Alex's defense attorney during his burglary proceeding), conferred with Hudock at the prosecution table. Both Seeley and Ornousky have long blond hair. Eventually, as the days of this trial went on, the view from the back of the courtroom came to resemble a sea of blond. There were the white-blond Bak sister, mother, and aunt, and rape crisis counselor on the left; Puccio's wife, Kathy (a former model with hauntingly deep-set eyes and a yard-long palomino-hued ponytail), and Melanie Kelly and Amy (when both were let out of witness-sequestration and allowed to view the proceedings*) on the right, as well as Seeley, Ornousky, and the light-haired court reporter. This prompted some silent what's-wrong-with-this-picture?s from the press, for whom the coverage of trials for violent, ugly crimes in the cramped chambers of seedy courthouses had never before put them in contact with so many principals more generally encountered in the giftware department of Lord & Taylor.

As for Alex, he sat twiddling his thumbs and absently playing with a pen. In due time, he would settle into a demeanor that combined polished charm with a guileless, eager-to-please

---

*Originally, Melanie was scheduled to testify; thus, she was barred from viewing the first days of the trial.

quality. He would start the day by unpeeling a fresh roll of mints and passing them to his counsel and his family. At recesses, he would lean over the rail that separated the defense area from the spectator section, clutching it with his notably strong hands, pursing his lips and raising his eyebrows like a helpful young junior executive pitching a new account.

But on that first day, he seemed nervous. So did almost all the family members: the Kelly family and supporters in the first two rows of the right aisle of wooden benches, and the Bak family and supporters in the first two rows of the left aisle. As the days wore on, the members of each camp would relax among themselves in clusters of conviviality. This was especially true on the defense side—with animated Kathy Puccio (a self-described born-again Christian whose daily appearance, she said, stemmed from her anger at the public's judgmental attitude toward her husband's client) a fulcrum of cheer and optimism. But on this first day there was tension. Everyone sat packed together: upright, dressed-up, high-chinned, as preternaturally attentive as a diver on the high board.

Clerk of the court Joe Williams, a charmingly gruff and stentorian courthouse lifer, invoked, as is his habit, the presence of "the ever-living God" in his calling the court to order, and demanded, "All rise!" Everyone clambered to full height for the entrance of Judge Martin Nigro. When Nigro ascended the bench, everyone sat down again. Then Joe reprised "All rise . . ."—and seventy pairs of shoes hit the floor once more as bodies rustled respectfully upward for the jury's entrance.

"Your honor," Bruce Hudock said, as the rearranging of limbs and jackets and briefcases and purses tapered into final silence, "the state calls Adrienne Ortolano."

It had taken almost eleven years before those seven words could be uttered.

* * *

Adrienne, dressed in a smart black double-breasted suit, her fine blond hair pulled back, strode to the stand, raised her right hand, and recited her oath.

She was deadly serious. You could see it right away. She was grave and wounded and blunt and cool—not a smiler, not an ingratiator. (Valerie Barnett, on the other hand, would present, Hudock knew, the opposite kind of victim-witness: warm and emotionally accessible.) How would she play to the jury, next to the handsome, exaggeratedly youthful, carefully winsome defendant?

Under Hudock's matter-of-fact questioning, Adrienne gave the rough outlines of the life she had lived before February 10, 1986—she'd gone to elementary school outside Chicago, then the family had moved to Darien when she was in the fourth grade. She had gone to Middlesex, then Darien High, then transferred to St. Mary's to help shore up her grades. She described her sports and her high-school daily routine.

She spoke of how she had arrived at Dan Anderson's party and had played quarters with the group assembled—that she had been picked four times to drink, and that when she had left the Anderson house for the basketball game, "I was walking fine, I was talking fine. I was in control. I knew there would be parents of friends of mine and teachers."

She testified about how the time spent back at Dan's house after the basketball game had been consumed by her trying to find a ride home in time for her curfew (no one wanted to leave the party to take her). She relayed her phone conversation with her father, whose offer to pick her up was as unwelcome as the curfew. And she spoke of Tom Kelly entering the party with two other boys, whom she did not know. One of the boys, she was told, was Alex Kelly.

Was the young man so identified in the courtroom? Bruce Hudock inquired.

Adrienne answered tensely and affirmatively.

Could she point him out, then?

Adrienne stood. In the tense stillness, and in seconds that

seemed minutes, she stretched out her right hand accusingly. She pointed straight at Alex. He was impassive. (She would later tell reporters that seeing him again, after all those years, brought the whole experience back to her.)

Standing fairly still, seeming to consciously refrain from the rhythmic pacing and lumbering that courtroom litigants often use as metronomes for their presentations (as if he knew his star witness's fragility required the anchor of his fierce composure), Hudock employed an interrogative style that might be called standard-issue civil-servant. In a voice oddly reedy for so large a man, he asked questions conversationally, sometimes clumsily, burying available drama. He projected sincerity, not polish.

Under his questioning, Adrienne outlined the rest of the evening. Her voice was terse. She persistently referred to Alex Kelly as "the defendant."

It had been snowing lightly outside when she got in the car, she said. She had remarked to the defendant on the Jeep Wagoneer—it was a nice car; was it his? No, he'd said. It belonged to his girlfriend Amy Molitor's family. "I said it was nice of them to let him use the car."

Did she notice anything unusual about the defendant? the prosecutor asked her.

"No," she said. He had seemed "pretty normal to me."

Did they talk in the car?

"It was just silent the whole drive."

Alex had braked at the stop sign about a mile and a half from her house, then leaned over and tried to kiss her. "I pushed him away. He tried to kiss me again and I pushed him away again. I felt like, what does he think he's doing? The defendant asked me if I wanted to go to his house to get stoned." She declined.

She had given directions to her house, but Alex had driven past her driveway. "I said, 'Stop! Wait! Pull in here!' He said he'd turn around." But he didn't.

About thirty minutes into her testimony, Adrienne breathed deeply and requested a glass of water. After swallowing and casting her eyes down to compose herself, she came to the heart of her testimony. "He stopped the car. He took the keys out of the ignition. He was on top of me, straddling me with one of his legs. His left leg was over both of my legs, pinning me. I asked, 'What do you think you're doing?' I started to be very scared.

"He put his left hand underneath my chin. He said I was going to make love to him or I was going to die."

"How did you feel?" Hudock asked.

Adrienne whispered, "Petrified. I could only see the ceiling of the car," she said. And then she broke down and cried.

Once she regained her composure, and in response to a series of questions put to her by Hudock, Adrienne testified that she felt for the door, then "he told me to get in the back of the car. . . . He held my throat. He started lifting my neck with his hand. . . . His hand never left my throat. . . . My back was pretty much level with the ceiling of the car."

When Adrienne said, ". . . and he told me to take off my clothes," Adrienne's mother and younger sister Kimberly were seen quietly crying.

The prosecutor asked the witness if she had ever been naked with a man before.

She replied, "Never."

Had she ever had sexual intercourse before?

"Never."

She paused, then continued: "I was frozen stiff. I was scared. He was starting to get mad at me. He was growling." (In retrospect, this revelation is jolting. Those who had watched Alex play football had also observed him growling.)

Adrienne then described the rape and the immediate aftermath.

Watching a young woman testify at the trial of her accused rapist (in other words, at *her* trial, since it is her behavior, character—and body—that is legitimate grist for aggressive deconstruction) is a little like watching a patient with an arcane disease, treatable only by experimental methods, submit to a physical examination in an amphitheater full of earnest medical students. They *have* to submit to indignity in order to have a stab at the deserved result (respectively, health or justice). And you are watching them struggling to maintain their dignity despite the public undressing, despite the excruciatingly condescending assault of well-intentioned curiosity.

Adrienne described going to Dr. Kessler and the police station the next day because she was too afraid to go immediately.

Those spectators impressed with Adrienne's very obvious pain and anger may have been surprised to know that at least one juror had already found two problems with her testimony. Why had this girl not fought off her alleged attacker? Not resisted more strenuously? And why did she wait until the next day to go to the police?

With or without these questions that we only know in hindsight (from published newspaper interviews with the jurors after the trial) that the jurors were privately mulling over, Thomas Puccio had just found, in the testimony, an arrow to put into his quiver. Adrienne had said that Alex's hand was around her throat the whole time—that he'd never removed it. "Always", "whole time": These were absolutes, and any first-year law student knows that absolutes were dangerous.

Didn't Bruce Hudock know that Adrienne had, inadvertently, contradicted this one detail in her own (ten-and-a-half-year-old) police statement?*

---

*In a newspaper interview after the retrial, Hudock would tell *The New York Times'* Monte Williams that although he realized the mistake, it was his practice not to point out inconsistencies in his own witness's testimony. And when this author sat down with Hudock in January 1997 he said he felt badly that he had made a "mistake" regarding that inconsistency.

In concluding her hour-and-a-half-long testimony, Adrienne identified the clothes she had been wearing the night of February 10, 1986. Then, item by item, the clothes were passed to the members of the jury: her white V-neck sweater, her long-sleeved Oxford cloth shirt, the purple ankle-zippered Guess? jeans borrowed from her older sister, Kristen. Finally, the jury handled the bloodstained white cotton panties with little purple polka dots. Some jurors seemed to recoil when handed the clear plastic bag which contained the undergarment. Whether they felt their privacy was being invaded by this gesture or whether they felt they were invading Adrienne's, the looks on several jurors' faces seemed to amount to distaste, as if a line had been crossed with the inclusion of this item of evidence.

After lunch recess, Adrienne resumed her seat on the witness stand. It was time for her cross-examination.

Some superstar defense attorneys—Bobby Lee Cook, Gerry Spence, Johnnie Cochran—specialize in the unctuous, showy, avuncular approach. They demand to romance you. Others— Leslie Abramson, Bruce Cutler, F. Lee Bailey—are flamboyantly sarcastic or imperious. They *like* being sonofabitches. The more they are feared or disliked, the better it is for their client. Thomas Puccio embodied a third style: the tough, impatient hitter. He was to criminal defense work what Yitzak Shamir and Bob Dole were to politics: no charm, no bullshit, no bedside manner. Just hard, blinding substance.

Puccio stood. Even standing, he appeared to be hunched-over—almost coiled to spring. "Uh, good afternoon Mrs. Ortolano . . ." he began, in a tone of voice that suggested he was getting right down to business.

Cross-examining an alleged acquaintance-rape victim who has just shed tears on the witness stand and who was a virgin at the time of the incident requires surgical precision. Puccio had to go after Adrienne's credibility without going after her character.

A clean place to start was Adrienne's college major: communciations. "Isn't the object of a communications degree to be able to get your point across?" Alex's attorney asked. "Don't they teach you how to act? How to dress?"

She answered in the affirmative, warily.

Hadn't she put her training to use recently—by "running through" the questions Hudock would be asking her . . . *with* Hudock?

"This past weekend, he showed me where I would sit," Adrienne admitted.

Only this weekend . . . ? Puccio got her to testify that she had had two other preparatory sessions, and that she had talked to the prosecutor six to eight times since 1986.

Rehearsal and possible prosecutor-witness collusion: These were the small balls Puccio had up in the air now. He moved on to the big item: inebriation.

"The object of the game of quarters is to get people drunk, is that right?" he queried.

"I guess," Adrienne allowed, flatly.

Puccio worked this vein—intoxication—for a while—as he would, elaborately and persistently work it, the next day, with the seven young adults (Sarah Marden Whitney, Andy Winebrenner, Tom Kelly, Dan Anderson, Mike Gedney, Kristin Stanley, Rob Jazwinksi) who, as teenagers, had been at the party.

Then he slid toward the issues of shame and deceptiveness. Adrienne had told the Darien police that she'd had about four beers, yet she had not told them she had played the game quarters. Puccio wondered, "Any *reason* you didn't?"

"No," Adrienne answered, tersely.

If she was so concerned about her curfew, why didn't she let her father pick her up? He could have just honked the horn. What was it that had persuaded her not to do so?

"My friends," she answered.

The witness was holding firm. A bit of jump-starting was required. "Did you hold hands on the way home?" Puccio asked, dangling an image of consent in front of the jurors' minds' eyes.

"No," she said sharply.

"Did it occur to you during this fifteen-minute ride that you might want to say something to Alex Kelly?"

"I didn't know him."

One hour and ten minutes into the cross-examination, with Puccio asking Adrienne details of "the incident" (as he called it), Adrienne began crying.

This was dangerous. Puccio backed off and returned to safe territory: the party. He compared her assessment of the time of Alex's arrival to the account she had given to the police in 1986, trying to show inconsistencies. Then, once the witness had safely regained her composure, he moved back to the incident itself. "Tell me how you got from the front seat to the back," he ordered.

"He grabbed me by the throat," she said.

"Using one hand or two?"

"One."

"Right hand or left hand?"

"Left."

And so, by her account, his right hand was left to manipulate the seat. Adrienne had already told Hudock that Alex had never removed his hand from her neck. The posited scenario would be very important to some jurors.

So would two other things be—two other things elicited in Hudock's direct examination of Adrienne: One was the fact that Adrienne had not fought Alex off. Of course, he had given her a good reason not to: He had threatened to kill her. Still in all, she hadn't fought. Did that still matter to a 1996 jury? Would only a kicking, screaming resistance mean that sex was not consensual?

But another image stayed in the mind of some others. Wasn't the sex consensual? Hadn't they kissed? Hadn't they held hands? Puccio had asked her.

Adrienne's answer had been swift and adamant: "It *never* happened."

The following day, the guests from Dan Anderson's party paraded on and off the stand for the prosecution and then the defense to question them. Faced with the necessity of slipping back into their teenage skins to recall a game of quarters during a desultory winter-break party, these young stockbrokers and sales reps (and one bartender-musician: Tom Kelly) seemed alternately bemused and put-upon.

Each side took from this group of witnesses what they needed and wished: The prosecution got affirmation that Adrienne had not flirted with Alex Kelly and that she had "desperately" (in Andy Winebrenner's word) sought a ride home. The defense culled the fact that the kids were playing a game whose purpose was inducing a "buzz" (Puccio seized on the generation-appropriate jargon with alacrity).

Next to testify were the police: Hugh McManus (then head of the Darien police's detective bureau, now the police chief), Lieutenant Ronald Bussell, and now-professor Rebecca Hahn Nathanson. Defense lawyers always enjoy catching police being sloppy. So when it was his turn, Puccio fired away: Why was there no police report? Why hadn't Adrienne's alleged injuries been photographed? How had the description of the alleged bloodstain started out as a description of a "red line"? Why such a casual instruction (as McManus indicated there had been) to the crime lab? Why weren't the victim's bra or coat or scarf recovered?

Still, it was these officers' words under Bruce Hudock's earlier questioning that seemed to resonate further than any lapses of textbook-perfect criminology. All the officers said that Adrienne had been "crying"—some said "trembling." As for why the police had not photographed the victim, McManus said, "She was highly emotional and fragile at best, and I decided it was in her best interest not to."

Dr. Henry Lee—America's most distinguished criminologist and, as the chief criminologist and director of Connecticut's forensic laboratory, the state's very own employee—did a largely irrelevant celebrity turn on the stand. More important, however, were the witnesses who told the human story: Adrienne's father, Bill Bak, and Adrienne's sister, Kristen. Kristen, who had comforted Adrienne and listened soothingly to her sister's horror story, provided, under Hudock's questioning, the most compelling corroboration of Adrienne's account.

But what was good for the goose was good for the gander. If Hudock had used Adrienne's look-alike sister to tell the victim's tale twice, Puccio would use that same victim-echoing witness to put across the defense scenario (which Alex, after all, would not deliver, since his eight-year flight left him a liability to himself as a witness) in the combative manner he would not dare have used on Adrienne herself.

In a detailed series of questions, lobbed over Hudock's objections, Puccio went after Kristen Bak aggressively, persistently mispronouncing the family name "Bock" instead of the correct "Back." Hadn't Adrienne said that she had *flirted* with Alex Kelly? That they had held hands? That she'd kissed him? That she had *voluntarily* entered the back of the vehicle? Each of these salvos that Puccio fired at Kristen Bak was immediately chased by "Objection!" by Hudock and "Sustained" by Nigro. But Puccio kept his unanswered questions coming anyway, in a strategic use of the simple trial truism, "You can't unring the bell." Puccio's other strategy was to appeal to the jurors to simply use their common sense and eyesight. Wasn't it likely that Ms. Bak's sister and this young man had flirted? Held hands? Kissed? If one moved from the suggestion (to Kristen Bak) of these possibilities to the visual evidence—and if the visual evidence was the extremely handsome, upper-middle-class, sweet-seeming young man at the defense table—then it would be hard not to infer what Alex's male peers had inferred right after winter break 1987: Why would Alex Kelly ever *need* to *rape* anybody?

Among the balance of the state's witnesses, the one that inspired Tom Puccio's most aggressive sarcasm was Dr. Marilyn Kessler. In a case such as this—where the alleged victim had never had sex before and where rape or consensual sex is the question the verdict hinges upon—the gynecologist becomes a forensic expert. She alone has seen the crucial physical evidence. She is to a rape what the criminologist and the DNA lab are to a blood crime and what the coroner is to a murder.

The fight with Dr. Kessler, a gracious-seeming if trial-naive doctor who had never before testified in a criminal proceeding, started before she ascended the witness stand—and while the jury was out of the courtroom. Puccio fought to make sure she could not use legal terms. Kessler could *not* classify the act as a rape, he insisted. She had conducted no internal examination.

Judge Nigro agreed. He ordered her testimony restricted: She could simply describe the injury. "The conclusion that there was nonconsensual intercourse cannot come before the jury," the judge announced. Now Kessler's forensic role had been stripped—she was simply a picture-drawer.

But Puccio would also fight her in this capacity.

Dr. Marilyn Kessler proved to be the kind of overenthusiastic witness that can sometimes turn out to hurt rather than help the side that calls her. Although much of what she had to say, in her direct examination by Hudock, was powerful prosecution testimony—that Adrienne had at first been afraid even of telling her Alex's name, for example; that she had seen "multiple cuts, lacerations, barely dried blood, black and blue areas, scrapes" on the teenager's genital area—some of the doctor's characterizations (she spoke of her young patient's "night of horror") made her sound less than objective. On top of this, Dr. Kessler had compensated for her investigative lapse (the lack of an internal examination of Adrienne) in a way that might be expected to raise any defense team's hackles: She had met—just a week before her testimony— with a medical illustrator to have a graphic drawing made of Adrienne's injuries "based . . . on my vivid recollection and also on my written report."

The sketch—so "lurid and horrible," one female spectator says, that some of the women viewers cringed for Adrienne— was presented to the jury. And while Adrienne's family seemed to swallow hard at the huge violation of her privacy (and as many women spectators began to grasp, by way of the drawing of genitalia, the indignity of pursuing a rape prosecution), Alex and Puccio became enraged at what they saw as a violation of *their* rights.

Why was that sketch—dictated from the ten-and-a-half-year-old memory of a clearly partisan witness—allowed in the courtroom? Jaw clenched, Alex leaned over and whispered furiously to his attorney.

When Puccio rose to cross-examine Kessler, he seemed ready to draw blood. It was often through doctors that reasonable doubt could be planted. Puccio had termed one of the von Bülow prosecutor's blood-sugar experts "Dr. One Hundred Percent" because of the man's excessive certainty. Dr. Kessler seemed here not so much excessively certain as excessively interested: interested in the prosecution winning; interested in her patient's testimony. In fact, in what looked like a possible violation of her sequestration order (witnesses in criminal trials are not allowed to view preceding testimony of other witnesses), her friend and lawyer, Mary Ellen Wynn, sat through Adrienne's testimony. If Puccio could raise the inference that Wynn had done so in order to give Kessler information that would help her tailor her testimony to suit the purposes of the prosecution, then he could score major points with the jury by proving that the doctor was overzealous and biased.

Puccio went after Kessler. Why was Mary Ellen Wynn in court during Adrienne's testimony? How many times had Kessler and Wynn talked since? When and where? What had they talked about? Didn't this show that Dr. Kessler had an agenda?

Yes, she and her lawyer had talked, Kessler admitted—but about something terribly innocent: what clothes the other witnesses were wearing.*

About *clothes?*

"She's primarily here for moral support," Kessler clarified.

Puccio moved on from Kessler's sympathies to her science. Why, he pointedly asked, had the doctor failed to conduct an internal examination?

The doctor's policy, she said, was to do what was "best for my patient." Besides, she said, "I will never forget Adrienne Bak's injuries."

To Hudock, Kessler had been poignantly blunt. "It would have been excruciatingly painful for me to do that exam in this case," she said. No point in opening the door for more such impassioned statements, Puccio may have felt. He changed the subject. Even if the bruises were seared in her mind, what did it all prove, ultimately? "Isn't it a fact that . . . *nothing* in the physical examination of the genital area can prove the inter-course was not consensual?" he demanded.

"It certainly did not look like consensual sex to me," Dr. Kessler responded.

But to somebody else, perhaps—to a more noted doctor, a

---

* Mary Ellen Wynn, considered one of the two top female lawyers in Stamford, was eventually subpoenaed by Puccio for possible violation of sequestration. At the hearing called to determine if such was the case, Wynn said that Kessler, nervous about testifying, had "wanted to have an idea . . . of how intimidating it was going to be." Wynn said she told Kessler that Adrienne had been "very composed and compelling. I was very moved by her testimony." Judge Nigro found no violation or need for sanctions.

more trial-savvy doctor—it *might* look like consensual sex. Puccio—the man who had hired Dick Morris—would have another big hire ready to take the stand, when the time came, to contest Dr. Kessler on that point.

The prosecution case ended with Lieutenant Ronald Bussell called back to the stand. He brought up Alex's flight from justice. On cross-examination, Puccio emphasized that his client had "surrendered himself" voluntarily to authorities in Switzerland.

The defense opened its case on Wednesday, October 23 with its glamour witness, Amy Molitor. A defendant's girlfriend always draws a jury up to full height. But, aside from her curtain-opener value, Amy had three real functions: One, she was there to show that this boy did not need to rape—"We had a serious and intimate relationship" before February 10, she said; two: she would show that the charge of rape was not at all believable at the time. ("Did you continue to see him and date him [after the charges]?" Puccio asked; "Yes," she answered.)

And, three—and most important—as the daughter of the owner of the vehicle in which the alleged crime had taken place, she could give the jurors instruction on how the seat back lowered.

"The latch for the backseat . . . to pull it down, you have to get out of the car," she testified. "You had to hold the latch down and use your other hand to pull the seat down."

Puccio seemed pleased with this simple testimony. Hudock didn't touch it.

Puccio's next witness was one that couldn't take an oath—or even speak. It was an exhibit—a 1983 Jeep Wagoneer. The jurors took a field trip to the garage of the Stamford Police Department parking lot. By using Lieutenant Bussell (a prosecution witness), the point Puccio was demonstrating now assumed a greater clarity and objectivity—you needed two hands, not one, to lower the backseat with one motion.

Lieutenant Bussell moved the seat back, with two hands, in one motion.

The jurors took turns moving the seat up and down, whispered among themselves. A few raised their hands, as if to ask questions. They were told by the judge that they could not ask them.

Lingering, unanswered questions are the checks defense lawyers can most profitably cash during closing arguments.

"I have no further questions for the car, Judge," Thomas Puccio said.

The next day, Joe Kelly took the stand. He was a commanding presence. The sheer force of his resolve—his unmovable loyalty to his son, his certainty of his son's innocence: These massed energies—so apparent in his intense, brooding manner—radiated from the witness stand.

Still, for all his commanding physical presence, his function seemed to be that of a stealth witness, one prepared to push testimony over, above, and through an anticipated barrage of likely-to-be-sustained prosecution objections.

He told of how he was awakened by a phone call at about 1:30 A.M. It was Bill Bak, his neighbor three houses down. As a result of the conversation the two men had, "I went in [Alex's] room and woke him up. I said—"

Bruce Hudock shouted: "Objection! Objection!" Judge Nigro sustained the objections, but Joe Kelly continued, loud and clear: " 'Alex,' I said, 'Mr. Bak says you raped his daughter.' He said, 'Dad, I didn't rape his daughter. We had sex. Dad, go to bed.' "

Key testimony. Emotional testimony. Alex's words on the night of the incident. His spontaneous plea of innocence: *"Dad, I didn't rape his daughter!"* Puccio needed those words in—and he pushed for them. It *is* admissable, he argued, because it fits the criterion of the main hearsay-exception: it is an *excited utterance.* Alex was awakened from deep sleep—it's spontaneous speech. It should be allowed in! Puccio argued.

Hudock took the opposite view. "It's a self-serving statement by the defendant, and an hour and a half after the incident," he argued.

Nigro ruled for the prosecution. It was the time factor—the hour-and-a-half delay after the act—that disqualified the remark as a hearsay exception. The remark was struck from the record. The jury was told to disregard it.

Puccio did not accept this ruling without contesting it. Such was his practice with all of Nigro's rulings for the prosecution. Consequently, over time, Nigro had developed a pattern of becoming short-tempered with the combative lawyer. At one point shortly after this ruling, out of the jury's presence, Puccio took issue with the judge's continued irritation with his persistence in questioning rulings.

"You have continually made your displeasure with me" known, Puccio complained. Nigro replied that Puccio had persisted in rearguing the same point, again and again.

Puccio told the judge that the judge's attitude toward him was telegraphing bias to the jury.

"I sometimes raise my voice," Nigro admitted. "That is improper."

When the jury returned, the judge turned to them and made a contrite confession. "I may sometimes appear snappish in my rulings," he said. "It is counsel's job to be persistent."

Thus, the long record for appeal that Puccio was establishing now included Judge Nigro's admitted irritation at the defense lawyer.

Puccio dealt with the flight issue creatively: He pinned it on Mickey Sherman.

Waiving his attorney-client privilege at his former client's request, Sherman took the stand and testified that, back in Colorado just before the February 1987 trial date, he had told Alex that he wasn't getting a "fair shake" from the legal system. When Bruce Hudock attempted, on cross-examination, to wrest other information about that infamous day at

Copper Mountain Resort from Sherman, the lawyer could not remember much.

Mickey Sherman, Joe Kelly, Tom Puccio, Alex Kelly: Together, they were powerful not only in what they did say, but in what they did not say and what they insisted on saying despite sustained objections.

Massed against all this collective machismo was the memory of Adrienne's quietly angry testimony. Her complete lack of desire to charm or persuade the jury. Her adamance about Puccio's suggestions of consensual sex: "It *never* happened." Her cold resolve. Her tears. The feelings, gleaned by many women in the courtroom at least, that she was being absolutely honest, and that the rape had left a part of her irreversibly bitter.

Was Adrienne's account receding or advancing in the jurors' memories?

In the event of the latter, Puccio was now going to wallpaper over that testimony with a long line of old men with academic and medical degrees, all of whom would render "expert" opinions.*

First came Dr. Robert Sadoff, forensic psychiatrist from the University of Pennsylvania, author of six books, physician to 8,000 patients, winner of many awards. Sadoff asserted that a five-foot, six-inch 135-pound sixteen-year-old female who consumed four to five glasses of beer over three or four hours would be affected in three areas: Emotionally, she might be catapulted into a state of euphoria; in terms of cognition, her critical judgment would be decreased; and, in regard to her actions, it would allow for "risk-taking behavior."

In terms of sex, specifically? Such intake of alcohol, in such

---

* Bruce Hudock had toyed with the idea of presenting a rape-trauma expert. (After the trial ended in mistrial, he even wanted to find a male rape-trauma expert, to deflect the anticipated perception that the criminalization of acquaintance rape was somehow the province of agenda-bearing feminists.) Ultimately, however, he decided that the clarity and integrity of Adrienne's testimony was best served unadorned by such props, which sometimes seem pseudo-knowledgeable and desperate.

a person "would lower inhibitions. Then it would allow a person to do things she would not allow herself to do without alcohol."

Next came the "sexologist"—Dr. Harold Lief, board-certified psychiatrist and professor emeritus at the University of Pennsylvania. (He proudly allowed that "all the major sexological associations have given me their annual awards.") Dr. Lief testified that girls who come to first-time sex from the "rather moral atmosphere where the emphasis is on not having sex in a promiscuous fashion" can become guilty and agitated about such an encounter. Further, Dr. Lief noted, rapists did not usually drive their victims home. And rapists almost never disrobe.

Another toxicologist, Dr. Kurt Dubowski, and another gynecologist, Dr. Samuel Ryan, took the stand. The former gave copious testimony about how neatly the effects of those four glasses of beer could dovetail into the conditions ("more manifested self-confidence and diminishment of inhibitions . . . lowered judgment, control, greater risk-taking") for consensual sex with a virtual stranger. The second expert discussed—in great, presumptuous clinical detail—the most intimate parts of the victim's anatomy . . . only to conclude absolutely nothing.

To watch a slew of jargon-spouting paid experts feast upon a young woman's intimate records with such numbingly pedestrian "expertise" is to understand a small piece of why so few young women ever press rape charges.

Puccio's star hired-gun was Dr. Michael Baden. The distinguished medical examiner with the unkempt appearance and heavy-breathing voice (whose casual allusion during his Simpson-trial testimony to his medical school's having been located in "the Harlem section of New York" was a laughable example of pandering to that jury) mounted the witness stand.

Bleeding, lacerations, abrasions: the symptoms Dr. Marilyn Kessler had found in Adrienne—were they also consistent with plain old nonrape first-time intercourse? Puccio asked.

"Yes, absolutely," the doctor cheerfully responded. "It is a normal part of intercourse to have scrapes and abrasions."*

Out of the presence of the jury, a series of hearings were going on and on about whether or not Dr. Fredric Rieders (yet another Simpson case alumnus) could present his tests to the jury, attesting that marijuana had been found in the blood in Adrienne's underwear.

Adrienne had adamantly denied that she had smoked marijuana.

Judge Nigro recalled Rieders and additional scientific witnesses to the stand in closed evidentiary hearings several times before concluding that Rieders' test of the bloodstain could not be presented to the jury because the manner in which the scientist had arrived at his result was contrary to the standards set in his own laboratory.

Even without getting Rieders' testimony admitted (and this would not be the end of Puccio's luck in the bloodstain drug-test department), Puccio had put on an overabundance of technical witnesses. He had also presented a committed father and a loving and beautiful girlfriend. He had unmasked a supposedly clinically objective gynecologist and had found an advocate; he had gotten Judge Nigro to apologize for his hot temper to the jury. He had presented a four-wheeled inani-

---

* Right after the mistrial, *The New York Times* published an opinion piece by Lynne Hecht Schafran, director of the National Judicial Education Project of the NOW Legal Defense and Education Fund, castigating Dr. Baden's "outrageous" assertion and making the point that Baden's conclusion was a "bizarre switch from the way the defense in rape trials usually deals with the question of physical injuries"—that is, to insist that a rape can't have occurred if there *aren't* injuries. The "erroneous notion that forced sex must result in visible trauma"—which Dr. Baden stood on its head—"is a powerful stereotype about rape," Schafran wrote. "Jurors often want such evidence, which they mistakenly perceive as proof of the victim's resistance and lack of consent." Baden's testimony, however, Schafran went on to say, made things more unfair and confusing by asserting that "the very type of injuries that rape-trial jurors typically expect" are "'a normal part of intercourse.'"

mate witness—a Jeep Wagoneer with a reclining backseat—
that had done a lot of talking.

On Tuesday, November 5, Bruce Hudock stood up to deliver
his closing argument. In it, he set out to dramatize the crime.
"A sixteen-year-old accepts a ride home from a party . . . and
within fifteen minutes she would be brutally raped." He asked
the jurors to "turn back the clock now to that winter night . . ."
and, in language a bit florid ("with all the speed and agility a
star wrestler can achieve. . . ."), he described the rape.

" 'I felt pain. I felt a lot of pain. . . . It hurt so bad. If I told
anybody, he would do it again and he would kill me. . . .': It is
Adrienne's voice the defendant fled in February 1987."

Hudock reminded the jury that the young people at the party
remembered that Adrienne was sober—*their* voices, too, he
suggests, are the voices Alex Kelly fled from. He reviewed the
police's assertions of Adrienne's fear, and Dr. Kessler's assertions. "On February 18, 1987, the defendant fled the voice that
accused him." But, more than that, Hudock said, attempting to
elicit the jury's indignation, he "ran from more than that voice.
He ran from *you*—the jury."

Alex's flight, Hudock said clearly, indicates his "consciousness of guilt." Speaking of his witness now, he said that "her
voice tells you . . . her pain has not diminished over time. . . .
The wounds have remained open and fresh." Anticipating
inconsistencies Puccio might find between Adrienne's police
report, early remarks, and her trial testimony, Hudock asked
the jury if any of them would have had the courage, at that age,
to tell "eight perfect strangers" about such an intimate violation. Of her police and medical interviews, "she told us the
truth as best a terrified sixteen-year-old can."

The only defense offered in this case, Hudock said, was that
the defendant was handsome.

In concluding his short—twenty-five-minute—closing statement, Hudock told the jury, "You will hear the voices—the

voices of all those who have been witness to" Adrienne's rape. Then he walked over and hugged Adrienne Bak Ortolano, who had sat crying and holding her husband's hand throughout the argument.

Five minutes after Hudock hugged his witness, in an abrupt shift of mood, Thomas Puccio rose and—energetically—asked the jurors to be not compassionate hearers of voices but, rather, "detectives in search of the facts." He urged them to draw "fair and logical inferences"—and he told them "there is not one reasonable doubt, there are *many* reasonable doubts."

As any defender of an accused rapist must do in these politicized times, he made sure the jury understood that he agreed that "rape is a horrible, horrible offense." But, he counseled, it is also "an inflammatory, emotional subject. It's a horrible thing if a twenty-eight-year-old man [Alex was actually twenty-nine.] is found guilty of something he didn't do." His voice thundered with horror: "It's as horrible as rape!

"Alex Kelly . . . denies each and every allegation in this case!" Appealing to the jurors' horror of false allegations, he said, *"Anybody* can walk into this courtroom and say anything they please!"

Was Adrienne Ortolano a liar? For now, Puccio waxed euphemistic. Her "performance was . . . beautifully scripted and rehearsed," he said.

Now Puccio got to the meat of those reasonable doubts:

First of all, the alcohol. Adrienne had not been candid, Puccio implied. She drank more than she said—people don't tell the truth about liquor consumption. He quoted Dr. Sadoff and Dr. Dubowski about alcohol's effects in releasing inhibitions and increasing risk-taking behavior.

Secondly, the story. Puccio told the jury that it did not make sense. Why didn't Adrienne ask Mike Gedney, whom she saw outside the party, for a ride home? And would the witness have you believe that Alex and Adrienne really drove fifteen minutes in silence? And the attack itself—Puccio mocked it. "Like a homicidal maniac, he jumps her and rapes her: Does that make sense to you?! Especially since Alex lived three doors away and knew Adrienne's brother and had disrobed. Dr. Lief, the sexologist, had said rapists do not disrobe!

"Where's the *proof?*" Puccio thundered. "Where's the proof you must demand to send this young man to prison?!"

There was no proof, Puccio continued, because Adrienne's story made no sense. Why drive across town, so close to your house and the girl's house that you're likely to be discovered? But the main problem with Adrienne's account, Puccio said, was that, as the Jeep demonstration showed, a person needed *two* hands to lower the seat . . . and Adrienne said Alex had never taken a hand off her neck. That story, Puccio contested, was a fiction created to obscure the fact that Adrienne willingly got from the front to the back of the car and helped Alex put the seat down, in fact.

There are *more* inconsistencies, Puccio went on, gathering steam. "Every garment is intact. Is *that* consistent with the sexual frenzy of a madman? Why is there no ripped clothing? Why no buttons torn off?" Puccio reminded the jury that Dr. Lief had said that disrobing is *not* consistent with rape.

Alex looked intensely and trustingly at Puccio through his passionate argument.

Now Puccio, having laid the groundwork, let loose the L-word. Adrienne, deeply guilty about having first-time sex in the back of a Jeep, was a *liar*. She "lied to her family on February 10" and, having given a police statement, she was "stuck with that lie she told ten years ago." The lie had taken on a life of its own over the years and continuing it had had no apparent consequences because "she didn't expect Alex Kelly to come back."

Adrienne, Puccio was telling the jury, was the one in denial. Out of necessity, she had convinced herself there had been a rape. That self-delusion is why "maybe those tears were real." But Adrienne's story was "a missile out of control."

Fleeing his trial was "the dumbest thing [Alex] has ever

done in his life"—but how could you blame him! His lawyer—at the time "the most important person in his life"—had told him he wasn't getting a fair shake.

Puccio ran through all of it again—the drinking, the science, the Jeep, Adrienne's account's inconsistency with Dr. Lief's scenario. As Adrienne sat gripping her husband's hand, Puccio insisted: "He didn't rape someone on Leeuwarden Lane on February 10, 1987! His life is in your hands. Based on the reasonable doubt that arises, return a verdict of not guilty . . . it's about this young man's life!"

At 2:30 P.M. Judge Nigro charged the jury with finding Alex Kelly guilty or not guilty for two different crimes: kidnapping in the first degree (abduction and restraint, here with the intent to violate and commit sexual abuse) and sexual assault in the first degree (compelling the victim to engage in sexual intercourse). The issue of Alex's flight "may justify a finding of guilt," Nigro said, although Mickey Sherman's testimony could be offered but "not for truth" but rather in terms of "the effect on the state of mind" of the defendant.

At 3:34, the jury began deliberations.

To the world outside the jury box, Alex's flight and the media-bandied details of his life of Riley abroad, plus the Jimmy's Seaside incident and especially the recent car accident had combined to make him not only guilty but a scorned and ridiculed man. (Even on Court-TV, which analyzes trials with professional dispassion, moderator Greg Jarrett would eventually, incredulously, say of the postsentencing bond renewal, "[But] this guy runs from *everything!*") He was the "preppy rapist." Thomas Puccio was right: All the coverage on his client was implicitly negative.

But, while the public watches and hears one set of events, a jury watches and hears another. We have seen that—in the first Rodney King verdict, in the first Menendez (another example of handsome, wealthy young defendants changing out of their customary clothes to relentlessly wear college-student garb throughout their two proceedings), in the first Crown Heights/Lemrick Nelson trial in New York. And in the fact that all of these *were* "first" trials—that justice in America in high-profile criminal trials has become a two-shot game for the prosecution (whether by mistrial—as in Menendez I—or federal civil-rights suit, as in King II and Nelson II).

The sign that this trial might go that now-common route was made evident with the first notes from the jury the next morning at 9:55 A.M. They wanted to hear Mike Gedney's full testimony, Tom Kelly's full testimony, and Adrienne's testimony—"from where she talks about Alex Kelly's arrival [at the party] until she arrives at her home," the note read.

To some, it seemed easy to infer from that note that this was a jury that *started* divided. They were asking for the heart of the consent testimony.

After the long readback—for which Adrienne, her husband and her sister were present—the jury resumed deliberations, then, at the very end of the day, requested to see the Jeep and the videotape of its backseat being lowered. Judge Nigro ruled that the Jeep itself was not evidence—they could see the video, but not the vehicle. Puccio pushed for letting the jury see the Jeep itself—*his* evidence. Nigro denied. Puccio pushed again. Nigro denied.

Even while this issue was being contested—and Puccio's conflict with Nigro had spilled over into Thursday—the jury had other requests: They wanted to hear Adrienne's cross-examination "from the point where he stopped the car to when she's in back of the vehicle," and they wanted to see the video of Ronald Bussell lowering the back seat of the Jeep. In that demonstration, of course, Bussell had done the lowering with two hands.

During the readback of her own cross-examination by Puccio, Adrienne sat and wept. Alex followed the court reporter's words by reading from his own transcript.

After lunch the jury asked for Dr. Kessler's complete testimony. Some of Puccio's strongest attacks were aimed at this witness. What did it mean that they wanted all of Kessler's testimony read back?

By now they had been deliberating almost fourteen hours, for over two days.

The next day—Friday, November 8—at 3:45 P.M., the jury delivered a note: "We are unable to reach a unanimous verdict on either count."

The prosecution side was dismayed. But to Alex and Amy, Alex's parents, and Tom Puccio, an enormous hurdle had been cleared. To have pushed that much reasonable doubt through so thick a scrim of public condemnation and negative press coverage was an extraordinary testament to the lawyer's skill, the defendant's handsome presence, and to the jury's commitment to the facts of the case as presented.

Judge Nigro, invoking the over-hundred-year-old "Chip Smith Charge," urged the minority opinion-holders on the jury to "seriously ask themselves whether in reason they should adhere to their own conclusions when those conclusions are not concurred in by most of those with whom they are associated."

Forty-five minutes after the minority was admonished to examine their opinion in this sterner light, the jury presented the judge with another note: "We want to hear Joe Kelly's complete testimony." Joe's outburst—"And he said, 'Dad, I didn't rape his daughter! We had sex . . .'"—had been stricken, of course. Yet the jury was now going back to Alex's most vigorous and unqualified champion: his father. What did this mean?

Deliberations adjourned for the weekend, with the defendant's father's words—and perhaps, in the memory of some jurors, his compelling physical intensity—left as the last piece of evidence they had discussed.

* * *

Since the court took Mondays off, deliberations did not resume until Tuesday, November 12. Now the jurors wanted to rehear the testimony of Ronald Bussell. He had testified, among other things, about Adrienne's tears and her fear. Ronald Bussell, a red-haired man with a ruddy complexion, had been fervently devoted to the prosecution of Alex Kelly for all these years. He attended the trial regularly—grim-faced and concerned—and when reporters asked him why he was there, he would answer that after all these years of counseling Adrienne through her terror, he was not about to abandon her now. Bussell had said to people that if freed to reoffend, Alex might well kill the next girl he raped.

Yet Bussell was a cop's cop, a meticulous professional. On the witness stand, his huge store of personal feelings about the danger of the defendant and his career-long obsession with seeing Alex prosecuted was hidden. Yet the jury wanted the policeman's testimony read. What did *this* mean?

During the readback, Alex looked from one juror's face to the next. According to one person who was covering the trial for the media, Mrs. Doubtfire first clasped her hands loosely, then held her hands as if praying.

After Bussell's testimony, they deliberated briefly, then sent a note to the judge. The judge, perhaps fearing the worst, dismissed them for lunch.

After lunch, back in the courtroom, waiting, waiting, Amy sat tapping her fingers on the rail.

The jurors, their communiqué had said, were still unable to reach a verdict on either count.

Judge Nigro grimly assessed the situation: "It doesn't seem to me there is any benefit to continuing."

Alex immediately turned around and looked, open-mouthed, at his parents. Adrienne and her husband walked quickly out of the courtroom.

When asked what Adrienne's reaction had been, Bruce

Hudock—the large, bearlike prosecutor—included himself in a three-word answer. He said, "We both cried."

The Kellys, of course, were quietly elated. Even though Hudock vowed to try the case again ("The victim is ready to take the stand again," he said), and even though retrials, civil wrongful-death trials, and federal civil-rights-violations trials had just become the faddish new judicial embodiment of "If at first you don't succeed . . . ," the jury's refusal to deliver the expected conviction confirmed to the Kellys that Alex could survive any trial, that others knew him to be as innocent as they knew him to be. And though the defendant becomes severely disadvantaged in a retrial (the prosecution spends the interim learning from its mistakes), one of the few well-known attorneys in recent memory to have pulled an *acquittal* out of a retrial was . . . Puccio himself. And, in that case (von Bülow), Trial I had not even been a hung jury but a *conviction.*

The Kellys and Puccio girded for continued triumph.

Perhaps it was this group hubris; perhaps it was just his combative style; perhaps it was his annoyance at political correctness, which put certain types of crimes out of bounds from the usual thrust and parry of lawyer talk; perhaps he just made a mistake. But, whatever the reason, standing on the steps of Stamford Superior—with Alex half-smiling behind him, his hand on Amy's shoulder—Puccio took a swipe at Adrienne and her family.

The Baks came to court every day, "Chanel clothing and all," he said, contemptuously. "They came here totally coiffed and dressed to kill. You might even say they *liked* being here. They were very unvictim victims, if you ask me."

Golub and Hudock, of course, each had an outburst—Hudock stepped up to the microphone and, referring to Alex and Amy, sarcastically apologized for not having anyone to hold hands with. Golub thundered that it was a "shameful outcome"—that Puccio had "pandered to every stereotype we have heard about rape victims." And Puccio and Golub attacked one another: Golub saying Puccio had lied about the earlier plea-bargain talks, Puccio accusing Golub of "ambulance-chasing" the case.

But it was Puccio's "unvictim victims" remark that was widely broadcast and incited a torrent of outrage. What did rape victims have to dress like to meet the (incidentally, impeccably dressed) lawyer's definition of a victim? commentators demanded. Sackcloth and ashes?

"We were totally appalled," said Carla Gisolfi, the executive director of Stamford's Rape and Sexual Abuse Crisis Center, who had one or more advocates attend every day of the trial (Puccio had complained about "all those victim's advocates" in the courtroom)—and had counseled and assisted Adrienne and Valerie ever since their attacks. "We felt [Puccio's] comments were insensitive, inhuman, and totally uncalled for."

Although Puccio professed that his remarks were "blown tremendously out of context" and were thoroughly appropriate "for a lawyer defending an innocent man," and although he seemed almost gleeful as he promised further aggressive behavior in the case (the retrial would involve "'a direct attack on [Adrienne's] credibility,' he said, with something of a chortle," to William Glaberson of *The New York Times*), one wonders if, privately, he was surprised at the public relations minefield he had stumbled upon.

He should have known better, says defense attorney Roy Black, who successfully defended William Kennedy Smith and is now defending Marv Albert, the sportscaster charged with biting a woman in a Virginia hotel room. He probably should have couched his remarks in a statement "saying he did not mean to disparage all victims. As the lawyer for the man in any kind of sex case, you have to be very careful what you say; everything you say about the victim is going to be picked apart. If you make too broad a statement, you're lending yourself to attacks." Black knows how Puccio must have felt after his "unvictim victim" remark. "This woman [*New York Post* columnist Andrea Peyser] wrote a poisonous column about the

Albert case, saying he deserves everything he gets because he's investigating this woman [the alleged victim]. In *every* case, a lawyer investigates the witness! You can't just give up! According to this woman in the *Post,* if you're a man charged with rape you should just plead guilty and go to the penitentiary and not say anything. You can't do that!"

Indeed, Puccio's tactics won him Alex's mistrial. He had kept Alex's entire criminal record—the burglaries, the Jimmy's Seaside incident, the car accident, and, most important, the second rape charge—out of the trial. He had opened the door to nothing incriminating about his client. This would not be the case the next time.

To the public, Alex might have looked ridiculous in that blazer day in and day out, but one juror said Alex's appearance as a "clean-cut guy" helped provide doubt. Another juror told the *Times'* William Glaberson that some on the panel—possibly influenced by Alex's appearance and demeanor—might have thought "there was a consensual element to it."

Three of the six jurors had originally held out for acquittal during the rancorous deliberations. Mrs. Doubtfire—whose name, it turned out, was Halina Farsun—was one; the jury foreman, a former executive named Robert Grimm, was another. And a male security guard named Connie Williams was a third. After Judge Nigro had given the Chip Smith charge, Williams changed his vote to conviction. But Farsun had apparently had trouble with the fact that Adrienne had not gone to the police until the next day. Farsun and the foreman would not change their votes. And so they had hung.

So shocked were some of the jurors to learn of the second rape charge that even Farsun came out of the experience believing—as she told William Glaberson—"there needs to be more information presented to juries. They have to do something to change the way the system is."

Juror Susan Kane, a businesswoman and mother of three, had left jury duty disheartened. When Puccio made his "unvictim" remark, Kane's feelings turned to outrage. Even though she and her fellow panel members had made a mutual decision not to speak publicly about the deliberations, so as not to prejudice the retrial jury, Puccio's remarks had prompted Kane to break her silence. She wrote a letter to Adrienne, telling the resilient victim how she felt.

"There was not one thing said or one 'expert' opinion that in any way impeached your story," she wrote. "Unfortunately," she continued, referring bitterly to the deliberations, "there are still people who actually believe that a woman should fight off her attacker despite the risk to her life. There are still people who won't believe that a woman has been raped unless they can see a black eye or a torn pair of pants. There are still people who can be fooled by a smooth-talking defense attorney who can weave a fairy tale that is in no way supported by the facts or evidence."

Kane ended her letter: "I am greatly relieved to be finished with this jury duty, though I am saddened by the outcome. Today, for the first day in five weeks I woke up without a knot in my stomach. Unfortunately, you must continue to live with a knot in yours."

Now that he had a client whom one half (before the Chip Smith charge) to one third (after) of the jury had found innocent, Puccio wanted Alex to be treated like an exonerated young man. So, just before New Year's, he submitted motions to Nigro for relaxation of Alex's bond. Filling out a schedule that included trips to a gym, to bookstores, to coffee bars, the dry cleaners, the bank, to church, and to do volunteer work "with inner-city youth." Puccio insisted that Alex be free of the "onerous" six P.M. to six A.M. curfew and the prohibition from leaving the house without his parents. Hudock, predictably, called the schedule "ludicrous" and said, "He's homebound and he can't take it anymore." Nigro yielded on only one issue: He would allow Alex to attend college classes alone. Otherwise, the restrictions remained. (Of Puccio's request that Alex go to church on his own, Nigro said dryly, "If I thought he was a devout churchgoer, I'd make arrangements. He can go with his parents.")

Having gotten Nigro to grant his client at least a modicum of freedom, Puccio next turned his attention to revealing the judge's alleged bias against Alex. A good lawyer investigates everything, and in the course of Puccio's investigation, he had discovered remarks that the judge had made after the mistrial. At a mid-January hearing, Puccio presented affidavits from the jurors, Farsun and Grimm, who had voted to acquit. They swore that after the mistrial Nigro had told them about the second rape allegation, the burglary arrest, and the car accident—and that someone in his courtroom had referred to Amy Molitor as "Amelia Airhead." In addition, Puccio's co-counsel Hope Seeley had come upon Nigro with prosecutors in the state's attorneys' office. (Nigro denied that this was an "ex parte conference," as Puccio claimed. But he did say that he was having lunch with the state's attorneys.)

Hudock did not want Nigro—a judge who certainly knew Alex Kelly's history—recused. So he stood up and argued that Nigro had not been biased against Alex—as a matter of fact, the prosecutor bellowed sarcastically, the judge had even allowed Alex to go to school "without an escort from mommy and daddy."

Hearing these ill-chosen words from the man he already considered his son's longtime tormentor, Joe Kelly leaned forward, coughed conspicuously, and smacked the wooden bar with his hand. He rose and stormed out of the courtroom, muttering, "You bastard." Later, as Hudock exited the court-room, Joe Kelly directed a *"You fuck!"* his way.

"What did you say?" Hudock asked Kelly. Puccio calmed his client's father down. (This was not the first fight between the two sides. During jury deliberations, Kathy Puccio's remark to Hudock that he should not have his middle-school-aged son in the courtroom led to Hudock touching her arm—whereupon

Hudock and Puccio had a loud verbal altercation out of sight, but not earshot, of many in the courtroom.)

Nigro stepped down, and was replaced by Judge William Hickey. All the more show of Puccio's strength.

Puccio kept filing motions—both before Judge Hickey and, when Hickey recused himself because of his participation in the October plea-bargain talks, in front of the new judge, Kevin Tierney. Puccio asked—again—for a change of venue (denied). He asked to bar the testimony of Valerie Barnett at the retrial in Adrienne's case (affirmed). When Hartford *Courant* reporter Lynne Touhy ran a story in March, asserting that three other women had sworn to police that Kelly had raped them,* Puccio, in a wildly showy gesture, subpoenaed Touhy, Hudock, and Golub to try to get to the bottom of what he implied was a prosecution-based news leak that would ruin Alex's chance for a fair retrial. (The judge ruled, in a brief hearing, that there had been no misconduct.)

Finally, in April, Puccio fought to make admissible tests he had commissioned on the bloodstain in Adrienne's underwear, which, Puccio claimed, indicated traces of marijuana found in the blood at the time of the rape. (Adrienne repeatedly and unequivocally denied that she had used marijuana.) Ever since the first trial, the finding, refining, and the admissibility of such test results had been a mission of Puccio's, and he had been unsuccessful once before (the test results were shown to be without merit). Judge Tierney said no—for now. But he left the door open for further offers of proof by Puccio that the test was valid. Puccio was *not* giving up.

Finally, when Bruce Hudock learned (through the Stamford

---

*Two of the women were Diane Sales (of the early January 1986 Vermont alleged rape) and the woman who claimed Alex had raped her when she was a thirteen-year-old visiting the Bahamas Club Med. The third woman referred to may have been Jillian Henderson, who was interviewed by police, but eventually (for reasons explained earlier in this book) decided not to testify. Puccio confirmed that the women had made statements but said he did not think the women were telling the truth.

Advocate's Dan Mangan, who had broken so many big stories on the case over ten years that he had become virtually synonymous with its coverage) that Alex had just been granted Irish citizenship, all Bruce Hudock's courtroom indignation—all his stated alarm that the citizenship could lead to a passport, which could lead, again, to flight—could not best Puccio's casually delivered arguments. First, his client had a Constitutional right to hold dual citizenship. Second, he did not have an Irish passport, so there was no risk of flight. With great frustration, Bruce Hudock saw his bid to double Alex's bond to $2 million rejected by Judge Tierney.

Some people who had watched their friend Adrienne endure what was now more than eleven years of frightened waiting were very worried. "Puccio is in a whole different league from Hudock," said one of the former quarters players who testified at the first trial and would testify again. "And this is Adrienne's last chance."

When jury selection for the retrial began in April, Bruce Hudock approached the task with fierce attention. He was looking for two things now—people with strong family values and people who could make a decision and take charge. Puccio, commensurately, was picking jurors who would be likely to hang a jury. In the panel of six plus two alternates, four men and four women, from their early twenties to late sixties, were ultimately seated in mid-May. Hudock was convinced that *this* jury would arrive at a decision.

On the witness stand, Adrienne was angrier this time. Some in the courtroom who had not seen her during the first trial were struck by how unapologetic her anger was. At times her irritation seemed to spill over to others—her friend Sarah Marden of eleven years ago, who hadn't given her the ride home from the party, and Bruce Hudock, as he questioned her. There were moments, in watching her talk of the events of that winter night long ago, that one feared that the jury would find her bitchy. And yet, when her face was in repose between statements, the sad, downcast eyes in her small, round face and her grimly closed mouth spoke volumes. The years seemed to have pushed her features closed and tight. Her face was a delicate map of bitter endurance.

"How long did it last?" Bruce Hudock asked her.

With the flattest, angriest misery, Adrienne said: "Forever."

Hudock had the benefit of cleaning up the memory lapses and inconsistencies in her former testimony—she now re-called that Alex had (as she'd originally told the police) taken one hand off her neck in order to put the seat down.

When Thomas Puccio stood to cross-examine Adrienne, his familiar irritated voice was ballasted by a new energy. If the retrial was a gift to the prosecutor in terms of cleaning up prior mistakes, it was also a gift to the defense attorney in the politically incorrect position of having to attack a rape victim: He could go after one neutral issue—the improvement of her testimony from the prior trial to this trial—repeatedly, without the sensitivity police running him out of town again, as they had after his famous "unvictim" statement.

So this was the theme he would pound.

But first, he was going to fire an opening salvo. Although expressly restricted by Judge Tierney from using the phrases "mistrial" or "hung jury" in front of the jury ("previous proceeding" was the allowed term), Puccio used one such term in his very first sentence to Adrienne. (Hudock shouted, "Objection!") The prosecution was on notice: Puccio had taken his gloves off.

Adrienne had said X in the first trial but Y in the second. She'd had time to reconsult with Hudock. She'd conveniently changed the troublesome passages. Well, which *was* the correct account, Mrs. Ortolano? Hmmm? Why the conve-niently elastic testimony and memory?

To this polished, weaving, supple dance, Adrienne Orto-lano's fierce honesty was a defiantly lead-footed partner. Her contempt for Puccio was palpable. The lack of ingratiation, the brittleness—the mien that had seemed, as she'd been questioned by respectful Bruce Hudock, offputting and ungrateful: All of this was now effective. She didn't give a damn about Puccio's games with her words. She knew what had happened to her. Puccio was simply a nuisance.

Puccio had a new revelation: Hadn't she been named "Biggest Flirt" in her class at Middlesex School? Here was the yearbook! See . . . ?

Adrienne did not dignify that piece of information with a reaction. It was irrelevant.

"I never 'ran through' testimony with Bruce Hudock," she said. When Puccio remarked that she had been concerned about her testimony about Alex's lowering of the Jeep's seat, she shot back, "No. I only heard *you* say that.

"I testified that because it's the truth! . . . I don't know what it takes the defendant [to lower the seat]. . . . *You* made an issue of its during the last trial."

When he pushed her all the more over details, Adrienne looked at the attorney with an effortlessly condescending glare; then she said, biting off each syllable solemnly: "I am *absolutely* sure of every detail of the rape and I'll *never* forget it."

When Puccio started suggesting that her police statement (from which it could be gleaned that Alex's hands might have left her neck to lower the backseat), might have been (since it contradicted her previous-trial testimony) untruthful, Adrienne was pushed to wearily challenge: "I gave that statement the day after the rape. *Show* it to the jury." I dare you, she was saying. I dare you to say that I was lying.

"Nonetheless," Puccio pressed on, "you made two statements to the contrary, to—"

"Yes!" she cut him off, wearily and defensively. "I made a *mistake* in the statement."

"But you testified without any hesitation that he never took his hands from your neck, correct?"

"I made a mistake!"

The imperious federal prosecutor had turned into a pesky

detail wonk, an irritant. And the pestier he got, the more eloquent and dignified Adrienne seemed.

Puccio pushed on. "Isn't it a *fact*," he asked, "that you were flirting with Alex Kelly?" Her whole thorax rose in revulsion and indignation. *"Absolutely* not!"

The whole ordeal—and, now, this second trial: It had scraped away at so much of the felicitousness that had been her birthright that what was left was the dead moral weight at the center of her story. Suddenly, Puccio's seizing on Adrienne's communications degree seemed amateur. (So what if she'd had that major; did that make her Sir Laurence Olivier?) His hairsplitting about the testimony inconsistencies seemed too petty for her even to be very bothered by. His brandishing of her "Biggest Flirt" award thirteen years ago served only to remind the spectators of how unflirtatious she now was.

Puccio had met his match this time around. Here was a woman who had been reduced by the games and delays and ironies of this feral lawyer's abundantly lucky client to a hard essence. She *was* her story: like it or not, take it or leave it. You could watch her and wonder why she had pursued this fight for so long. You could watch her and wonder if she would ever get over her anger.

But there was one thing you could not do. You could not watch her and wonder if she was lying.

Thomas Puccio, be careful what you wish for. Here is your unvictim victim.

Hudock had cleaned up his case nicely. Dr. Marilyn Kessler was no longer painted as the florid victim's advocate with the lawyer who doubled as wardrobe consultant. She emerged in the second trial "so professional," one media person observed, "he damn well turned her into Hillary Rodham Clinton."

But one of the big changes in the second trial was the testimony of Tom Kelly. For years now, he had been carrying around the memories of Alex Kelly's statements to him—from both the day after the rape and the week after Alex returned from the Bridgeport jail. While Alex was in Europe, Tom would have dreams that his former buddy and neighbor would suddenly appear in town to get rid of the loose ends, Tom being one of them. Most of all, though, Tom felt guilty. Was silence collusion? No one from the prosecution side had ever *asked* him what happened next, after the party—never asked him if Alex had ever asked him to cover for him or if Alex had ever said anything self-covering.

The defense side had asked. Mickey Sherman had sent a private investigator around once and taped Tom on the subject. But lawyers for charismatic, athletic, wealthy male defendants are funny ducks. They can get cocky about the stupidest things. They've hung out in too many locker rooms. They seem to think male bonding, loyalty, and jock admiration is some Arthurian code of honor. O. J. Simpson's lawyers had been completely astonished and unprepared when Ron Shipp, displaying an integrity so alien to that trial's preceedings it seemed from another country, got on the witness stand and told the truth about their client. As for Tom Kelly, he listened to his mother. His mother always said, "You're only as good as your word."

Tom Kelly got on the witness stand in the second trial and under Hudock's questioning told the jury that the day after Dan Anderson's party, when Alex had come over to go sledding with him, Alex denied taking Adrienne home. (He was prevented from testifying that Alex, after getting out of Bridgeport, had asked Tom to tell the police he had come back to the party, because the judge felt the phrase "the party" was too vague and could have referred to Steve Devereux's rather than Dan Anderson's party.)

Tom Puccio was probably so angered that Hudock was able to present this incriminating material, that he went after Tom Kelly's ponytailed, hey-dude style rather than his testimony: acting sarcastically surprised that Tom Kelly was wearing a suit, asking him if he'd smoked marijuana earlier. This frantic attempt to make Tom Kelly look noncredible to the jury backfired on Puccio: In the course of questioning, he gave Tom the opportunity to say that, the morning after Dan Anderson's party, he and Alex were "probably smoking pot when we were sledding behind those cars."

Months and months—and all the navy blue gabardine, gold buttons, and khaki that Brooks Brothers had to offer—had been spent reducing his client to the incandescent image of preppy decorum and yet Tom Puccio himself had ended up opening the door on his own client's secret history.

The defense case went well. The testimony and evidence that worked the first time was reprised and polished. For Jeep Demonstration II, Bussell was out and Amy was in. Who needed a dour male cop when the defendant's beautiful girlfriend could do a Vanna White turn? Joe Kelly, again, shouted Alex's protestations of innocence through Hudock's heated objections (though, this time, Hudock objected faster, so fewer people heard it). Dr. Lief was back playing Dr. Ruth, as were many of the other expert witnesses. Mickey Sherman uttered his "fair shake" line and, afterward, shuttled off to do television commentary with his buddy Geraldo Rivera. Most important—most triumphal: Judge Tierney dismissed the kidnapping charge. He just threw it out as wrongly conceived. This was as much a blow to the prosecution (for having brought it) as a boon to the defense. A defendant who gets a major charge dropped well into his second trial has powerful ammunition for declaring—in appeals—that he was unjustly charged (something Alex always claimed): hunted by the prosecution.

Puccio terrified the court administrators when he sleuthed out a loophole in Connecticut procedure that made the compensation by the state for in-state witnesses' work-days-off improper. (Dan Anderson and Tom Kelly had been compensated thusly.) He even went after Tom Kelly's IRS declarations.

Before the first trial began, Puccio had complained to *Vanity Fair* that the Stamford courthouse world was so small and incestuous, with prosecutors' and judges' offices so close together. (That point had been borne out in Judge Nigro's self-recusal.) Now, the cramped quarters were truly taking their toll. The small courtroom, the small lobby area, the floor's single pay-phone booth, the tiny bathrooms, the limited choice of lunch spots (jury, media, prosecution, and defense often rubbed elbows in the cafeteria line of the local yogurt parlor)—how long could the intense passions remain under wraps with such inevitable jostling and mixing between the two enemy camps of this tortured proceeding?

The answer, of course, was: not long. Puccio and Hudock had already had their fight (during the last trial's jury selection). Hudock and Joe Kelly had had *their* fight (during the hearing on Nigro's recusal). Now, on June 7, the incident that was just waiting to happen happened: Chris Ortolano, Adrienne's husband, walked into the men's room while Alex Kelly was in one of the stalls. A radio reporter who was also in the bathroom at the time heard Chris ask, "Are there any paper towels here?," whereupon Alex—apparently feeling that the sudden presence of his accusor's husband was a violation, reportedly said, "Hey, pal, I'm just trying to [go to the bathroom]." Alex came out and complained to Puccio that he had been threatened. Reporters and spectators were abuzz—Adrienne's husband and Alex had gone head to head! Puccio heatedly complained to the judge that the Ortolanos, when entering the courthouse, did not have to go through metal detectors. Alex called the reporters who were present "vultures" looking for a new "angle" to get him on. In time, tempers subsided.

Puccio's tour-de-force close was the presentation Dr. Kurt Dubowski, who had testified in the first trial about alcohol's effects on teenage girls' judgments. But now he was here for a different reason. In a three's-the-charm example of persistence paying off, Puccio had finally gotten his controversial drug test on the bloodstain admitted by Tierney. This stunned and dismayed the prosecution. Adrienne had unequivocally denied (and does to this day) that she had used marijuana— but some arcane lab test had been hunted down that could be used to posit such claim.

And so, based on his conclusions on blood testing on Adrienne's panties performed by Dr. Kevin Ballard of Baylor University, Dr. Kurt Dubowski got on the stand and testified that Adrienne had ingested marijuana on the night she was raped.

If the jury believed the expert, then they were free to conclude that Adrienne had taken the illegal drug and worse, much worse, that she was a liar.

In closing arguments, Hudock projected a reflective, muted confidence. As with his witness, the weight of it all—the years of it all—came out in the simple, earned gravity of his words and his body language. "Adrienne is a survivor of rape," he told the jury, in a tone of voice that presumed that they had already sensed this about her. "She will always feel the same. The fear of rape still grips her, and her testimony shows it. No matter how loving her marriage, no matter how many children she has, she will always be a rape victim.

"Based on the facts, there is no reasonable conclusion but that Alex Kelly raped Adrienne Bak." He reviewed the facts, the testimony: the curfew, the party, the offer of a ride by Alex, the rape itself. The testimony of Adrienne's family. The injuries. The police testimony.

Then he mocked the defense's expert witnesses' theories. "Did *any* one of those 'experts' *see* Adrienne Bak? Did they talk to Adrienne Bak? All the defense offers you is speculation, guesswork, and sloppy science. And that is not reasonable doubt."

Hudock spoke of Alex's fugitive flight, then he addressed his biggest stumbling block: Alex's appearance. "We may not want to believe that that handsome eighteen-year-old down the street can rape. The evidence shows he did. A verdict that runs counter to the evidence erodes our system of justice. The citizens of this state rely on you to honor your oath and return a verdict of guilty."

Puccio rose and addressed the jury. "There are two diametrically opposed sides" to this case, he began by saying. "My function is to draw inferences that arise from the evidence in this case—evidence that is reasonable. Think about this case in detail, because my client's life is involved in this case. . . .

"I want you to be thinking adults. What's not evidence in this case is sympathy for anyone involved. . . . You need only find one reasonable doubt to find Alex Kelly not guilty of this single charge. . . . You are . . . to find what happened between two teenagers in a car outside a house eleven years ago. This case depends on the credibility of this story.

"Do you believe Adrienne Bak's words beyond a reasonable doubt?" Refering now to the discrepancy between Adrienne's original police statement (about the hands on her neck) and Adrienne's first-trial testimony, Puccio waxed casually erudite: "There's a famous European statement: 'Paper is very patient.'" In other words, that police statement had waited eleven years to tell its story. And it was capable of waiting another eleven, if it had to.

"If you listen carefully and if you analyze the evidence carefully you will see the telltale signs . . . that there are many, many, many instances of deception."

In a skillfully reasoned, dramatic argument, he went through her entire testimony about the rape and picked it apart,—mostly on the basis that it did not fit the crime's "classic" pattern—interweaving the same rhetorical line: *"Adrienne Bak lied. And when she lies, she always lies for a reason."*

Puccio called his client's accuser a liar about thirty times in his stemwinder. It was an effective, sophisticated, tough closing argument. It was expensive-lawyer stuff, all right. For those who were on the prosecution side, it was frightening.

The only thing is, the argument worked in the abstract, but not in the concrete—in the hypothetical, but not in the real world of this case and this witness.

You had to believe that Adrienne Bak had been lying.

"The clothing! It looks like it came out of a store! Does that sound like sexual frenzy?!" Puccio massed all his witnesses and inconsistencies, all the investigative lapses together and then he said it himself: "All roads lead to her. You have to believe her beyond a reasonable doubt and there are lots and lots of reasonable doubts."

Pounding the lectern and pleading and nearly crying, the father who lost his own son in a fluke accident implored: "This boy's life is involved! He came back here! He voluntarily surrendered in Switzerland to seek justice and I know you'll find it! I thank you and my client thanks you. This is the most serious thing in this boy's life. I leave it in your hands. Thank you."

Tears were streaming down Melanie Kelly's face when Puccio finished. A few minutes later, proffering a paper cup of water, Alex turned and, seemingly frightened by her grief, said, "Here, Mom."

Every mother of a son in that courtroom must have thought: Some things are wild-card genes. Just dumb luck. There but for fortune. Oh, that poor woman.

On Thursday, June 12, just after lunch, after deliberating only eight hours, the jury had a verdict.

Everyone crammed the courtroom. The jury entered, inscrutable. They sat. The foreman, Robert Derleth, remained seated as he delivered the jury's verdict: Guilty.

For a second or two, there was silence. Then the supporting characters reacted—three pointed claps from David Golub, a fist thrust in the air from the Rape Crisis Center's Carla Gisolfi—while the principals digested the information. Adrienne sat crying gratefully. Her husband and family embraced her. Melanie and Joe slumped in their seats. Amy sobbed uncontrollably. Her mother, Bobbie Dee, leaned over to console her. Kathy Puccio's head went into her hands. Tom Puccio was stoic.

Then Alex stunned the courtroom. His voice had never been heard in this chamber—not once. Now he leapt to his feet and emotionally shouted, "Are you serious? But I'm not guilty! I'm not guilty! I'm not guilty! Are you serious? I'm innocent. I didn't do this! I want to speak!" He turned to Adrienne and angrily asked: "Why are you doing this to me?!"

Through Alex's exclamation, Judge Tierney admonished him: "Sit down Mr. Kelly." Sheriffs descended upon Alex and began to handcuff him. He asked, "Can I hug my girlfriend for a minute?" The sheriffs did not permit this request. Amy sobbed as Alex turned around and said, "Amy, I love you. Mom, Dad, I love you guys."

The mystery of it is: He had always been able to express love, shamelessly and freely in his letters to his parents, and now verbally. Why did there also have to be so much cruelty and violence?

Alex was led away to a holding area, but not for long. Puccio went right to Judge Tierney. Alex's bail bond was stayed. He was rereleased, free on the 1-million-dollar bond until sentencing.

Bruce Hudock demanded rescinding of the bond. But Judge Tierney emphatically defended his controversial decision to allow Alex to stay free until sentencing, citing the recent reversal of a Connecticut ruling by a state higher court to affirm that to do otherwise was to violate the Constitution.

The verdict, juror Robert Landress later said, had been "certainly unanimous."

Adrienne issued a statement, through her husband, thanking her supporters. She also thanked the press—collectively and in gracious handwritten notes to individual reporters—for doing an almost unprecedented thing, especially in these times: unwaveringly refusing to reveal her identity, over eleven and a quarter years of coverage.

Then, in order to give back to others in a most meaningful way—to give courage to other rape victims—she broke that long-protected anonymity. She gave an interview to the Stamford *Advocate, The New York Times,* and the Associated Press. Her name was used and her photograph was emblazoned on the covers of the *Advocate, The New York Times,* the New York *Daily News* and other publications. Then she resumed her privacy.

In a very real sense, Adrienne had stood trial on behalf of all the other girls, over all the years. It was she who finally stopped Alex Kelly—who said: Enough silence; I don't care how hard this is—I'll do it. She had endured more than most eventually successful accusers in rape cases endured: almost a dozen years and two trials; but, then, she was carrying other silenced voices with her.

Some in the prosecutor's office and Darien Police Department expected Alex to flee before sentencing. In fact, they even had a date predicted: Thursday, July 3. Since a judge would be needed to issue warrants enabling the police to meaningfully pursue him and compel his parents to answer questions, it was thought that the eve of the Fourth of July weekend—with no courts open—would be a perfect time for any would-be fugitive to choose to make a run for it.

But he did not flee. This time, Alex Kelly stayed and faced the consequences.

On July 24, Alex Kelly was sentenced to the maximum term allowable—twenty years—to be suspended after sixteen. By suspending four years, the state was able to impose an unusually long period of probation—ten years—onto his sentence. This move allows Connecticut to exert more years of control —twenty-six—over Alex Kelly than would have been possible with a straight maximum sentence. The length of the sentence surprised many trial insiders, who, although they had long ago stopped trying to predict Judge Tierney's decisions, felt the stringency of the sentence was unusual, given the judge's several significant rulings for the defense.

Before Judge Tierney announced the sentence, Adrienne Bak Ortolano read a long and emotional victim-impact statement, which she had submitted to the judge beforehand. In it she recounted her years of fear and nightmares. She spoke of the rape as having permanently affected her life and her marriage. Adrienne's statement included statements written by her husband and family. (The judge disallowed them from presenting them themselves.) Adrienne's voice broke as she read her younger sister Kimberly's words: "We cannot get back the time he took from us, time that he is not worthy of taking or occupying." The statement drove home to many just how emotionally costly rape can be, to an entire family.

After the sentencing, Judge Tierney said his stiff sentence was based not on Alex's flight, not on Darien's reputation, but on the impact of the rape on Adrienne.

About one hundred of Alex's friends and neighbors had written letters in his behalf, begging the judge for mercy and speaking of Alex's virtues: Junius Clark, the neighbor whose sons (Cy and Junie) were among Alex's best friends. Elisabet Jansson and her parents. Bobbie Dee Molitor. A number of friends from Chamonix and La Grave. Amy wrote: "I always felt safe and secure [with him]. . . . He was a young man who wanted to excel in life. . . . We want to share a life together. . . . I beg you, Judge Tierney, to truly bring these dreams to life. . . . to show mercy."

When it was his turn to speak at his sentencing, Alex rose and placed his right hand on his forehead and his left hand on his hip. He took a deep breath, as if he was struggling for words and for composure. Then, in an emotional voice, he told the judge:

"The prosecution may have already read this [statement] to you. I want you and Mrs. Ortolano to hear it from me. I have learned lessons that are indelibly marked on me, that have changed my life forever. . . . I know it was wrong to run. There are many reasons why I ran. None of them are right.

"I know now you can't run from your problems. You have to stand up for what you believe in, no matter what . . . I apologize to the court, to my family and especially to Mrs. Ortolano and her family for not showing up."

Thus having apologized specifically for the failure to appear in court, he made no such apology for the rape. Rather, "People all have their own perspectives. My perception may be different from Adrienne Bak's. I never meant to hurt her."

However, he conceded, "During the trial, I heard her perception. I now know that I hurt her." Now came the apology. "I never meant to and I'm sorry."

Then Alex said: "I hope we can stop destroying ourselves and start healing each other. The teenagers of eleven years ago have grown up." Indeed, they had. It was only now, all these years too late, that he had joined them.

"I know I'm not a threat to society or to Mrs. Ortolano," he said. Now he began crying. "Please, your honor, give me that chance!" He wished to become "a contributing member of society." Tragically, he had many of the qualities that could have allowed him to become a sterling contributing member. But other forces had eclipsed them.

Thomas Puccio has filed an appeal of Alex's sentence, listing over fifty appealable items. He believes there is ample doubt in the case, and he has asserted that it was his client's flight, not the facts of the case, that had hurt his case. ("It made it difficult to get an untainted verdict," he said, noting that the public attitude seems to be that "once someone hears that he didn't show up in 1987, they've made up their minds.")

Though many insiders believe that a plea bargain is imminent, as of early September 1997, the second *State* v. *Kelly*—Valerie Barnett's case—goes forward.

* * *

All stories about young people who were born and raised with every possible good fortune and advantage and yet who persistently misused these qualities are, at their hearts, mysteries. This is why they are compelling, and this is why they are tragic.

Why did flawed but essentially decent people like Joe and Melanie Kelly transform themselves into parents who flamboyantly refused to acknowledge their son's problems? Who never seemed to focus on getting him help for those problems, and who, in supporting his flight from justice, simply helped to make his eventual conviction so much more certain? And— the more essential and mysterious question: How did that much pathology spring from this particular family?

Some things are unknowable. And those who choose to live in communities that have long been elegant hiding places tend to keep their deepest secrets better than others.

On September 10, 1997, Alex Kelly was committed to MacDougall Corrections Center, a maximum-security prison with a hardcore population. Many of his old friends imagined that he would fall prey to fellow inmates. But this may not be the case. One of Alex's friends has heard that, in the Walker Classification Center in Suffield, Connecticut (where Alex spent interim time while being evaluated for permanent prison placement): "They were in awe of him. If you get on *America's Most Wanted* four times, you're, like, a big deal in prison.

"It's just like in high school. Alex is a star, man."

ACKNOWLEDGMENTS

This is the third book I have written in which I have approached a community of the close friends of the principals in a social tragedy—and we have told the story together. Of my fifty or so sources within the world of this story, special thanks to these now older-and-wiser onetime Darien teenagers:

A.: As with so many young men in this story, you are appalled at the crime of rape and you wanted justice. You opened doors for me. "Kathy Bishop": The story achieved a new depth when I got on the phone with you. You drew me right into the experience of being a girl in that crowd and saw the larger meaning of growing up in that time and place as keenly as any sociologist. Thanks for your spirited truthfulness. "Rick Dawson": Your theatrical presentation of the tableau of characters made so much come alive for me. I laughed through all our interviews. "Cory Johnson": You supplied the moral outrage. Hats off! "Margaret": You survived events that crush the spirit, yet remain triumphantly exuberant. I am immensely grateful to you and your husband for trusting me. Mrs. D.: Appreciation for the witty candor. You were brave in wanting to go all the way in breaking the silence. Brad Lareau: Gratitude for sharing that painful memory. "Julia West": You are a person of great dignity and insight. Your chilling articulation is something so many can learn from. My charming pub-lunch partner: Thanks for your skillful service as local social analyst. T.K.: What you did took guts. That was (how can I use any other adjective?) awesome. "Jim Hunter": I know it was not easy reliving that year of your life, but you did so so vividly, I could almost hear you bawling in that jail cell. The "Bushes": You were always so welcoming and upbeat with my phone calls to your house. Thank you for those vital, sensitive revelations.

A character known as the Hero Cop finds his way into each of my books: someone who has managed to implant a moral perspective upon the troubled world he patrolled and the crises he intervened in. Becky Hahn Nathanson, thank you for forever changing the gender of the pronoun in my archetype. I admire you enormously.

Great appreciation to the educators of the area, and to one in particular, for speaking with such astute authority.

Gary Bigham: Thanks for insisting that I come and see it all for myself, and for putting me up once I got there. Mark Hanson: Your difficulty in reconciling the good friend you admired with the rape defendant you heard about resonated soulfully through our New York/Japan phone calls. Thank you.

Steve Silberman: Thank you for the perfect book title.

Carla Gisolfi, executive director of the Stamford Rape and Sexual Abuse Crisis Center: The support, advocacy, and protection your center provided to Adrienne Bak Ortolano and her family for almost a dozen years drove home, to everyone who watched the trials, how profoundly important is the service you render to sexual assault victims in your community. (I hope potential benefactors are reading this.) You are a warm, generous, and very courageous woman.

Elizabeth Hilts: I admired your *Fairfield County Weekly* features. Let's do another lunch . . . *if* they ever do let me eat lunch in that town again.

I owe a debt to the local media—the Darien *Times* and *News-Review*, the Norwalk *Hour*, and the Stamford *Advocate*—whose ongoing coverage of this story provided the historical record. In following the trials, News-12 Connecticut's Audrey Honig, the Kelly case's very own Christiane Amanpour, and the undisputed dean of the saga's print reporters, Dan Mangan of the *Advocate*, made the work for us tagalongs easy.

The Darien Public Library is a beautiful facility whose librarians are equally helpful with sleuthing out the town's exemplary history and its dark police blotter listings.

Stamford/Norwalk Trial Court Administrator Lorraine Murphy

ACKNOWLEDGMENTS

personalized the experience of covering *State* v. *Kelly* and showed Stamford Superior to be not just a court but also a humane community.

To my publishers: Pocket Books publisher, Gina Centrello: Thank you so much for trusting me, again, to find the hidden story. Jack Romanos, President of the Simon & Schuster Consumer Group: Gratitude for the early interest. To my wonderful editor Nancy Miller, who brought a refined literary eye and a heart-lifting enthusiasm to my manuscript: I can't believe it— we made the deadline! Scrambling toward that end, assistant editor Dan Slater was an island of calm and a whiz with flying inserts and kamikaze script versions. Simon & Schuster counsel Jennifer Weidman: Thanks, again, for working that wizardry. Associate director of publicity Amy Greeman: Gratitude for all the savvy, energetic attention. Nathaniel Bisson: I love the jacket copy.

Ellen Levine: No matter how famous and busy you get, you still act as if each of us is your most important client. I am so lucky to have you as my agent. And thanks to the splendid Diana Finch, Jay Rogers, Deborah Clifford, and Bob Simpson.

Esmerelda Agosto ran dozens of errands, cut up and assembled 100 interview-transcript files, conducted interviews with Swedish sources—and that's not even half of it. You are, as John says, one of life's great top sergeants. Ace research aides David Newman, Claire DeBruner, Ken Hyman: There was no hockey-brawl arrest, Revolutionary War fun fact, or famous-recent-crime detail you could not dig up for me. My private-investigator buddy, Richie Haeg: Appreciation, once again, for volunteering your sleuth-power. Heather Alberts: Thank you for getting such great photos so quickly. Anderson at Hotaling's: Thanks for having a Stamford *Advocate* waiting for me daily.

John Kelly supported and commiserated with me in that weathered shorthand empathy that only another workaholic writer and a partner of twenty-two years can provide. I watched you put your heart and soul into the writing of a magnificent book while I was writing this one. The energy we give each other comes out on the pages.

ACKNOWLEDGMENTS

While writing this book about an extremely handsome, macho young athletic star who veered one way in life, I watched my own extremely handsome, macho young athletic star become a high school freshman and, now, a sophomore. Jonathan Daniel Kelly: I am so incredibly proud of how you are continuing to develop your character—not just in terms of how diligent, sensible, and creative you are, but how you handled your own recent loss and grief, and in the fact that most of your trusted buddies and confidantes, with whom you chew up that phone line all night, are female. Dad and I look at you and say: Boy, did we get lucky. And—as you get older, you see—luck is so much of it. Be humble and sensitive and responsible with that luck. You are my greatest triumph.